The Rug Book

Lillian Mary Quirke is an instructor at De Anza Community College, California in rugmaking, general crafts, screen printing, design, weaving, and stitchery. She belongs to many professional organizations, her screen prints have won awards, and several have become collector's pieces.

BOOKS IN THE CREATIVE HANDCRAFTS SERIES:

The Art of Woodcarving, Jack J. Colletti
Clothesmaking, Linda Faiola
*The Craftsman's Survival Manual: Making a Full- or Part-Time
   Living from Your Craft*, George & Nancy Wettlaufer
Creative Embroidery with Your Sewing Machine, Mildred Foss
The Denim Book, Sharon Rosenberg & Joan Wiener Bordow
Designing in Batik and Tie Dye, Nancy Belfer
Designing and Making Mosaics, Virginia Gayheart Timmons
Designing in Stitching and Appliqué, Nancy Belfer
Experimental Stitchery and Other Fiber Techniques,
   Arline K. Morrison
Inventive Fiber Crafts, Elyse Sommer
Jewelry-Making: An Illustrated Guide to Technique,
   Dominic DiPasquale, Jean Delius, & Thomas Eckersley
Needlepoint: The Third Dimension, Jo Ippolito Christensen
The Needlepoint Book: 303 Stitches with Patterns and Projects,
   Jo Ippolito Christensen
New Dimensions in Needlework, Jeanne Schnitzler & Ginny Ross
The Perfect Fit: Easy Pattern Alterations, Jackie Rutan
The Quiltmaker's Handbook: A Guide to Design and Construction,
   Michael James
The Rug Book: How to Make All Kinds of Rugs,
   Lillian Mary Quirke
The Sewing Machine as a Creative Tool, Karen Bakke
Soft Jewelry: Designing, Techniques & Materials,
   Nancy Howell-Koehler
Teach Yourself Needlepoint, Jo Ippolito Christensen
Tailoring the Easy Way, Lucille Milani
Weaving, Spinning, and Dyeing: A Beginner's Manual,
   Virginia G. Hower
Weaving without a Loom, Sarita S. Rainey

The Rug Book

HOW TO MAKE ALL KINDS OF RUGS

LILLIAN MARY QUIRKE

photographs by Shirley I. Fisher

A SPECTRUM BOOK

PRENTICE-HALL, INC.
Englewood Cliffs, New Jersey 07632

Library of Congress Cataloging in Publication Data

QUIRKE, LILLIAN MARY.
   The rug book.

   (The Creative handcrafts series) (A Spectrum Book)
   Bibliography: p.
   Includes index.
   1. Rugs.   I. Title.
TT850.Q57 1979   746.7   79-15121
ISBN 0-13-783712-7
ISBN 0-13-783704-6 pbk.

Editorial/production supervision
and interior design by Carol Smith
Page layout by Jenny Markus
Manufacturing buyer: Cathie Lenard

Cover photograph: "Czechoslovakian Romance,"
work in progress, edition of twenty tapestries,
Robert Freimark, 1973;
photograph courtesy of Shirley I. Fisher

A SPECTRUM BOOK

Printed in the United States of America

10 9 8 7 6 5 4 3 2 1

PRENTICE-HALL INTERNATIONAL, INC., *London*
PRENTICE-HALL OF AUSTRALIA PTY., LIMITED, *Sydney*
PRENTICE-HALL OF CANADA, LTD., *Toronto*
PRENTICE-HALL OF INDIA PRIVATE, LIMITED, *New Delhi*
PRENTICE-HALL OF JAPAN, INC., *Tokyo*
PRENTICE-HALL OF SOUTHEAST ASIA PTE., LTD., *Singapore*
WHITEHALL BOOKS, LIMITED, *Wellington, New Zealand*

To Annie Bird Plumb

Contents

Preface xv

CHAPTER ONE **Introduction** 1

CHAPTER TWO **Starting Points** 7

PAINTED FLOORCLOTHS, 8
Making a Floorcloth 11
PIECED CARPETS, 22
Judy Miller Johnson 22, Making a Rug Collage 23
FELTED RUGS, 25
Samantha Cochran 27, Making a Felted Rug 27,
Robert Freimark 31

xi

CHAPTER THREE

Traditional American Rugs 35

HOOKED RAG RUGS, 36
Annie Bird Plumb 36, Making a Hooked Rug 40
BRAIDED RAG RUGS, 50
Making a Braided Rug 50, Berkeley Cooper 50
WOVEN AND COILED RUGS, 60
Woven Rugs 63, Naturalistic and Geometric
Designs 81, Regional Designs 84,
Pile Rugs 87
CROCHETED AND KNITTED RUGS, 94
THE CROCHETED RUG, 103
Making a Hexagonal Crocheted Rug 104,
Making a Circular Crocheted Rug 106
THE KNITTED RUG, 119
Making a Knit Throw Rug 128

CHAPTER FOUR

Other Types of Rugs 130

RYA RUGS, 131
Making a Rya Rug 131
LATCH HOOK RUGS, 136
Making a Latch Hook Rug 143
PUNCH HOOK PILE RUGS, 144
Making a Punch Hook Pile Rug 144
NEEDLEPOINT RUGS, 156
Making a Needlepoint Rug 158

CHAPTER FIVE

Meet Some Fiber Artists 176

CROCHET RUGS, 176
Nancy Koren 176
SHUTTLE HOOK AND LATCH HOOK RUGS, 179
Howard Milton Warner 179
ELECTRIC SPEED TUFTED RUGS AND TAPESTRIES, 182
Patti Henry 182, Lynden Keith Johnson 184

CHAPTER SIX **You're on Your Own** 191

Design 192, Texture 195, Color 197,
Finishing Techniques 202, Caring for Your Rugs 203,
Marketing, the Law, and the Craftsperson 206,
Appraising and Photographing Your Rug 209

A Final Word 211

Appendix 213

Glossary 215

Sources of Supplies 218

Bibliography 222

Index 229

Preface

Work done well for its own sake—the well-formed object—is art. Earlier in this century, Louis Sullivan, Frank Lloyd Wright, Le Corbusier, and others proclaimed that the form of the artist's work follows its function. Certainly making anything that is both functional and beautiful with your own hands can offset the effects of the so-called impersonal forces in the world. An artist and craftsperson is one who can make the artifact work *with* these forces, not against or in spite of them. In this book we shall explore rugmaking as an art and a craft (as opposed to large-scale manufacturing of rugs), to discover the joy, beauty, and satisfaction that can be derived.

With an emphasis on both esthetic and technical considerations of rugmaking, we shall explore the foundatin for learning how to make several of the many kinds of floorcoverings.

The chapters are divided into three major areas: how rugmaking is done generally, how others do it, and how you might do it. Chapters One, Two, Three, and Four give you background information, with full details on process, color, texture, and design, as well as the *do*'s and *don't*'s that ensure perfect results each time. Several rugmakers, who represent all levels of creativity and methods of working, are interviewed to give you first-hand insight into the creative process of making a functional form. In Chapter Five, several fiber artists present their views. Chapter Six contains ideas and sources for creating the finished product and enhancing your home.

Throughout, you will find ample illustrations of tools and processes for braiding, crocheting, felting, gluing, hooking, knotting, needlepointing, painting, making tapestry, weaving, wrapping, and coiling. Step-by-step instructions guide you through the process of making a specific rug, and numerous photographs illustrate the text. The color insert presents the artists' rugs in room environments in vibrant color.

Think of yourself as a pebble dropping into the mainstream of the fiber arts. Just as the ripples move out in ever-widening concentric circles, so will you move from the small first plunge and reach out to expand your skills, interest, and knowledge. No matter what your level of expertise—whether you're a newcomer to rugmaking or a designer-craftsperson—you're bound to find something that will catch your eye and that you'll want to try among the wide range of rug techniques. Anybody of any age can make a rug. What could be more enjoyable or relaxing on a quiet evening or a rainy day at home? And, whether you want to make something for yourself or for your friends, I hope you will enjoy yourself.

Acknowledgments A silent army helps an author write a book, from the typists to the publisher's editors to the many people who contribute information about and examples of the rugs and techniques.

Special thanks go to Samantha Cochran, who edited the text and saw to it that I managed to eat, to Nora Bartine, who gave advice about grammar, and to Carole Greene, who wrote the section about Annie Bird Plumb in Chapter Three. In addition to the artists whose interviews and comments appear throughout the text, I would also like to acknowledge Maggie Brosnan, who shared her knowledge of the art of dyeing, and Deborah Q. Graham, who contributed valuable information about resources for the craftsperson.

Many talented artists designed and made the rugs that appear in this book, and many students tried out the techniques and made samples of the rugs: Annie Bird Plumb, Mortimer F. Quirke, Berkeley Cooper, Nancy Koren, Howard Milton Warner, Patti Henry, Lynden Keith Johnson,

Judy Miller Johnson, Anna Marie Lininger, De Anza Community College students, Joyce A. Hupp, Jean DeMouthe, Thelma Bailey, Joy Sinderson, Jane Fowler, the Peninsula Rug Guild, Amy Schaible, Constance Chase, Patti Jauch, Laura Dahlke, Stephanie Thomas, Judy Chargin, Josephine Lee, and Dorothy P. Cutler. Special thanks also to Doris Beezley, Valarie Cummings, Deborah Hayes, Barbara Hill, Nancy Kind, Patricia Skillcorn, Dorothy Y. Thomas, Mark Daly, Beatriz Uribe, Marion Windsor, Barbara Lyman, and Nancy Perry.

For the illustrations, I extend my thanks to Samantha Cochran, Kathy Puccio, Tim Mitchell, and to Mortimer F. Quirke, whose drawings, though unattributed, appear throughout.

Shirley I. Fisher, my colleague and photography instructor at De Anza Community College, is responsible for most of the photographs showing the rugs themselves and the specific processes. Not only did Terence M. Campbell contribute photographs but he put in many hours of organizing them. Others who contributed photographs are: Maggie Brosnan, Samantha Cochran, Berkeley Cooper, Jane Fowler, Robert Freimark, George M. Craven, Jack McConnell, Deborah Graham, Patti Henry, Judy Miller Johnson, Lynden Keith Johnson, Nancy Koren, Norman L. Koren, Ellen B. Quirke, Mortimer F. Quirke, Howard Milton Warner, Caroline Wigginton, John Pirro, and Anna Marie Lininger.

I am indebted to the many craftspeople who allowed me to interview them and to visit their studios, homes, and shops.

Finally, my gratitude to Annie Bird Plumb, my aunt, who taught me her skills and creative outlook and her philosophy that beautiful things ease the pain and hardships of life and help us to share the joys.

The Rug Book

Introduction

In this last half of the twentieth century, interest in and attention to crafts is reawakening. Approximately two out of every five Americans are involved in handcrafts. Many of us want to make beautiful things to decorate our world; we want relaxing and enjoyable outlets for creativity. Rugmaking is one of the most popular crafts because the rug can be seen and appreciated every day.

Kits and patterns, tools and equipment for making rugs are appearing everywhere. Latch hook rug kits, for example, stand among the groceries in the local supermarkets, readily available to the beginner. (Of course, there are many other ways to make floorcovers.) More and more people are exhibiting rugs at county and state fairs, at church bazaars, at city cultural centers, and in juried exhibitions of guilds and galleries and museums.

Rugmakers are textile artists who study and analyze rugs and techniques in an effort to improve the quality of the useful object. These artists recreate forms and designs, an essential role in a functional craft like rugmaking. Each textile artist contributes a new look using traditional forms and

1

techniques, and it is this bond with the past that keeps rugmaking endlessly alive. On the other hand, the fiber artist, who often works on large productions, is not as interested in historical forms as in breaking boundaries, surprising us when he or she goes beyond traditional limits of scale, technique, or form. Both types of artist begin with textile or fibrous materials and techniques but each sets up a different esthetic problem or goal. One emphasizes the useful object (i.e., a rug), the other emphasizes the decorative, contemplative object (i.e., a tapestry). The origin of rugmaking has been lost in the dim past of history and in decayed natural fibers. The Middle Eastern craftsperson who lived a thousand years before the Medieval crafts guilds testifies to the integrity of work done well. This lasting art depends on such elements as appearance, quality of materials, durability, and attention to finishing details; at the same time, it reflects a belief that a creative object belongs to an overall ideal—a votive gift to God and to beauty. Even if we don't know the exact origin of rugmaking, our heritage of information—from anthropology, history, contemporary guilds, exhibits, television programs, adult education classes, periodicals, and books—is extensive.

Historically, rugs were not used solely as floor coverings. American Indians used buffalo hides, decorated with paintings of battle scenes, as robes on cold, snowy nights as well as covers for the earthen floors of their tepees. The rya rug of the Norseman protected his bed from the winds creeping through every chink in the door of his home. Each English or Colonial American sailor was allotted a rug as part of his gear on trading ships to serve as a blanket for the voyage.

Although a great abundance of material things has been made possible through industrialization and technology, something of our relationship to the various crafts and to craftsmanship in general has been lost. Our lives and livelihoods tend to be fragmented. When life and livelihood were identical, as in Puritan New England or in the Mesa Culture of Arizona, people were at harmony with the natural world. Craftsmanship was a life-enriching activity. Today, your interest can lead you to an understanding of the meaning of craftsmanship as a life-enriching activity and can put you in harmony with your natural gifts of curiosity and creativity.

What do you want to know about rugmaking? The purpose of this book is not to exhaust one technique but to provide basic knowledge about constructing, finishing, preserv-

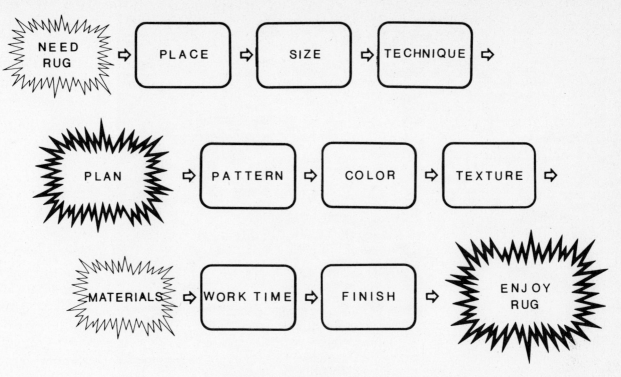

FIGURE 1-1 The process of making a rug (illustration by Samantha Cochran).

ing, exhibiting, and selling. It provides a foundation for learning how to make several of the many kinds of floorcoverings: carpets, area rugs, and those too-precious-to-walk-on wall hangings. Skill improves with practice and by deciding how the basic fibers and construction methods can be varied in color, texture, pattern, and use. Although rugs or floorcovers are the specific subject of this book, the methods of construction and the ideas can be used to make many other kinds of covers for seats, walls, tables, beds, bunks, and trunks, to name just a few. What you learn will be up to you.

How do you know if you will like making rugs? Only by handling the materials and actually trying to make something can you become involved in the functional and creative aspects of rugmaking. Begin by *looking* at rugs. For instance, in Figures 1-2 through 1-5 you will see four rugs made by using four different techniques. Which one appeals to you? Do you find yourself captivated by the design pattern, the textural qualities, or the techniques involved? Figure 1-2 shows a hand-hooked rug made by Annie Plumb; the naturalistic flower-shaped design motif was inspired by her garden. (This rug is discussed in Chapter Three and is shown in the color insert in Plate 18.) Figure 1-3 shows a braided rug by Berkeley Cooper, with a richly varied yet simple geometric line

FIGURE 1-2 Detail of hooked wool rug, naturalistic design motif, 156″ x 132″ (396 cm. x 335 cm.), Annie Bird Plumb; photograph courtesy of Ellen B. Quirke.

FIGURE 1-3 Braided wool rug, striped design motif, 76″ x 46″ (115 cm. x 190 cm.), Berkeley Cooper; author's collection.

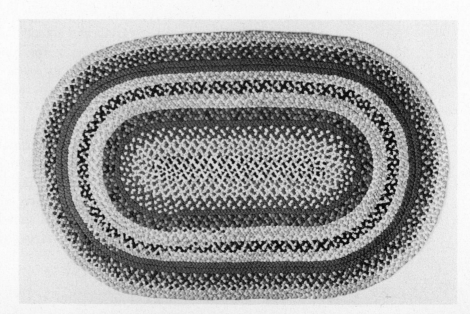

FIGURE 1-4 Knit, crochet, woven rug of handspun Irish wool, Aran knit pattern, crochet and woven design, 54″ x 36″ (135 cm. x 90 cm.), Jean De Mouthe.

FIGURE 1-5 Woven tapestry rug, 33″ x 24″ (84 cm. x 60 cm.), Egyptian youth; author's collection.

design. The knitted and crocheted rug of handspun Irish wool in Figure 1-4 was made by Jean De Mouthe, with a crochet mesh worked in off-white yarn. The sculptural quality of the knit motif creates a shadow pattern, making this handsome piece look as good on the wall as it does on the floor. Figure 1-5 is a woven tapestry made by an Egyptian youth, who wove the birds and trees with handspun wools and without a cartoon or drawing of his idea. (See detail in Plate 1, color insert.)

These black-and-white pictures do not show the rich variation of colors each craftsperson used. Yet the dark and light values of the fibers create patterns that dramatize the rugs. And several secondary patterns of grey areas carry the eye around the design, adding subtle variations.

You may be inspired by any of these designs. Or you may be inclined to draw inspiration from other sources. Geometric designs, for example, may be variations of linear patterns, straight lines, curving lines, thick or thin lines; or they may play upon squares or rectangles of various proportions and sizes. Hexagons, honeycomb shapes, triangles, and diamonds can also provide inspiration for a single unit motif. Any of these shapes may be repeated in a wide range of colors to create a floorcover of striking beauty. In addition, the mechanics of construction might lend special interest in texture and pattern.

The scope is limitless. Rugmaking provides an outlet for creativity. No matter what you are looking for—a quick, easy way to make a rug out of scraps or a method for making a larger, more expensive looped rug or stimulation to create an elegant effect with little effort—you'll find plenty of examples. Even if you have a physical handicap, the many varieties of floorcoverings will allow you to explore the rugmaking process.

CHAPTER TWO

Starting Points

Look around your home. Wouldn't you love to have a rug somewhere in your house that you had made yourself? Do you think it would be too costly? Too difficult? Surprisingly, it's not because you don't have to invest in large machines or expensive tools to produce your own artifact.

A painted floorcloth that repeats your favorite pattern from quilts, towels, or other items might be just the thing to satisfy your needs. You can glue together commercial carpet remnants for a quick, colorful carpet. If you like to work on small sections at a time, you can join together units of felt by stitching or crochet.

This chapter is designed to help you create these floorcovers, which will take from five to thirty hours to produce. Step-by-step instructions are given for painted floorcloths, pieced carpets, and felted rugs. Interviews with rugmakers will give insight into these methods and their rich and interesting tradition.

PAINTED FLOORCLOTHS

Painting on cloth is as old as weaving. Anthropology museums, national museums of decorative arts, and museums of history and technology show examples of painted surfaces that were used as wall, floor, or body covers.

Wealthy shipowners of New England, as well as owners of tobacco and cotton plantations in the Southern states, could afford to import many of their household luxuries. Pile rugs and painted canvas floorcoverings were valued imports because they added warmth, color, and elegance to a home. However, imports were rare among the majority of the three-millions of colonists and pioneers living in America before the Revolution. How could those people cover their hard-beaten earth or sanded wood floors? With straw? Yes. With sand? Yes. With nothing? Certainly. Yet, where could someone buy a rug before carpet factories were built in eighteenth-century America? Professional painters and paperhangers advertised painted canvas, sailcloth, or burlap. Enterprising women would even weave coarse cloth and paint their own carpets.*

In the British Museum of London you can see a fragment of linen votive cloth showing a man bearing an offering to Hathor, the cow-shaped god. The coarse cloth of ten threads per inch has a ground cover of white. Dark earth-brown pigment outlines the figures, jar, and god symbol. Other colors used in this 1500 BC work are brick earth-red, dark blue-green, light blue, light brick-red, and earth brown.

Skins painted with decorative patterns or battle scenes are in the National Museum of American Indians in New York City. In the South Sea Islands, tapa or felted bark cloth was painted or printed using wooden stamps.

Several tribes in Africa decorate cloth that is sometimes used on ceremonial occasions as an earth covering under the leader's chair (see Figure 2-1).

A few museums and historical sites exhibit handpainted reproductions of eighteenth- and nineteenth-century painted canvas floorcloths. The Smithsonian Museum mounts a traveling exhibit called "America Underfoot," which features a rug designed after an American primitive painting, "Girl With a Dog."

The Ulster Room of the Henry Francis Dupont Winterthur Museum (Wilmington, Delaware) exhibits another re-

*Roth Rodris, *Floor Coverings in 18th Century America* (Washington, D.C.: Smithsonian Press, 1967).

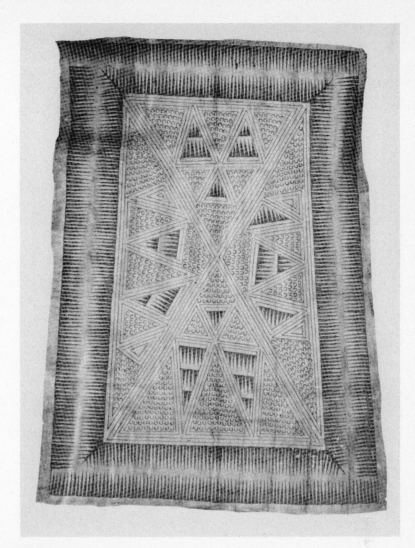

FIGURE 2-1　Beaten bark cloth rug (from *Contemporary African Arts and Crafts* by Thelma R. Newman. © 1974 by Thelma R. Newman, used by permission of Crown Publishers, Inc.).

production. Winterthur Museum had only fragments of floorcloths in 1960. Leonard C. Crewe, Jr., now president of Floorcloths, Inc., took his problem of creating authentic floorcloth reproductions to the Maryland Institute College of Art. From a search for authentic floorcoverings to furnish a small eighteenth-century home grew a new business, which produces a rug that can be easily cleaned and that carries a ten-year guarantee against surface wear, fading, or mildew damage.*

Figure 2-2 shows the beautiful painted floorcloth in the Brush Everard Dining Room in Williamsburg, Virginia. It's not difficult to make your own however. The painted and printed floorcloth made by Thelma Baily (Figure 2-3) may tempt you to try.

*For a catalogue and sales material, write to Floorcloths, Inc., 37 West Street, Annapolis, Maryland 21401.

9

FIGURE 2-2 Painted floorcloth in Brush Everard Dining Room. Colonial Williamburg Foundation (photographed by Colonial Williamsburg, Williamsburg, Virginia 23185 and used with permission).

FIGURE 2-3 Painted and printed floorcloth, acrylic, string print border, 42″ x 25″ (107 cm. x 63 cm.), Thelma Bailey.

Making a Floorcloth If you're interested in producing your own floorcloth, you should be aware of the limitations posed by the materials available. Floorcloths, Inc. uses 40-weight canvas and their own line of permanent oil colors, which are unavailable to the general public. You can make your own floorcloth, using common 10-ounce canvas and acrylic paints, but it won't be as durable as those produced professionally. For a quick solution to covering a floor, you can make a painted rug at home, with these materials:

- heavy cotton duck canvas, 24″ × 36″ (60 cm. × 91 cm.)
- ruler
- pencil for sketching and marking pattern
- sketch paper
- cartoon paper: shelf paper, newspaper, brown bags pasted together to size
- sharp scissors to cut out geometric design
- stiff bristle brush, 2″ (5 cm.) for lines and small areas of color
- acrylic polymer paint: 1/2 pint of a color; 1/2 pint of white; 1/2 pint of black or dark brown, used as a contrasting color or a darkening or dulling agent (1 pint usually covers 50 square feet)
- 1 pint water clear varnish, interior and exterior; nontoxic, nonyellowing, acrylic polymer
- varnish brush, 5″ (12.5 cm.) for water base paint
- white glue for hemming edges, pasting up large cartoon
- newspaper for protecting work surface

This project should take about five hours, plus the time involved in applying a second and third coat of varnish and allowing each coat twenty-four hours to dry. Be sure you work in an area that is large enough to allow you to stretch out the canvas.

Preparation "But I can't paint!" you exclaim. Don't worry; a few household items can help you. Masking tape gives you sharp, straight edges. A stencil made from a file folder guides your brush. Good old common sense comes to your aid. Forget any worries and plunge in! Decide where you want to display and use your rug and how large you want it.

While on a trip to London I got a sudden inspiration for making a hall carpet. I was on Doughty Street in London on my way to see the house where Charles Dickens wrote *Oliver Twist*. I noticed that the coal chute covers had beautiful designs and thought what nice patterns they would be if used as a motif in a rug (see Figure 2-4). Later, I gathered up the necessary tools for making a rubbing:

- white paper with a hard slick finish
- wax rubbing sticks
- masking tape
- scissors
- stiff brush
- handkerchief and tissues.

I went back to Doughty Street, brushed off one of the cast-iron coal chute covers, taped paper over it, and creased the paper around the raised design. Then I rubbed with strong, slanted strokes, side by side covering areas of 4 inches at a time. Why work on small areas? There is less chance for the paper to slip as you work. I held the paper down with one

FIGURE 2-4 Coal chute covers, photograph courtesy of the author.

hand and with the other hand pressed on the tip of the wax rubbing stick, depositing a solid black line. Were my fingers tired when I finished three-and-a-half hours later! It was a tedious afternoon, but I felt great satisfaction as I rolled up the four rubbings to take home to California. I knew they'd make unique designs for a floorcloth.

Choosing the Area for the Rug

Once home, I spread the rubbings on my dark oak parquet floor. Common sense or instinct told me to look at my hallway with the flower-like rubbing in mind. The hall is 3′ × 9 1/2′ (85 cm. × 381 cm.). One side has a closet and a folding door that covers the washer–dryer area. The other side has double-doors leading to a studio–work area. During the winter months I cover the floors with handmade rugs to keep the rooms warm and ward off the California chill from the concrete slab on which the house is built. The rubbings from the coal chutes of London, I thought, would be perfect for this hallway. Yes, I'd make a runner.

Deciding on a Method

The two major factors in my decision were time and money. Lack of time being my problem, I decided the fastest way to make a 2 1/2′ × 9′ (76 cm. × 274 cm.) rug was to paint one. A large scrap of cotton duck canvas was rolled up in a closet. Latex indoor house paint was left over from painting three accent walls, as were brushes, rollers, and trays. A dark color pigment or a bright accent-color paint might be the only purchase necessary.

Besides the main materials and tools, the accessories were readily available in my garage/workroom: yard/meter stick, scissors, pencil, chalk, masking tape, 4″ nylon bristle brush, 1″ bristle brush, 8″ roller and cover, roller pan, satin finish clear Varathane plastic finish, paint thinner, white glue, compass, scissors, water, newspapers, paint rags, T-square, or triangle—and time. Fortunately, work space was no problem even for such a large piece. I used the garage floor. When I chose to stand up and paint, there was the garage wall. I could even use a well-protected rosewood dining room table. As luck would have it, I broke out with a red rash from the latex paint. Oh, well, I put on rubber gloves when I worked! Open doors and windows provided ventilation while the paint dried.

Preparing the Canvas

I had 5′ wide canvas on hand to use. What could you use? You could use decorator's burlap or any evenly woven and sturdy cloth, cotton monks cloth, or basketweave material. The best backing is heavy duck canvas.

Because any cloth shrinks when latex or acrylic paint is used, you will need to cut the material 1″ (2.5 cm.) longer and 1″ (2.5 cm.) wider than the desired rug size. Cut through the selvedge (tightly woven) edge, place thumb and forefinger of each hand astride the cut, and tear along the line of the woven thread. This tear along the grain gives a rectangular shape. In order to get the size I needed, I put two lengths of canvas together, overlapping the selvedges. Then I machine-sewed them.

The material can be handsewn or even glued together. When gluing fabrics together, it is necessary to clamp the surfaces using books, clothespins, or weights of some kind until the glue has dried. A flexible white latex rug glue that does not leave the hem stiff is available at hardware stores and craft shops. Barge cement, a flexible glue used on leather, can also be used, but it has a dark color and should be used only if the rug will be painted a dark color.

Shrinking. All woven materials should be pre-shrunk before using. Washing and rinsing remove any sizing or starch-like fill so the cloth will not ripple when painted. Duck canvas must be ironed dry and shaped into a flat unwrinkled cloth. Remember, I had my two pieces sewn together before I pre-shrunk, but you can also pre-shrink before cutting and joining together.

Hemming. Now you're ready to hem the actual rug-sized piece of material. Each of the four edges is mitered, pinned, and sewn. The cloth is cut away at right angles or mitered to produce a sharp, flat corner. A glue joint can be used for hemming the material. It is tacked or pinned to a board, door, or wall before painting. Pins inserted every 1/2″ (1.25 cm.) around all the edges stretch the canvas into a smooth surface for applying the latex or acrylic paint. When the board is not as big as the whole cloth, sections are stretched and painted.

Squaring up the canvas. The cloth must be straight and squared before starting any work. There are many ways to square the cloth: a T-square with a yard/meter stick or a page from a newspaper with a ruler. In our example, I used the lines of the parquet floor in the hallway where my rug was going to be displayed to square off my canvas. The short end of the canvas was selvedge and straight, so I stretched the cloth along the wood line and taped it firmly. By holding a ruler perpendicular to the uncovered straight line of parquet, I measured from that line to the narrowest part of the cloth.

Placing a ruler perpendicular at the 1″ (2.5 cm.) mark, I placed a dot on the cloth at the narrowest distance measure. Continuing along the length of canvas, I marked dots as I went; a line drawn through the dots results in a straight edge. I cut carefully with sharp scissors. After this, I hemmed the duck canvas on my grandmother's treadle sewing machine, using #40 cotton thread and a heavy-duty needle.

Designing the Pattern

My idea was to use the center flower-liihehofthnoal chute design for a component of the pattern. Deciding the layout of the pattern wasn't difficult. I made small, thumbnail sketches in the shape of the rug. After examining the thumbnail sketches, I drew a circle on the actual cloth to symbolize the circular form of the pattern units. The dark and light cross-hatched areas planned the light, medium, and dark pattern I thought would look good.

Selecting and Using Color

There are many types of pigment color hues and only general guidelines for their use. The way you see colors in relation to each other—the tints and shades, amounts and placement, dull or grey tones, vibrancy and brightness—is automatic. The way you plan to use colors is often the result of trial and error and of personal taste. Each of us has some color preference—reds, pinks, oranges, blues, greens, yellows, or earth tones.

There are many aids for selecting color combinations. Hardware stores have paint chips that show related or harmonizing colors in the same family. Color wheels are available. Artists' pigments found in art supply stores have the basic color hues of the Munsell Color Theory—red, yellow, green, blue, and purple—as well as the in-between hues. Take a trip to your local hardware or art supply store and look at color wheels, charts, and guides.

One rule is that complementary colors are color opposites. One color has none of the other color in it: for example, red and green, blue and orange, purple and yellow. To create a vibrating accent, both colors should be either of the same brightness or intensity or of the same value of greyness or lightness. For a better depiction of color usage, see the plates in the color insert.

The important criteria are the contrasts of light and dark, bright and dull, warm and cool. Choose the colors you really like to work with. Don't worry about logic because any combination of these contrasts looks good if the area of each color is not equal.

In our example, the leftover latex paints in my workroom

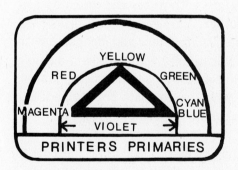

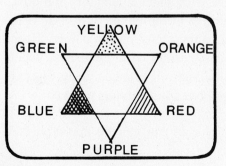

were a greyed brick pink, a medium greyed yellow-orange, and a light greyed avocado green. Since these colors had been used for accent walls in my home, I knew that repeating the color hues on the floor would be perfect for achieving a calm harmony. But something was missing: there was too much of the same medium greyish tone. I decided to achieve a color contrast by painting grey-green rectangles on a field of greyed pink. These colors from opposite color families, red and green, provided a nice contrast.

For the designs, which were shapes copied from the rubbings, I chose dark colors to accent the lighter backgrounds. I used ultramarine blue and burnt sienna to paint the geometric lines in the center. I combined lines of burnt sienna and bright red in the two outer designs; for the ends, to paint chevrons I used bright red and burnt sienna.

The paint. When selecting paint, be sure to choose only one type: latex, acrylic, or oil. The coefficient of molecular expansion is different for each type of paint. For example, oil-based paint cannot be used underneath latex or acrylic without resulting in a cracked or peeling surface because acrylic and latex paint dry faster than oil paint.

The latex paint that I used has rubber latex as its binder. Water thins the paint and cleans the brushes. This kind of paint dries in four hours and the surface is water-resistant in twenty-four hours.

The finish. I had a choice of two finishes: one, an acrylic polymer emulsion varnish, thins with water and dries to a low sheen or matte finish; the other, Varathane liquid plastic exterior clear satin finish, dries in five hours and cleans up with paint thinner. I chose the Varathane, which gives a durable coating with an ultraviolet absorber. This finish resists water, salt spray, and sun fading when three coats are applied. Directions for use are on the can.

Applying the Color

Brushes and roller covers may be used, although roller covers are not recommended for use with shellac, lacquer, and often solvent-based varnishes because of bubbling. Synthetic bristle brushes may be used for almost any paint project. However, they do not give the best results with varnishes, which are best applied with soft, long-haired brushes. (See Figures 2-5 and 2-6, which show methods for applying paint).

Brush size. Painting on any size rug can be accomplished with the following brushes:

FIGURE 2-5 (left) Applying paint texture to the canvas using a sponge and cardboard stencil.

FIGURE 2-6 (below) Using a brush to paint a sharp edge with paper stencil—brush from the stencil out to the canvas.

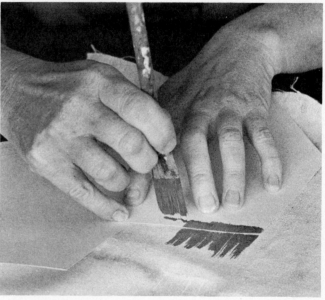

- a 5″ (12.7 cm.) brush for priming large areas
- a 2″ (5 cm.) or 3″ (7.6 cm.) brush with a chisel edge for cutting in sharp edges
- a 1″ (2.5 cm.) chisel-edged, flat brush for outlining and making narrow lines.

Narrow lines on a rug should be at least 1/4″ (6 mm.) wide. Otherwise they look lost on the floor or look as though a thread or piece of yarn had not been picked up.

Natural or synthetic bristles. The important thing to remember when deciding between a natural or nylon bristle brush is that natural bristles are never used to apply latex or water-thinned paints. The bristles of these brushes absorb excessive amounts of water and become limp and hard to control. Choose a quality brush with full flagged, tapered

17

bristles to obtain a better and neater paint job faster. Fullness of bristle can be judged by squeezing gently. The bristles should feel full and somewhat spongy. Look at the bristle ends: the fine branch-like split ends or flagged ends will hold a good amount of paint and cover the surface with fewer passes. A tapered bristle brush has more bristles at the metal banded base and less toward the tip end; the paint flows more evenly as the tip variance in bristle length provides new tips.

Roller and pad applicators. Rollers are a time saver when covering large areas. Flat rectangular foam pads also give the speed of a roller and the smooth finish of a brush, especially on smooth surfaces. Usually they cost less than a quality brush. The Mohair, Dynel, or Super Dynel covers can be cleaned thoroughly by soaking and rinsing. Store them standing on end near the clean floating cap roller frame or threaded handle of the push-button release pad.

Testing the paints. Since all the latex house paint I had on hand was medium light in tone and greyed, I had a choice of bright and medium or light and dark accents for contrast. Excluding white because the rug would be in a heavily trafficked area, I tested the paint color with its top finish coat on a scrap piece of canvas.

Acrylic polymer matte varnish will not change the colors. However, Varathane liquid plastic exterior satin finish has a slightly brownish cast. A test strip of the colors with the finishing varnish helped me decide that the greyed pink and grey-green background looked best with the blue, red, and brown accents in acrylic. The Varathane gave a pleasant brightness to the colors.

Enlarging the Motif

An opaque projector can be used to enlarge parts of a pattern, but I didn't have one. Without a projector, the rubbing could be ruled off into blocks and the small center sections enlarged. However, coal chute designs are circular, and the block method didn't apply, since the rectangular block grid method requires a lot of free-hand sketching to draw in the curved lines. I chose another method.

The curved forms in the center part of the coal chute cover design are even and regular. I found I could abstract the petal-shaped arm or star-shaped arm and make accurate drawings to transfer to the prepared rug canvas. Here's the method I found works best.

Finding a repeat. Take a ruler or a piece of writing paper with a straight edge. Lay it on the design so that the edge passes through the center point and divides it vertically in half. If this is still a complex shape, lay another sheet of paper horizontally and at right angles to the other. Now one-fourth of the circular shape shows. Divide this quarter into two equal wedge shapes and a one-eighth, pie-shaped segment of the circle remains. This isolated design section can easily and accurately be drawn and enlarged.

FIGURE 2-7   *Left:* mechanical copy of a rubbing made by enlarging the circular motif and finding the repeat. *Right:* segment of the central design, which has been enlarged and traced to make a pattern.

A compass and protractor can be used to locate the radii for enlarging the segments. However, the enlargement of the circular petal shape can be made by folding a square of paper. Half of the width of the square is equal to the longest segment. Figure 2-7 illustrates how the repeat is found.

Here is another way to enlarge the circular pattern.

• Cut the paper into a square.

• Fold the paper on the two diagonals, crease it both times, but leave it open in a square.

• Fold the paper in half both ways and leave it open in a square.

• Pencil in a line from the center to the paper's edge along a half-way (not diagonal) crease. Now eight radii divide the points of the flower-like motif, one of which is traced in pencil.

- Make a detail of one branch. Draw one-half of it along the penciled radius line.

- Fold the paper over. Trace the other half, and the points will be symmetrical

To enlarge this, cut a large square bigger than the final size of the circle. Fold on the diagonals, then on the halves to obtain the radii. Use a compass to draw circles in the center to give the edges of the design. Fill in and enlarge the segments free-hand until the pattern is symmetrical and regular. After taping the segment to a window, place tracing, shelf, or typing paper over it. Center on the middle of the segment and trace. Moving the top paper around to center each spoke, continue tracing the pattern. This is the master drawing for a stencil or a tracing onto brown wrapping paper. Tape the motif to the window, pencil marks against the glass. Trace the line with soft pencil or charcoal. This will transfer by tracing with a wide ballpoint onto the background.

All the preparations of cutting, hemming, shrinking, laying on the background color, enlarging the pattern of the design motifs, and making the paper pattern or cartoon have been finished. The rug canvas is ready to be painted.

Painting the Canvas   The thumbnail sketches are guides to tone and pattern. The color placement is arbitrary. Sketches can be made with color crayons, always bearing in mind that some colors are going to be greyed darker or lighter. Small shapes or lines of the complementary color add sparkle to the final rug.

I laid out newspapers on a dining room table, and I applied the base coat to my canvas. Then I drew in the border lines around the grey-green rectangles. The paper cartoons were laid down to see how the 18″ (45 cm.) circles looked. Each was a different design, with the pointed angular one for the center and largest rectangle. At both ends a chevron was drawn to attract the eye toward the central patterns by repetition of the angles. (Figure 2-8 shows a section of the painted floorcloth.)

In Colonial times a varnish coat was applied between each layer of color after it dried. This prolonged the durability of the cloth. However, I chose to paint two base coats of the greyed pink latex, then applied accent colors using the smallest chisel-edged flat brush, which was the same width as the

FIGURE 2-8 Section of the painted floorcloth.

lines. To obtain straight lines along the edges of the rug and the borders, I rubbed masking tape down and painted in the darkest color last. The dark color against the medium light tone had to be a straight edge because it stood out by contrast.

Finishing the rug required two coats of Varathane. This clear, lustrous finish—desirable on heavily used floorcloths—can be applied by roller on a long hallway rug. Moving the roller at a moderate speed helps to avoid frothing or air bubbles which show in the finished film.

I chose to brush on the finish using a "follow-through" motion during the brush stroke. It's an easy technique. The rug was laid on the garage floor over protective newspapers. I began the motion without touching the cloth at first; then the tip of the brush lightly released the plastic varnish onto the surface. As I brushed on the varnish, I stroked away from my body without slowing or stopping the motion. Few brush marks show this way. Each successive stroke overlaps the previous one and is applied in the same horizontal direction. The rug should dry for twenty-four hours between coats. Each coat should be lightly sanded when dry and the dust wiped off so the finish adheres well to the surface.

Cleaning the brushes. If you plan to use the brushes again soon, they can be suspended in old cans or jars full of the correct solvent. Latex and acrylics are water soluble. Paint thinner cleans plastic varnish brushes. By swishing the brushes in hot water or thinner, most of the color comes out. To protect the bristles, wrap newspaper around them and secure it with a rubber band. This keeps the bristles from curling.

After all the water-base painting is done, rinse the brushes thoroughly. Dry them with paper towels, then wash them in warm water and soap. Rinse again thoroughly, making sure all paint is out of the brush, especially up near the metal holder. Cut pieces of light cardboard to lay over the bristles to keep them flat and protected in storage. Keep your brushes covered and they'll last for years.

The Finished Floorcloth

You can now try the rug on the floor and decide if a rubber pad is needed underneath to keep it from slipping. Smaller rugs may be anchored by cementing scraps of rubber bathmats underneath. I bought remnant rug backing at a carpet discount store. Now I have a rug to remind me of my walk down the street where Charles Dickens once lived.

PIECED CARPETS

There are other ways to make an inexpensive room-size carpet or area rug. You can design a pieced carpet from new carpet scraps. Carpet scraps are available in many fibers, textures, and colors: long wool shags, long twilled shags, shiny plush pile, indoor–outdoor carpeting, short shags, sheep skin, and long furry pile. Most of us have cut out pictures and pasted them together. Using this same collage technique, we can easily make a rug with cloth backing, rug scraps, and a latex-based, multi-purpose adhesive.

Judy Miller Johnson

Judy Miller Johnson is a printmaker who sends her etchings, woodcuts, and serigraphs to local and regional competitive exhibitions. She also exhibits her rugs in an invitational sale held in her home twice a year. The rugs on exhibit have prompted some people to commission her for custom-made rugs, which are priced by the square foot. Judy got started in rugmaking when, dissatisfied with the choices in the local carpet stores, she decided to make her own rugs.

I recently visited Judy's home to see her rugs. The family room, which is two steps below the dining room, overlooks a grassy yard, a fish pond, and a redwood deck area bordered by pots of bright red geraniums. The browns and beiges of her wall-to-wall rug flow away from the comfortable couch like a wandering brook. A variegated shag in dark burnt orange adds a colorful, textured accent in a few areas of this rug (13′ × 17′, or 396 cm. × 518 cm.). Judy's two children romp and play on this earth-colored rug, which doesn't show dust and wear as quickly as lighter colors would.

In the living room, an area rug in various reds accents the Danish modern furniture. Another rug of yellow and green shag scraps contrasts with the short plush pile of the other spring colors in the bedroom. Sunlight bounces off the sculptured surfaces in a rhythmic flow.

Judy said that planning her family room rug was an evolutionary process. It developed as the carpet was constructed. This method required more time and concentration than the predetermined plan used to make the yellow and green area rug. The 10′ × 7′ (304 cm. × 213 cm.) carpet required about sixty hours of working time. A quick summary of Judy's working methods may encourage you to try making this type of rug.

Making a Rug Collage

First, measure your room. Add 2″ (5 cm.) for a border on all sides. Cut and sew cotton duck canvas to size. Fold back the 2″ border and then glue it down with adhesive. Lay the rug backing out on newspapers to dry.

The materials you will need to make a rug collage are:

- jute burlap or cotton duck canvas for rug backing; 39″ × 78″ (1 m. × 2 m.)
- 6 cardboard squeegees, 3″ × 6″ (7.5 cm. × 15 cm.)
- 1 pint multi-purpose latex adhesive
- razor-sharp mat knife
- pencil and indelible marking pen
- sketch paper
- brown paper bags for stencil patterns used in cutting rug scrap shapes
- glue or tape, used to hold stencil shapes together
- rug scraps (choose contrasts of texture and color)—A checkerboard patchwork design is easily cut, arranged by contrasts and made for the first rug.
- newspaper for protecting work surface
- rubber gloves for applying adhesive

The collage should take about eight hours. Be sure you work near an open window or in a well-ventilated area.

Designing the Pattern

Select pieces of long shag or a combination of high–low shag and loop for best results. The long pile will overlap joints and hide less-than-skillful cutting or gluing, as well as adding texture in pattern and color development, depending on the amount of pieces available. Often colors may be selected from one multi-colored carpet's range of colors. Solid color carpet scraps echo colors of the mixture and contrast visually to establish a color pattern. A monochromatic color scheme in the brown family from light to medium to dark is an easy carpet to make for a first attempt.

Lay out the areas of the carpet to feel the compatibility of the colors and to judge the relative amounts of each color you'll need. Decide in the beginning which color will predominate and which will be repeated in smaller amounts. Make sure the nap all runs the same way, as light reflects differently off pile, depending on the direction in which it falls.

23

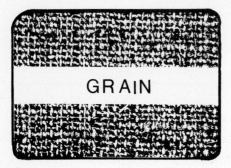

GRAIN

When working with a sketch, enlarge it and make the cartoon or rug design on heavy paper or grocery sacks. Draw the cartoon exactly to the size of the finished rug with a waterproof marking pen. The cartoon must be marked on the reverse side for the design to face the direction you had planned.

Cut each pattern segment apart, marking each pattern piece both "front" and "back" and also indicating on the back what color of rug material it's intended for. You might also mark the grain line, as in a dress pattern, on all segments before cutting apart the design.

With grain consistent, place the rug material face down on a cutting board and lay the appropriate pattern piece on it with the "back" side up. Trace around the pattern with your indelible marker. Carefully mark each segment.

Once each segment is marked you can begin cutting. Using a sharp mat knife, cut each piece from the back, taking care to cut around *outside* the line.

Once all the pieces are cut, it's a good idea to lay the rug out as it's supposed to look before you glue, in case you need to make any changes. Fit the edges together without gaps. Even a quarter-inch, or 6-mm., gap shows as a line in the finished carpet (Figure 2-9). Be sure you've cut each shape to fit.

Gluing the Pieces   Make a spreader from a piece of cardboard or mat board, about 3″ × 6″ (7.5 cm. × 15 cm.). Using this cardboard squeegee eliminates brush or roller clean-up. You'll also be able to spread a thicker layer of adhesive with this homemade tool.

Cover the exposed pile on the cut edges of each carpet piece to prevent the glue from smearing on it.

Lay the canvas backing on a clean, flat surface in a well-ventilated area, someplace where it won't be disturbed for several days.

You'll be filling in one edge at a time. Spread a thick, even coat of multi-purpose latex adhesive, following the directions on the can, on one big piece at a time with your cardboard squeegee. Wipe away all excess at edges. Do the large areas first; you can insert small pieces into the larger areas. Press each piece down firmly on the backing. If the piece won't lie flat, walk all over it until it's glued into place. Or weight it down. You can also try sitting on it while working on another section.

If you've accidentally dropped glue on your rug, don't panic. If it's a small drip, merely cut off the affected tuft. If it's a larger area, remove it at once and cut another replacement. Keep your hands as clean as possible.

Whenever you get tired, stop working and avoid mistakes.

Variations This type of collage can be used to make large wall hangings. Areas of the wall hanging can have long knotted pile set into shapes on the plush carpet, with painted areas for a striking contrast. An electric rug punch can make looped areas. A wall rug allows you more freedom to vary fibers, to experiment in shapes with holes or with other geometric and biomorphic shapes, because you need not worry that someone will trip. Diamonds, dodecahedrons, waves, shells, and other forms can inspire new ideas. This quickly and easily made carpet or area rug brings enjoyment because of the variation in texture. Hence its name.

Incidentally, the moths will probably never eat this carpet. Commercially woven and fabricated wool carpets are moth-proofed at the factory.

FELTED RUGS

Once upon a time, long, long ago a woman was washing her clothes in the Nile River in Egypt. There, among the papyrus where she worked, she noticed masses of soft whitish material floating in the eddies of the current and coagulating in the shallow pools. She scooped up this soft substance, placed it on a rock, then turned back to do her laundering. After the heat of the sun had dried the pulpy mass, when she lifted it off the rock, she found that she had a white, hard, thin cast of the top of the rock. She had paper!

How true this and other legends are doesn't really matter. The process of felting is an old method of making a material for many uses. For example, tapa cloth consists of the beaten fibers from the inner lining of bark, with water to aid the process. Paper is macerated wet cotton fibers that are dried on a large screen. Felt is made of teased woolen fleece, usually from sheep. All these fabrics are made by wetting layers of natural materials with fibrous or thread-like characteristics, then beating and applying heat to them. The process of felting results in thick or thin water-resistant material. It may be dried flat for rugs, blankets, or clothing fabric. It may also be shaped over forms to make hats and other objects.

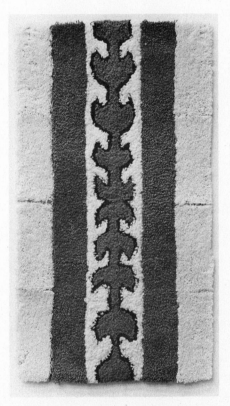

FIGURE 2-9 Pieced carpet showing a poor joint—electric punch hook and pieced carpet rug, 36″ × 24″ (90 cm. × 60 cm.), Joy Sinderson, 1977.

Two areas in the world famous for felted fabrics are India and Russia. The natural, light-colored woolen Numdah rugs from India are embroidered with a floral motif in a couching stitch. They have been imported to the United States from the Numdah area of India, especially since the sixties. Figure 2-10 shows an example of this type of felted rug, with its pattern worked in dark, medium, and light colors using a

FIGURE 2-10   Numdah felted rug, wool, 69″ x 43″ (175 cm. x 109 cm.).

linear stitch and its tree of life design. This rug can be seen in the color insert, Plate 13. Feltmaking has become a highly developed art in the Russian state of Georgia, which borders on Czechoslovakia. Its cold climate requires warm clothing, rugs to cover the legs when driving carts and sleighs, and blankets for the people and their animals.

In the twentieth century, mechanical methods were developed to produce felt rapidly. With technological advances in chemical dyes, felt could be colored more permanently. Still today there are artists who enjoy making felt in a more primitive manner, as well as artists who have gone beyond the process that creates the material commonly in use these days.

Samantha Cochran

Samantha Cochran, a college student, sells her homespun yarn and other fiber art. Her baskets and weavings have been exhibited in Pasadena and Cupertino, California. Tired of spinning, she wondered what she could do with her leftover fleece. Seeing felted rugs in import shops in San Francisco gave her the idea to try a new technique. She learned to make felt from Maggie Brosnan, her textile arts instructor.

Felting is easily done at home with simple equipment. For rugmaking purposes, it's best to work in sections or make small area rugs. Samantha likes to create modular units of felt which she later pieces together like a quilt.

Where does Samantha get her designs and pattern ideas?—from "nature and science books; cave art, too. Sometimes I cut out sections from colored photographs in magazines—anything that has interesting color combinations. I like to juxtapose bold contrasting areas or remarkably subtle ones in a nonobjective way. Large companies send brochures and advertising materials to potential clients and stockholders. The quality of the photographs is excellent. For example, in the background of a photo of a steel mill worker, the colors of the molten metal are already organized and beautiful. They might inspire a pattern of warm colors for my felted sections."

Making a Felted Rug

A sectional rug is easily made of felt. Each piece can be embroidered or, by using dyed fleece, can have areas of color incorporated into the overall pattern. The irregularity of the edges of the felted section can be emphasized in the joinings or cut into precise geometric shapes. Pictures of American piecework quilts can inspire a pattern of shapes and arrangements that can be adapted to your design (Figure 2-11).

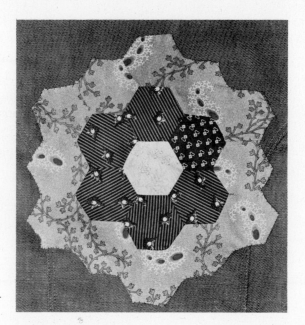

FIGURE 2-11   American piecework quilt patch, printed textiles, 8″ (20 cm.) hexagon; c. 1907, artist unknown.

The supplies that will be needed for felting a small rug or pillow top are:

- 1 pound or 1/2 kilo of wool fleece, which has been teased by hand or drum carded
- a needle and thread or several safety pins
- two pieces of muslin or an old pillow case, about 25″ × 25″ (62 cm. × 62 cm.)
- a washboard
- heavy mallet or rock
- five large safety pins
- a dishwashing pan
- scissors

Making a Section of Felt   Making the sandwich of cloth and fleece is easy to do. Lay one piece of muslin down and place the fiber on top, teased or fluffed up to about 12″ high (Figure 2-12). The mass will be about 18″ high. For added color, loosen and fluff any pre-dyed fibers and lay them gently on top of the white fleece. Any decorative yarn is placed down last, with a very thin membrane of plain fleece spread over it to keep it from moving out of position while you wash it. Then the top piece of muslin completes the sandwich. (If you don't have muslin and you're making the felt in a pillow case, slit open the closed end so you have a tube; then carefully lay the teased fleece, topped with your design of colored fleece, inside the tube.)

28

FIGURE 2-12 Fleece is teased to about 12″ high.

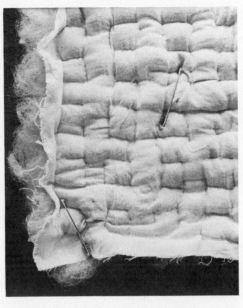

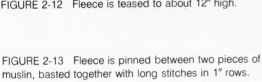

FIGURE 2-13 Fleece is pinned between two pieces of muslin, basted together with long stitches in 1″ rows.

Next you'll want to compact the fibers. Starting at the center, pin through the sandwich with a large safety pin. Then fasten each corner. You can then begin to sew through the layers if you're working with two separate pieces of muslin. Thread your needle with a knot at one end. Using a long basting stitch, 2″ (5 cm.), sew several 1″ rows in each direction. This holds all the layers together (Figure 2-13). For the pillow case method, stitch or pin the ends closed.

The actual felting process takes place because wool shrinks from the application of boiling hot water and the shock of cold water. The fibers, which look like barbed wires when magnified, shrink and interface into a compact mass. First, pour boiling water over your fleece; then add a little soap, using a spoon or tongs to push your fleece around. Rinse with cold water (Figure 2-14). All this water can be saved and

FIGURE 2-14 Fleece is washed in hot, soapy water alternated with cold.

recycled if you live in a drought area. Repeat the hot, soapy water washing and cold water rinsing to shrink and mat the fibers together. Then wring the fleece out.

Then beat the fleece. If you have an old-fashioned washboard, scrub the sandwiched mass of fleece on its rippled surface. You can also place the fleece bundle on a concrete walk or garage floor. Pound it with a rock, mallet, hammer, or wooden spoon, or even stamp on it with your foot. This beating interlaces the fibers and compresses them into felt.

Take the sandwiched felt back to the washing area and rinse it in cold water again. Roll it like a sleeping bag and wring it dry (Figure 2-15) to mat the fibers more thoroughly. Open it up. Hold it up to the light. Look and see how evenly it is matted: Light will show through the less dense areas. Pull or beat the denser mass to even up the felted layer.

Now you're almost finished. Before the stitches come out and the cloth layers are removed, dry this mass. If you put it into an automatic dryer immediately, you'll waste a lot of heat because the mass is still very wet, even after wringing. To avoid waste, place the felt on a fluffy bath towel or absorbent paper and dry it like a sweater. Or, place the felted sandwich down on a towel, and put another towel and a book or weight on top. It should be dried flat. After a few hours, change the towels or heavy paper and weight the top board down again. Remove the weights after a while and let the felt dry in the sun or automatic dryer. The dryer, by the way, will really help to compact the fibers if you're looking for a tougher felt.

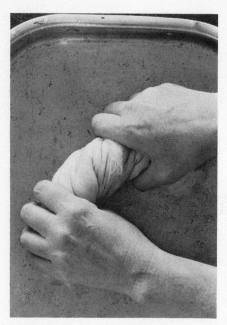

FIGURE 2-15 Fleece is rolled up and wrung out.

FIGURE 2-16 Remove muslin when fleece is dry.

To finish the felt process, remove the thread or pins and cloth (Figure 2-16). Iron it smooth if desired. Figure 2-17 shows what the finished sample looks like. The whole process takes about three hours, including drying time. No great strength in your hands or arms is necessary for this process. No fine finger dexterity is needed if you use safety pins. So, anyone from a child to a grandparent can make felted rugs.

FIGURE 2-17   Finished sample of felted piece.

Large felted fiber pieces can become wall hangings and ceiling covers. These tapestry-like hangings can be a soft, warm, and colorful complement to contemporary architecture, especially well-suited to office buildings of concrete, steel, and glass.

Robert Freimark   San Jose State University art professor Robert Freimark uses the Czechoslovakian Art Protis method for felted tapestry making. "Czechoslovakian Romance," which can be seen on the front cover of this book, is the first tapestry he made in 1970. It is from an edition of twenty works, all the same size and color, made by him personally at the Art Protis factory in Europe. He describes its content as "an expression of my feelings as an American in a foreign element. You become more aware of being an American when overseas." He has since then made more than two hundred tapestries, which can be seen in the National Gallery in Prague, the Smithsonian Institution in the United States, and the British Museum. The Brenton Bank of Des Moines, Iowa, American Micro-Systems, Inc. in Santa Clara, California, and the Desert Museum in Palms Springs also house some of his special tapestries.

Freimark has been returning to Czechoslovakia annually since 1972 to produce his felted tapestries. A skilled lithographer and printmaker before he was invited to try this process, he approaches this art–craft medium as an artist in charge of every creative step. As he says, "The process is related to painting. The felt looks like water color or dye color painted on an absorbent surface . . . I make hundreds of sketches during the year. I order materials and have my plans drawn out so I don't waste time when I arrive there." You may wonder, after all the sketching and planning, how many tapestries he works on at the same time. He usually has several large ones going simultaneously. And he says, "If I can't see a thing clearly in my mind, I let it percolate. If you force it, it looks forced."

Freimark had planned another of his works for months—see Plate 16 in the color insert—a section of which is shown in Figure 2-18. He said, "I kept seeing the advertise-

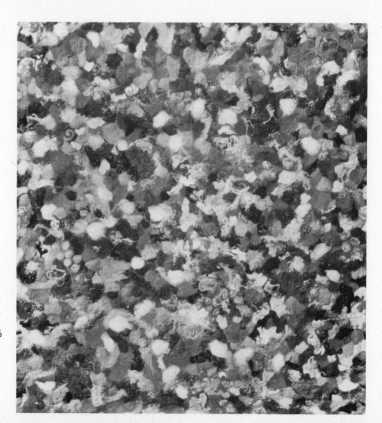

FIGURE 2-18 Detail of "Flowers Wired All Over the World," 108″ x 88″ (274 cm. x 223.5 cm.), Robert Freimark, photograph courtesy of the artist.

ment, 'Flowers Wired All Over the World,' and visualizing that effect." The finished tapestry shows us how he decided it should look.

Extending the Felting   The Art Protis process of creating tapestries that Robert Freimark uses, which employs products from the felting industry, is not available to artists in any factory in the United States. It was invented in the late 1960s by the Wool Institute of Brno, Czechoslovakia. This new textile machine is power-driven. Woolen fleece is blown out of an oriface into a thin blanket, which falls on a flat surface. Pressure and heat crush the long fibers into large, thin translucent sheets. This fleece is pre-dyed with one of one hundred and twenty standard colors. Because the sheet is thin (1/2″ or 1.5 cm.) and translucent, it can be cut and stacked in layers. The translucent quality permits gradation of color tones.

A cardboard base is then placed on a large 8′ × 10′ (240 cm. × 300 cm.) table on rollers. The cotton or linen backing sheet for the wall hanging is laid down. About seven layers of dyed felt are built up in the pattern. Other textile-related materials may be incorporated into the design.

You cannot step back and view these large forms as you would easel paintings. Instead, a plexiglass sheet is placed over the felts and the artist climbs a 12′ ladder and looks down to see if the areas of color and pattern are complete. Any weak areas of little tone contrast can then be seen and corrections made.

Assistants sew this 4″ (approx. 10 cm.) layer of felt to the cloth backing sheet with a long running stitch (later removed). The felt is placed on a moving bed to be carried through a pressure and heat treatment to the sewing arm. A thousand needles, 1/8″ apart and operating independently of each other because the felt is uneven, sew a zigzag stitch through the entire tapestry. This zigzag stitch adds a subtle texture when examined closely. It holds the felt to the backing. Sewing also prevents sagging when the large, heavy tapestry is hung on a wall.

A cotton dust jacket is sewn on the back to finish off the tapestry. Then a 1/2″-wide, woven tape is sewn across the top two inches of the back to permit insertion of a strip of wood for a hidden hanger. Each piece has a woven registration identification sewn onto it with the name, edition number, fiber content, artist's name, and Czechoslovakian registration number.

When the rolls of tapestry arrive at his home in California, Freimark evaluates each again. Some tapestries have metal or other materials added to enrich the fiber surface with the contrast of material, texture, color, and pattern. Once in a great while, a felted piece may be scrapped. Because the dye is permanent, any piece to be hung in a public place may be fire-proofed to meet local city building codes.

This extension of felting requires the Art Protis process. However, some techniques that the rugmaker can experiment with are building up the rug with felted thin layers of dyed fleece, and sewing the backing in an all-over regular repeated stitch using a contrasting thread. Sewing tapes on one end permits hanging the rug, and identifying each piece with title, artist's name, fiber content, and size adds a professional finishing touch. If you run out of materials or patience, the felted piece can become a pillow top, a stuffed toy, a pocket, or a framed picture. Pieces of felt can be combined with other techniques, like crochet or latch hook.

You, as the rugmaker, have endless variations available to you. You are limited only by your skills and your eagerness to explore new ideas.

CHAPTER THREE

Traditional American Rugs

The traditional American rugs evolved from the knowledge and traditions that the early settlers of the United States brought with them when they sailed to the New World. The Pilgrims brought precious cloth from Europe, as well as a knowledge of weaving, plaiting, knotting, crocheting, knitting, spinning, and dyeing. When materials were unavailable to them, they adapted what they had, using and reusing cloth for strands in braided, crocheted, or rag rugs; they also invented substitutes.

The native American Indians, using indigenous materials, also had knowledge of and traditions in lacing, plaiting, coiling, and weaving. The Indian civilizations of Central and South America had been making beautifully designed cloth long before the arrival of the Spanish explorers. The adventurers who migrated from Mexico to the southwestern United States brought new skills in weaving to the Hopi and Navajo Indians of the Southwest.

Out of roots such as these grew a uniquely American style of rugmaking. This chapter will give you some examples of how several artists have designed and made such traditional hooked, braided, woven, coiled, crocheted, and knitted rugs.

FIGURE 3-1   Early American style hooked rug, 36″ x 21″ (91 cm. x 53 cm.); Peninsula Rug Guild, 1973, collection of Caroline Wigginton.

HOOKED RAG RUGS

Annie Bird Plumb   Annie Bird Plumb lives in an old New England farmhouse, built before the Civil War and located in Prospect, Connecticut. During the unusually long, cold New England winters, she keeps herself busy raising indoor flowers and hooking rugs. At first the rugs were for the men to wipe their feet on when they came in from the barns or from the cold storage cellars.

When she travelled to the city, Annie bought simple patterns that were preprinted on burlap. Food and grain stores sold patterns, such as "Grapes" or "Log Cabins," and Montgomery Ward Catalogues were full of stamped rug patterns.* People didn't have washing machines fifty-eight years

*Today, commercial patterns are referred to by the designer's name. For instance, rugs and wall hangings designed by Alexander Calder—the noted American sculptor who invented the mobile—and hooked by his wife or friends are known as "Calders." His initials "A.C." are hooked into the background.

36

ago, so Annie took old burlap feed sacks and washed them by hand. She then tacked them to an old, broken mirror frame, enlarged the picture of an embroidery pattern, and copied it on the burlap. Old woolen clothes cut into strips were used for hooking with a metal crochet hook into a straight loop pattern on the burlap. She worked from the top side of the fabric, leaving the loops uncut and about 1/2″ high. She used strips of 12″ to 15″ long and about 1/4″ wide. She cut these strips by hand with a very sharp pair of scissors. The looping process involved such close work (every hole in the burlap had a loop) that the side pressure kept the loops in place without the need of a latex backing, which is commonly used today for punch or loop hooking. And she used a rug pad underneath the finished rug. It was a long, hard process (although after twenty-five years of hand-cutting, she rewarded herself with a heavy-duty strip rug cutter that enabled her to work with wider strips).

With her artistic nature, Annie soon grew tired of the artificial-looking rug patterns and went to her brother-in-law, Mortimer Quirke, for help. A commercial artist, he was able to advise her about how to make flowers that were more

FIGURE 3-2 Early American style hand-hooked rug cut from woolen fabric strips, Annie Bird Plumb, c. 1920; photograph courtesy of Ellen B. Quirke.

FIGURE 3-3 Hummingbird and flower hand-hooked wall decoration, 52″ x 28″ (105 cm. x 70 cm.), Annie Bird Plumb, designed by Mortimer F. Quirke; photograph courtesy of Ellen B. Quirke.

"real" and colorful, like the ones she loved so much that grew around her farm. He showed her why photos of flowers in a Burpee's Seed Catalogue looked so real—at least five different shades of the same color were needed to give the flower more form and to make it look more rounded and alive.

She experimented, finding that with some fabric colors, such as green, it was possible to get as many as eleven different shades ranging from warm and bright to cold and dull; with other colors, such as pink and red woolen cloth, color variation was more limited. She used men's old pants for darker border colors and went to rug mills in Rhode Island to buy remnants and blanket mill ends. She always worked with fabrics rather than yarns, and she discovered which weaves worked best. Being innovative, Annie learned how to dye her own fabrics in kettles with mordants.

38

For years, Annie worked at her rugmaking and became very proficient. She even immortalized her quaint white farmhouse with the red barn in a hooked rug (Figure 3-4), which she originally intended as a floor covering but turned into a wall hanging when she discovered that "it's too good to wipe your feet on."

When her children grew up and moved away, Annie was left in the rambling old farmhouse with many empty rooms. One day, she decided to refurbish the front room, a parlor that hadn't been used in years except for formal occasions. It seemed to her a wonderful way to invest her time because, as she said, "I like to work in the winter on something that's cheerful when it's cold and icy out." She brought her Victorian furniture down from the attic—including Hitchcock chairs that had been presented to her grandfather by "old man Hitchcock" himself as a wedding present. And, to add the finishing touch to the room, she decided to hook a rug.

FIGURE 3-4 New England farmhouse, hand-hooked wall decoration of cut fabric strips, 24″ x 36″ (60 cm. x 90 cm.), Annie Bird Plumb, 1957, designed by Mortimer F. Quirke; photograph courtesy of Ellen B. Quirke.

Making a Hooked Rug After mastering the art of making hooked rugs, Annie helped Jane Fowler, a painter, get started. Jane cuts her wool rug strips with a machine and hand hooks her original designs on burlap or monks cloth. Figure 3-5 shows one of the designs, and Figure 3-6, the steps she follows in hand hooking a rug.

FIGURE 3-5 "Angel" rug, hand-hooked on burlap backing thumbtacked and tied to rug frame, Jane Fowler, 1976; photograph courtesy of John Pirro.

FIGURE 3-6a Hand hook pulls a loop of cut fabric up through the weave of burlap from the underneath strand.

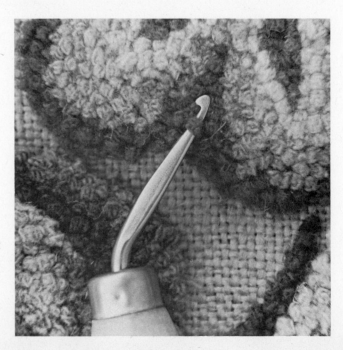

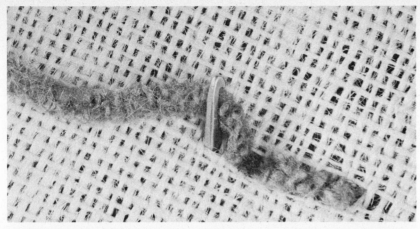

FIGURE 3-6b   Underside of burlap, showing the hook grasping a thin strand of fabric.

FIGURE 3-6c   Side view of hooking. Loops are placed close together. Side pressure holds them securely.

FIGURE 3-6d   Shading of flower and leaves. Use five values of one hue to give form to flower or leaves. Hooking follows the contour of the shapes. Lighter value of green on leaves on right indicates highlights.

"Primitive type hooked rugs," Jane says, "simple and reminiscent of old and modern starkness, are my best designs. Because hooking is a simple, creative craft, I taught all my children to hook rugs or pictures when they were five years old. I treasure all these funny, simple designs they drew and hooked on burlap, choosing their own colors and exaggerating patterns as only children can."

To make a hand-hooked rug, the following materials will be needed:

- burlap backing
- frame
- woolen cloth
- sharp scissors or a heavy-duty strip rag cutter
- sketch paper
- shelf paper or large paper for the pattern cartoon
- a pounce wheel or tracing wheel
- fabric carbon or chalk dust pounce bag
- indelible black or grey marking pen (for drawing outline on burlap)
- heavy-duty sewing thread or button hole thread
- needle or heavy-duty sewing machine (for stitching burlap together for a large room-size rug)
- rug binding (to sew around turned-back edge)
- rug yarn of border color or very thin rug strips (to overcast around folded edges)
- 64-72 loops per square inch: 1/8″ (4 mm.) wide fabric strip × 1/8″ (4 mm.) high

Perhaps the best way to demonstrate how to use the materials to make a hand-hooked rug is to follow the steps Annie did in making her rug.

Designing the Rug   Once Annie had decided to make her rug, the logical person to make the pattern was her brother-in-law, affectionately called Mert. A collaboration was born between Annie, the craftsperson, and Mert Quirke, the artist. The results of that collaboration can be seen in the color insert, Plate 18, and in Figure 3-7.

Mert asked Annie what kind of a rug she wanted.

"You know me, Mert. I don't want any of these crazy modern designs. I like flowers."

"Well," Mert said, "how big do you want the rug?"

FIGURE 3-7 Hooked rug with borders of randomly scattered flower motifs and directional hooking, 156″ x 132″ (396 cm. x 335 cm.), Annie Bird Plumb, 1959–1961, designed by Mortimer F. Quirke; photograph courtesy of Ellen Bird Quirke.

"I'd like it as big as the room, but I don't know how my hands'll be 'cause I think it'll take a couple of years, and I only work in the wintertime."

So Mert sat down with a paper and pencil, and Annie sat down next to him. "Well, let's see what we can give you, Annie. Do you know how big the room is?"

"Sure, Mert! It isn't even straight. I'd like something like eleven by twelve, eleven by thirteen, something like that. I want it to cover the floor because it's got those great big wide boards with the cracks between, and the dust gets in between them." So it was settled—the rug would be 11′ × 13′ (330 cm. × 390 cm.).

Mert Quirke was familiar with Persian rugs, with their center motifs and two border rug bands, a rug-on-a-rug-on-a-rug concept. That seemed to him a good idea for Annie Plumb's rug because if the proportions were figured out correctly, at any place that she stopped she would have a good-looking completed rug with a patterned center and borders. The next time he saw Annie, Mert said, "I knew you liked roses and pansies, Annie, and those colored flowers will look best on a dark background—maybe black or grey. So let's make a nice-size rug and use your favorite flowers. I'll start with flowers in the middle and something besides plain edges that we usually use because if you work on plain borders for too long a time on too wide an area, you'll get tired, and you

FIGURE 3-8 Detail of flower motif of hooked rug.

might run out of colored material. Then you'll have to dye in the middle of winter and that would be a mess."

Mert sketched a center section of 5′ × 7′ (150 cm. × 210 cm.) with three 2′ (60 cm.) borders around that.

"Annie, let's do something different with the outside border. You like dogwood because it grows around the farm. So we'll make the outside border of dogwood blossoms and the state flower, mountain laurel. With the pansies and roses in the center, you'll have bright color in the middle and bright color in the border. I really think that bright colors in the other bands will make the rug too busy. I saw that you had some nice grey flannel rags in your rug pile, and if you make the other two bands a middle grey and a darker grey, the neutral middle background will be a good accent for the bright flower colors. And also, the furniture will probably look a little better on the neutral areas of the rug."

Soon after, Mert went to New York to look more closely at rugs in the Metropolitan Museum of Art and other places and share his ideas with Annie. The middle bands of grey in Annie's rug pattern ended up with a cornflower design of light grey on darker grey and of medium grey on the darkest grey in a scattered design. The design was not drawn on the burlap. My father said to Aunt Annie, "Whenever you get tired of doing the grey background, hook in a flower in darker grey." With forty years of experience in hooking, she was used to filling in another leaf here and there, "to carry your eye around the design."

Making the Pattern and Transferring to Backing

Mert next took a piece of butcher paper (the kind that Annie used for wrapping vegetables) and sketched with a soft lead pencil. He put the central design slightly off-center because placing the largest flower off to the side gave the basically symmetrical design more subtle variety. Also, if Aunt Annie stopped at any border, it would look complete. Because of thread count and breakage of the burlap, it's easier to work asymmetrical patterns if you run out of color. One flower shape can be hooked in a smaller size, and a leaf shape can be added for balance.

On this paper pattern, Mert used a pounce wheel (or tracing wheel) which is like a pie edger. It punched little holes in the paper over the line design as it was rolled along. Then he took chalk dust, wrapped in several thickness of cheesecloth or an old stocking, and transferred the yellow chalk dust through the holes onto the burlap backing. (The dust bag is called a pounce bag because it is pounced or bounced up and down in order to sift the chalk dust through the holes in the

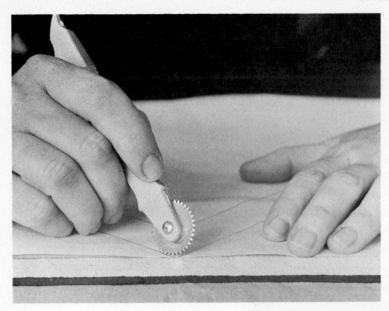

FIGURE 3-9a Tracing wheel marks the cartoon placed over a dressmaker's carbon tracing tissue.

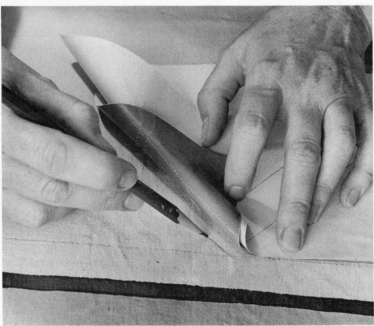

FIGURE 3-9b Pencil lightly marks the design after the tracing wheel has dotted the line on the canvas.

paper.) Then, the design was drawn on the burlap. Mert used an indelible black marking pen.

Hooking The base of the rug was three widths of burlap, but two of the widths were not sewn on until the middle portion was completed over a rug frame. This middle section took one whole winter; the other two bands were sewn on by machine. The artist got out his ruler and measured out the 2′ bands after the three widths had been sewn together. There was a 1/2″ section left between each band for a color accent strip. One was a grey-blue-green band; the next was a maroon band; and the last was a yellow-orange-gold color. The grey border took another winter to complete.

For the outside border, Annie used Grandpa Plumb's black serge wedding-funeral-church suits from the attic. When she ran out of funeral rags for the outside border, she had to dye more black rags. The 22″ × 18″ (55 cm. × 45 cm.) area that remained had been left with an irregular edge so that the old color and the new color would blend together when the area was filled in. After the fabric was dyed and hung out to dry, Annie said, "Oh dear, I should have kept it in longer!" The new dark color didn't match. She re-dyed it in the spring of the third year, and today, you can't tell where the new corner is.

Annie, who was concerned about having to stop working at some point, completed her room-size rug in 1960. Since then, she has made twenty-six smaller rugs. They all reflect her love of flowers, birds, and life in general.

Finishing the Rug   There are three ways to finish a hooked rug: overcast the hem, use rug binding tape, and overcast the edges. The fastest finish for the edges (though not the most durable hem) is to turn the burlap backing under and hem, using a long cross stitch (see Figure 3-10). The overlapped corners make a slight bump on the surface. This is a suitable way to edge a rug which you plan to use as a central motif in a braided rug. The rug can be enjoyed and used while you braid. The last rows of loops wear out quickly, in about five years. A better and more durable edge is made using rug binding tape. (See Figure

FIGURE 3-10   Quick finish for hand-hooked rug. Turn the burlap backing under and hem.

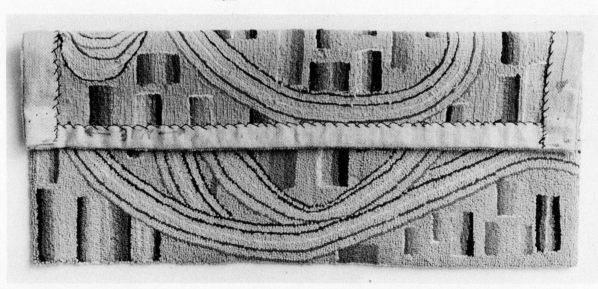

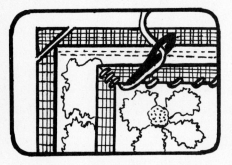

3-11.) A miter or 45° diagonal line is drawn on the face of the rug. Some fabric is left between the loops and the angle. Fold the cloth along the line to the back. The fold of the fabric should not twist the edge row of the loops. Keep the cloth fold centered at the corner. Fold the long edges to the back and pin. Hand stitch rug binding tape to burlap and to the rug with strong buttonhole thread or linen rug thread. The rug binding tape may be sewn on the face side with a sewing machine. Leave 1/4″ (.7 cm.) between the loop and the tape for the fold. Then miter, cut off excess burlap, fold back, pin, and

FIGURE 3-11a Begin sequence for a mitered corner. Draw the line at a 45° angle across the end of the fabric. Leave some fabric between loops.

FIGURE 3-11b Fold miter back on diagonal. Be careful not to twist the edge row of loops.

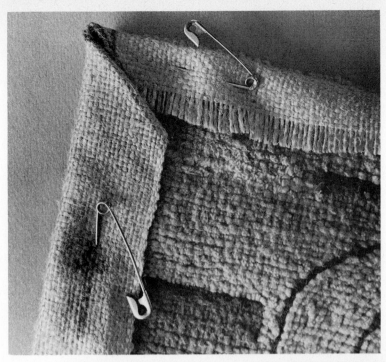

FIGURE 3-11c   Pin rug binding tape to back.

FIGURE 3-11d   Hand stitch in place, to burlap and into the back of the carpet.

FIGURE 3-11e   Finish edges with a whip or overcast stitch with yarn that blends. A blanket stitch may be made along the edge instead.

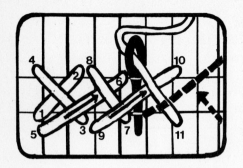

stitch with a running stitch or a long legged cross stitch. This is the usual ending for the rug.

For more durability, finish edges with an overcast stitch, a whip stitch, or a blanket stitch. This edge made of yarn the color and value of the background takes the wear off the pile. The edge can be replaced when frayed. Your heirloom can be passed along to your heirs.

BRAIDED RAG RUGS

Another traditional American rug, one that is still quite popular, is the braided rag rug. This casual sturdy type of rug is well-suited to recreation areas and children's rooms. Smaller braided rugs can become placemats and seat covers on trunks and benches.

Making a Braided Rug

In order to make a braided rug, you will need to have the following materials and simple equipment on hand:

- sharp scissors or rug strip cutting machine
- strong fingers or three triangular metal braid aids
- 100% wool cloth of firm close weave in two colors and a plaid, check or tweed—to calculate, figure that 1 yard (1 m.) of 54″ new woolen material makes approximately one square foot (slightly less than 15 square cm.) of rug braid.
- C-clamp
- tapestry needle or cotter pin
- linen carpet thread
- safety pin

A detail of a rug created by Berkeley Cooper can be seen in Figure 3-12d and in the color insert, Plate 10. Talking with Berkeley about how he made this rug can be helpful to a beginner.

Berkeley Cooper

Berkeley Cooper, a retired foreman in a tool and die making company, braids rugs for fun and profit. It all started when his doctor treated him for phlebitis. What does an active man—the kind who paints the kitchen in one evening as a surprise for his wife—do when confined to a chair for three months with his leg elevated? What does he do during long winter months? Berkeley Cooper used this time to learn how to make Colonial American braided rugs from strips of old clothes and remnants of blankets.

When he was asked about braiding rugs, he said, "I like to watch the rug grow. When people asked me to make them rugs, I realized that I had found a hobby that matched my antique business."

Planning the Shape and Colors

Berkeley began by making a 3′10″ × 6′4″ (115 cm. × 190 cm.) oval rug with braided strips 3/4″ (1.8 cm.) wide. The color of most of his woolen material was a medium warm brown. Other autumn colors—golds, reds, oranges, and brown tweeds—made a warm-colored area rug. He planned the pattern of this rug with a light-colored, hit-and-miss center oval, two rows of darker braid, a medium light hit-or-miss section, another two rows of darker braid, a medium dark section, and a border of darker toned braids. This resulted in the traditional dark braided areas being repeated. The color sequences carried on in the folk craft tradition were comprised of a light strand of one solid color, a medium-toned strand of patterned material, and a dark strand of one solid color family. The dark solid strips of brown ended with black. The light strand started out gold and continued with orange. The patterned strand moved from brick red to maroon. The speckled strand twisted through the braid, creating a nice textural contrast with the solid strands.

Estimating the Amount of Fabric

When the size and shape of the rug were decided, a rough estimate was made of the amount of fabric needed. Each square foot (slightly less than 15 square cm.) of rug requires either 1 lb. (1/2 kg.) or 1 yd. (1 m.) of 54″ new wool material or old coat-weight wool. Berkeley needed about 24 lbs. (12 kg.) or 24 yds. (24 m.) of material for the entire rug.

How do you estimate the amount of each color you'll need? Estimate the length of each strip needed for one row. Approximately one-third to one-half the length of each strip is taken up in braiding, depending on the tightness and tension control of the individual braiding. About 7″ (15–20 cm.) of tapered braid ends the rug. Generally, the following amounts of fabric are required:

- 3′ (90 cm.) × 5′ (150 cm.) uses 8–12 lbs. (4.6 kg.) or 15 yds. (1,250 cm.)

- 4′ (120 cm.) × 6′ (180 cm.) uses 14–18 lbs. (6–8 kg.) or 24 yds. (2,060 cm.)

- 5′ (150 cm.) × 7′ (210 cm.) uses 20–24 lbs. (10–12 kg.) or 35 yds. (3,150 cm.).

For a first rug, the hit-and-miss design is easiest, using the light, medium, and dark strips to control the pattern, rather than trying to plan the design's outcome exactly. Gather your tools and equipment, and you're ready to start.

Preparing the Balls of Woolen Strips

You can purchase an automatic cutting machine at a rug shop or tear strips from tightly woven, heavy-weight woolen cloth. Though it's a simpler process, tearing or cutting your strips crosswise doesn't give you as elastic a braid as cutting the fabric on the bias or diagonal. The crosscut strip is used for the traditional rug.

Berkeley bought his wool from a retail outlet of a woolen mill. It was washed and shrunk by his helpful wife before cutting. Each piece was torn from selvedge to selvedge. A cut was made in the selvedge to make tearing easier. These 1 1/2″ (3.8 cm.) wide strips were pieced by cutting the ends on the diagonal and seaming them together.

Your light, medium, and dark rolls don't have to be the same color, but one strip should be close in value. The other strips are made of random color strips. When you've finished joining your strips, they should be 8′ to 10′ long (3 m.). Roll them and stack them together. The color variations create the hit-and-miss pattern.

Braiding the Three-strand Traditional Braids

Berkeley Cooper does not use the flat triangular braid aids which make braiding easier. He finger-creases the strips flat, folding the edges 1/4″ in toward the center, then folding the strip in half. Berkeley begins by overcasting the top edges of the three strips of material together. Then he turns the seam inside so it will be hidden.

The three strips are secured to the table with a C-clamp. Braiding as one would braid hair, Berkeley moves the outside strands to the center, alternating right and left sides, folding the raw edges of the wool strips in and under.

Braiding close to the clamp, he maintains an even tension. He makes sure the edges are turned all the way to the center so that there are four thicknesses of wool making an even braid. Keeping all the open sides to the same outside makes a more uniform braid and a reversible rug because the joining covers the edges. As Berkeley works, he pulls the braided strip through the clamp to maintain an even tension.

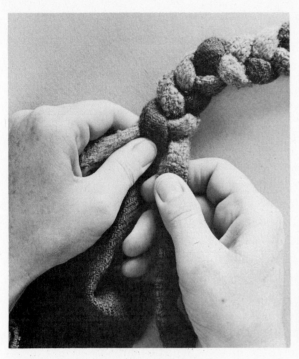

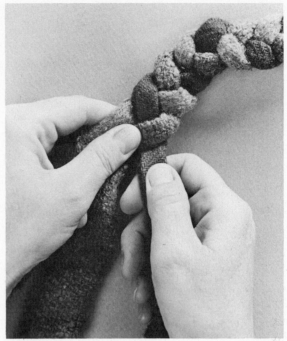

FIGURE 3-12a Folding raw edges of wool strips under and braiding right over left, then left over right.

FIGURE 3-12b Textured strip with raw edges folded into center is braided over the dark center strip. Folded edge is kept to the same side on all strips.

FIGURE 3-12c Lighter strip is braided over center strip to the right and pulled tight.

FIGURE 3-12d Detail of braided rug showing change of colors within braided sections and the tapered edge.

When he stops braiding, he secures the cloth with a safety pin.

Tension problems. Both a tightly braided strand or a loosely braided strand cause problems. The tight braid makes joining difficult and often causes a rippled surface because the braid cannot be eased around corners. A loose, limp braid may ripple because of the strong joining thread. It also permits dirt to penetrate the folds, making cleaning more difficult.

Shaping the Oval

Begin a curved rug at the center, spiralling outward. The rule of thumb is to decide the length and width of the oval rug, then subtract the smaller number from the larger number. This figure gives you the length of the center braid strip. Berkeley's rug is 3′ × 6′ (90 cm. × 180 cm.). The central braid before it was turned was 3′ long (90 cm.). To turn a neat, flat corner, Berkeley marks the end of the center strand of braid with a pin. On the outside of the turn, the outside strand is slightly looser to accommodate the turn. He pins this flat, next to the center. The strand on the inside of the turn is pulled a little tighter than the rest, and is also pinned flat. Usually, one double right-hand braid is enough to turn the braid. If the new row doesn't lie flat against the first, braid and pin another double right-handed joint, ending with a tight left strand.

The open edges on the same outside edge of the braids are covered as braiding progresses.

Joining the Braid

Berkeley joins the braid together by lacing. He uses a double strand of carpet thread or linen lacing thread, about a yard long (1 m.), knotted at the end. A blunt cotter pin, a wide-eyed tapestry needle, or a lacer from a braid kit can be used. He uses a tapestry needle. Pulling the needle through the starting end of the braid hides the knot. The braid is laid on a flat surface and gently shaped into a spiralling oval. A safety pin holds the ends of the strands securely so they don't come undone. He laces through each loop of the braid, from one row across to the loop in the adjacent row (Figure 3-13). The thread cannot be seen when it is pulled tightly enough to interlock the loops. The lacing continues, alternating from loop to loop until coming to a turn.

Increasing the Oval

When lacing the rest of the oval, you have to increase the material around the curves—a special method used only for turning sharp corners. The braid, joined to the rug at the

FIGURE 3-13   The finishing nails show how lacing through the loop on one row pulls the loop on the adjacent row tight. The braided loops are alternated and slightly offset.

curves, is laced through every second or third loop, while still laced through each loop on the previous row to which the braid is being attached. Pull the thread taut every two or three loops; the tight lacing retains the shape of the rug. Whereas uneven tension or too many loops can cause ripples, skipping too few loops on corners may cause the rug to pucker. Working on a flat surface allows you to see how the rug lies.

When Berkeley adds to his lacing thread, he makes a double strand, threads it in through the needle, and ties it to the old strand with an overhand knot.

Carrying Out the Traditional Pattern   In the traditional braided rug pattern, the light central area is surrounded by two or three rows of darker braids. Then alternating rows of dark braids are used, followed by light, darker, medium, and dark rows. Changing the colors from light to dark looks best when done at the oval ends, rather than along the straight sides. The expert braider adds the new or darker colors to the outside strand, braiding one or two loops before adding the other strands, one at a time. The prejoined strands may therefore have to be cut and sewn on the diagonal again at the joints to permit the gradual transition from one color or shade into another (Figure 3-14). Make the color transition happen at alternate ends of the rug. The hit-and-miss pattern looks delightful and dappled, like a garden of flowers under leafy shade trees, or the glorious warmth of fallen autumn leaves.

FIGURE 3-14   Gradual color change in braid strands.

Ending the Rug   The end of an oval or circular rug should be tapered. Berkeley loosely lays his ending row around the rug. He wants the long side to have a complete braid and the taper to happen at the curved end. About 15″ (38 cm.) from the ending point, he cuts back into the three strands, tapering each down to a point. He then folds the raw edges in and braids to a point. The lacing cord is wrapped several times around the point and tucked inside the braid or a loop so it won't show. This lovely rug is reversible because all the lacing is hidden in the loops of the braids.

Variations   The traditional braider uses no aids, but excellent braid-aids are available that speed up the braiding process. One of the easiest to use is triangular-shaped (see Figure 3-15). The flat strip, threaded into the wide end of the tool, comes out with both raw edges turned in, and folds together naturally.

FIGURE 3-15   Triangular-shaped braid aid. The raw edges are folded under.

Rags are not the only things used for braids. Rectangular rugs braided of straw were used in English homes during Shakespeare's time. Corn husks can be braided, as well as the dampened fibers from plants. Today braided rugs can be made of yarns and strips of fur, felt, old stockings, newspapers, even plastic bags. Each material presents a challenge to the skill of the craftsperson.

Persons who have arthritis or who are bedridden can do braiding with simple aids devised at home. Frank DeMouthe, for example, invented a stirrup-style brace for his wife who was recovering from a back injury (Figure 3-16). The braid was held securely with a Rigby clamp that is at the top of the center post. She could adjust the tension while working. Lying in bed, she placed both feet astride the center post. Bending her knees allowed her to hold the post in place, providing a work area from shoulder to waist; she was able to pull the completed braid through the braid clamp. Working about ten minutes at a time and resting often, she progressed slowly and carefully. Scissors, needle, thread, ruler, and balls of wool can be kept in a basket within easy reach of the bed. Naturally, a room-size rug would be too cumbersome to work in a reclining position. However, table "rugs," doormats, or rectangular and square rugs done in strips are easily made this way. This device can also be used sitting up in a chair.

For your first project, try a small mat. Once you learn the braiding technique and get the feel for the correct tension, and after you develop a good working rhythm, you can attempt a large rug.

Deliberate patterns can be incorporated into your rug (Figure 3-17). While lacing, you might notice that by stretch-

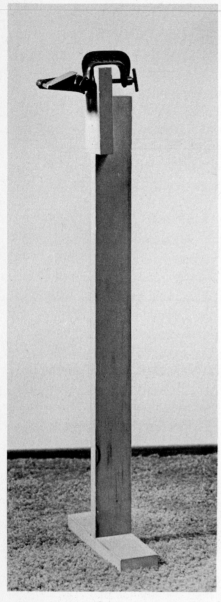

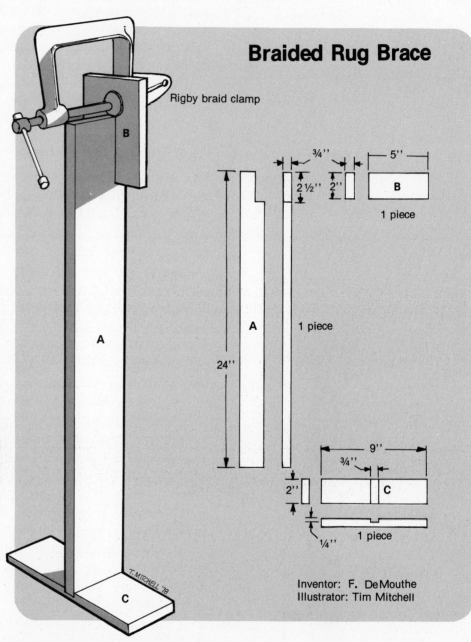

FIGURE 3-16a Stirrup braiding aid brace with Rigby clamp attached, designed by Frank DeMouthe. The gate in the clamp keeps the braid taut.

Braided Rug Brace

Rigby braid clamp

¾''

5''

2½'' 2''

B

1 piece

24''

A

1 piece

9''

¾''

2''

C

¼''

1 piece

Inventor: F. DeMouthe
Illustrator: Tim Mitchell

FIGURE 3-16b Diagram for building a braided rug brace (illustration by Tim Mitchell).

ing or compressing the braid slightly, loops of the same color can be joined, forming a zigzag pattern. Usually, to turn a curve smoothly, two strands are braided twice, then three strand braiding continues. However, *no* increases can be made for four turns at the oval ends when you are matching

58

color loops to form the pattern. Using two strands of the same color combined with another, a different pattern evolves. Geometric patterns can be figured out on graph paper. The traditional colonial rug materials, tools, and methods can be adapted to your color choices and life style—it's up to you!

FIGURE 3-17   Three different patterns of braided rugs, from *How to Make Braided Rugs* by Salley Clarke Carty. Copyright © 1977, McGraw-Hill Book Co., photograph by Martin Iger. Used with permission.

WOVEN AND COILED RUGS

Basket weaving was one of the first crafts developed by primitive people. In most areas it predates pottery and cloth weaving, as in the Tehuacan Valley, Mexico, and the Hopi Reservations in the United States. The first kind of basketry was wicker weaving, the intertwining of sticks and twigs to make huts, fish weirs, and traps.

Later the discovery of better basket materials led to the creation of other useful items: clothing (such as hats), furniture (stools, chairs, hammocks), beehives, baskets to carry loads, floor mats. In some parts of North America and Tasmania, the craft developed to the point where baskets were woven so finely as to be watertight! They were even used for cooking—hot stones were dropped into the water to make it boil.

In different parts of the world different materials were used for basket weaving—grass, straw, flax, cane, and bamboo. Colors were produced by dyeing the materials. Decorations were made by incorporating leather strips, beads, feathers, and other ornaments into the baskets. In some regions, each family or town had its traditional exclusive designs and pattern motifs.

Pottery developed from basketry. A basket lined with clay was accidentally left too near the fire, and the basket burned off. There was the first pot, a hard fired pot with basket marks on the surface. For a long time people used baskets as molds for their pottery. From the imprints on these pots we have learned the weaving patterns used by prehistoric peoples. Anthropological collections in museums are sources for visual reference.*

People developed cloth by adapting basketry techniques to new raw materials, such as fleece, cotton, silk, and linen. By 6000 BC or possibly earlier, ancient farming communities of the Near East were making cloth. It seems to have been invented in many other places and at different times. You've probably already seen some rugs made of basket materials. Import shops have mats for sale made of grass, straw, flax, cane, and bamboo. More rugs are made by weaving than by any other process.

Making a Basket   There are three ways to make a basket—plaiting, coiling, and weaving. From these three ways, many methods can be learned and applied to make floorcoverings of various kinds.

*Ben Burt, *Weaving: Museum of Mankind; Discovering Other Cultures* (London: The Trustees of the British Museum, 1977).

60

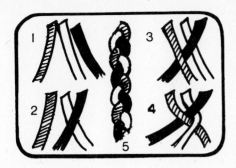

Plaiting. Plaiting is a braiding method. The warp and weft are interlaced diagonally from the outer strand toward the center. Traditional American braided rugs are examples of this technique.

Another example of a braided rug is the commercial product from Taiwan shown in Figure 3-18: a small, three-strand braid of sea grass is placed on its edge and sewn in an oval, 4 1/8″ × 5 3/8″ (10 cm. × 14 cm.). The oval motif is repeated twenty-five times in an alternated pattern with parallel stripes of a darker-colored grass plait sewn in between the motifs. The border around the edge is one-half the width of the oval and sewn around with a pinched turned right angle. The narrow braid—5/16″ inch (7.9 mm.) wide—when dampened for plaiting, can be pinched into a right angle turn rather than double braided on the outside edge of a turn, as a rag braid is.

FIGURE 3-18   Taiwanese braided rug of sea grass, three-strand braid is placed on edge and sewn.

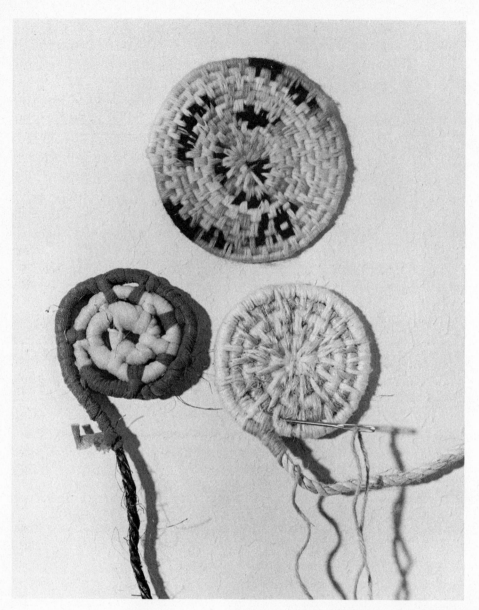

FIGURE 3-19   Three examples of coiling. *Top:* Peruvian coil stitch of variegated wool over plastic clothes line. *Bottom left:* Nylon stocking cut on bias and laced in the Mariposa stitch over a filling of jute rope. *Bottom right:* Peruvian coil stitch of cotton cord over jute rope.

Coiling. Coiling is a wrapping technique. The center core is wrapped by overcasting another set of threads called *weft material*, forming spiraling coils. These coils are wrapped together in various patterns, like the Lazy Stitch. The weft is wound three times around the exposed core, then wrapped around both the exposed core and the round already covered. Usually the wrapping material, or weft, is threaded on a large-eyed tapestry needle, and the stitch is quickly executed.

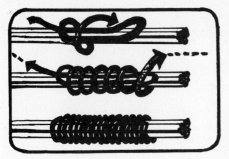

Adding more material to the core is easily done by tapering the ends of both strands to be joined. When wrapped in a figure eight, over and under motion, both tapered ends are covered. To add weft material for wrapping, hold the free end of the new piece along the central core and enclose it as the wrapping continues. The end of the old strand is tucked into the core and incorporated as the wrapping continues. Tapering all strands when joining them creates an invisible connection.

Coiling can also be used in crochet techniques, which will be discussed in detail later in this chapter. The coil can also be stitched or laced together.

Weaving. Weaving is an interlacing method. This is an important technique for rugmaking and is explained in the following section.

Woven Rugs

Weaving, whether done on simple hand looms or in large factories, is a technique involving two sets of thread. One set, the warp, is strung up in a "north to south" direction. The other set, the weft, can be passed from "east to west," or back and forth at right angles. The weft is passed over and under alternate warps to form the cloth. Simply stated, the horizontal filling thread goes over and under the vertically stretched warp threads.

Paper Weaving

When I was a child, I used to be overjoyed when drops of rain trickled down the window pane because our mother always had something for us to do. She taught us how to weave paper placemats and folded hats. Paper weaving is a good way to begin getting into rug weaving because it makes it easier for you to visualize patterns and colors for your rug. Why not try it? You will need:

- lined notebook paper
- scissors
- advertising section of the newspaper (to make weaving strips) or comic page (for colored strips) or colored paper

Begin a small sample showing plain weave. Fold a piece of lined notebook paper in half vertically. Unfold the paper. Then begin a series of nine horizontal cuts along the lines, from the outside edge into the folded line. You should have eight strips attached at one end. Turn the paper. The uncut edge is at the bottom. The cut spaces run vertically. Number the strips from one to eight on the uncut edge, beginning at the right-hand side. These are your *warps* (Figure 3-20).

Cut the strips you will weave with from newspaper. An easy way to assure they will all be of equal width is to lay another piece of notebook paper on top of the newspaper, cutting through both thicknesses along the lines. These strips are called *weft*.

Visualizing Weaving Patterns

Rugs need to be strong and durable. Loose threads will catch and pull out. The strongest flat weave is a fifty-fifty weave. This plain weave alternates the fill thread or weft over every other warp.

Let's see what the paper weaving can show. *Tabby* or *plain* weave is easy to make on your paper sample (Figure 3-21a). A diagram of this looks like the illustration next to the paper sample. There are eight columns in the grid. The X in the alternating squares of the diagram (Figure 3-21b) indicates the order in which the paper strip or warp should be picked up so you can weave the *pick* (weft strand) through the opening or *shed* between the warps. To interlock the weave, the second row of filling material goes *under* the X warps indicated in the next row of the diagram. This is repeated throughout.

How can a bolder, wider pattern be made? Try weaving under two and over two to make a *basketweave* pattern (Figure 3-22).

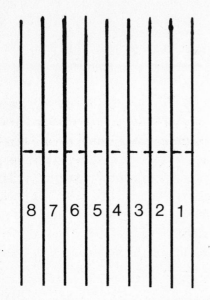

FIGURE 3-20   Paper warps for plain weave.

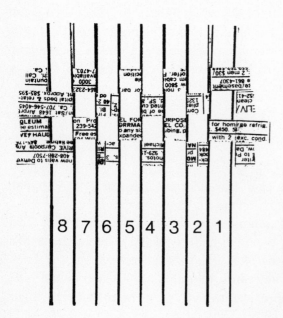

FIGURE 3-21a   Plain weave (tabby) using strips of paper.

FIGURE 3-21b   Draft for plain weave.

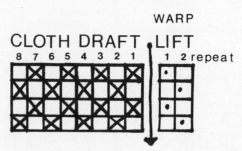

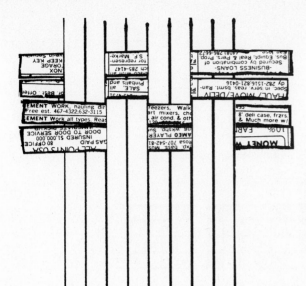

FIGURE 3-22a   Basketweave using strips of paper.

FIGURE 3-22b   Draft for 2/2 Basketweave.

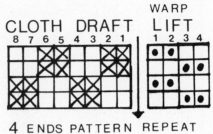

A diagonal pattern can be woven into the structure. Read the pattern draft and try your paper weaving. Lift the warps marked X. Place the filling strip underneath and across three paper warps. The long weft steps over one warp at the next row. This creates a diagonal. The pickup repeats at the fifth row (Figure 3-23).

FIGURE 3-23a   1/3 twill pattern.

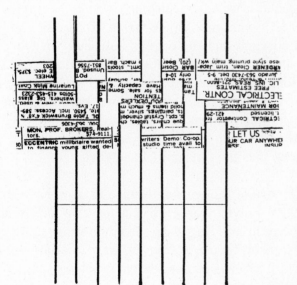

FIGURE 3-23b   Draft for 1/3 twill.

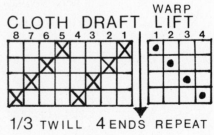

A sturdier weaving, one with an equal distribution of warp and weft in the diagonal light and dark pattern, is made by weaving under two and over two vertical warps in the *twill* pattern. The double pickup moves over one weft for four rows. The fifth row begins the same sequence as the first (Figure 24).

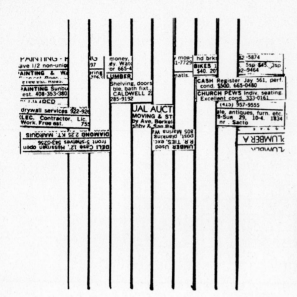

FIGURE 3-24a Sturdier weaving of twill.

FIGURE 3-24b Balanced twill weave.

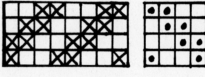

2/2 TWILL 4 ENDS REPEAT

The structure of the rug can be varied by other arrangements of lifting the warps. It can also be changed by the use of darker and lighter colors in various patterns. In *plaid* weave, the repeated colors of the warp and weft make the blocks of the design. Can you figure out how to weave a plaid?

Your paper weaving used single strips of colored paper. This left an open and loose edge which needs paste or staples to hold it in place. Sometimes single strips of rag are used when making a doormat and the edge is stitched. However, weaving is usually made using a continuous strand of weft.

Now let's think about making a rug. It needs to be sturdy to withstand foot traffic, easily cleaned, and expressive of your choice of color and pattern. The personal touch you give is achieved by the variation in dark and light colors, the pattern, the textures, and the finishing of the edges.

Designing the Pattern The color and texture of the yarn determine the emphasis in the pattern. When weaving a rug, do not use two different thicknesses of warp thread. Rug warp should be either tightly twisted cotton twine or linen or cotton rug warp. Variation in thicknesses of warp threads causes tension problems that result in slack and rippling areas. A sturdy warp adds to the durability of the rug.

You may use recycled rags as weft, as well as woolen rug yarns, rayon, and acrylic. Synthetics often pill from wear or washing. Wool is recommended, as it is more resilient. Further, it doesn't matt together and flatten down as quickly as synthetic yarn.

You can visit weaving supply shops to get an idea of the

yarns that are available. And much can be learned and many ideas triggered by visiting galleries and exhibits—for example, the beautiful woven rug shown in Figure 3-25. But the best way to learn about the texture of a yarn is to use it.

FIGURE 3-25   Serpentine rug by Martha Stanley, photographed by Josephine Coatsworth, courtesy of Richmond Art Center, Richmond, California.

Plain weave or *tabby weave* is the rug weft pattern most often used. It is probably the most durable weave, excellent for stripes and for holding the looped rya knot. When weaving the tabby weave, the filling yarn goes over every other thread.

Plaid is a variation of plain weave. The crossed bands are created because the warp is tied on with the same colors and often in the same sequence that the weft is woven. It is only plaid if the weft and warp are evenly exposed; covering the warp by beating harder or setting the warp wider apart results in stripes.

Stripes in their infinite variety can be made using the plain weave. One color, or a monochromatic plan, can be used.

Eleven or twelve light and dark yarns of the same color can be found at most weaving stores. Use your favorite color with a neutral black, off white, or grey yarn in different widths of stripes. Combine textures, such as soft mohair yarn, with rug yarn in the same shed for an accent. Somewhere in the stripe pattern, thick, fluffy yarns can also be introduced, adding surface variation to the piece.

Columns or vertical stripes require the use of two shuttles of contrasting dark, light, bright, or dull colors. First one shuttle carries across a color, which is beaten down to cover the warp. The second color is then placed in the alternate shed and beaten down to cover the warp. By alternating the colors, vertical rows or columns are made. Using an over-two/under-two weaving pattern (or over-three/under-three), wider stripes result.

Varying tabby weave is easy. Examine some woven cloth closely. Does each weft thread go under, then over, then under, as in tabby weaving? You may see a different arrangement of the weft. The weft might skip over two, then under one, then over two again. Or the weft may go under one, then over three. You can discover patterns through observation or by unravelling a swatch of cloth carefully.

Interesting things are done with tabby weave in Guatemala in making clothing. The weaver wraps parts of the warp strands and sometimes the weft strands before the cloth is constructed. The strands are dyed, and the wrapped areas resist the color, producing an alternating pattern of color on each strand. The decorative motifs, therefore, have irregular outlines on the woven cloth. The pleasant softness of detail brought about by the warp ikat or in compound or double ikat blends into the folds of the woven garment and ripples with the movements of the wearer. This technique can be used to make a beautiful flat rug, but because tie-up is difficult, you should have some experience.

Estimating the Amount of Yarn When weaving your rug, you have to figure out the amount of rug yarn you need to buy. You can use the following method if you like to estimate materials yourself.

How to estimate the warp ends. First, decide the dimensions you would like your finished weaving to be. For example: your frame loom is 20″ × 26″ (50 cm. × 66 cm.). If you are planning to make three pieces of fabric 12″ × 24″ (30 cm. × 61 cm.), you will lace them together at the 24″ selvedge edge. The warp ends will become fringe or braids on both sides.

Then, decide the number of thread ends per inch for the width of the loom and the rug piece. A rug with thick hand-spun weft or 1/2″ rag rug strips for fill usually has four ends per inch (2.5/cm.) of warp. The example uses four thread ends per inch or two per centimeter. Add 1″ to the width of the final size to allow for take-in caused by the release of tension when the warp is cut off the loom.

Multiply the number of ends per inch by the number of inches in the width. The result tells you how many warp ends need to be cut, or the length of each in continuous warping. For example,

12″	wide		30	cm. wide
+ 1″	tension take up		+ 2.5	cm. tension
13″	of warp ends		32	cm. of warp ends
× 4	ends per inch		× 2	ends per cm.
52	ends to cut		64	thread ends

Note: Though the length is the same in both examples, the number of thread ends is not. Four ends per inch actually equals 1.60 per cm., but it is easier to use whole numbers to multiply. A rug doesn't need to be that exact in dimensions.

Add two thread ends, one on either side, to add a thickness to the edge or selvedge and to prevent wear. Thus, in our example, you need to cut 54 ends if your dimension is in inches, or 66 thread ends for metric unit.

52	ends to cut		64	thread ends
+ 2	extra for selvedge		+ 2	extra for selvedge
54	ends		66	ends

To estimate *how long to make each warp thread*, take the number of inches (or centimeters) in the length of the piece—24″ (60 cm. in our example). Add 12″ (30 cm.) for tie-up. If you plan a continuous warp, allow extra rug warp for going around the thickness of the frame, dowel rod, or door. You can't make a 24″ (60 cm.) fabric on a 24″ (60 cm.) loom, because part of the space is taken up by the heading and the extra warp used for finishing ends.

Most rug warps of cotton and linen are sold on spools that indicate the weight of the thread and the total number of yards on the spool. Use the heavier cotton rug warp, 400 yds.

per spool. Rounding off the length of each strand of yarn to yards or meters usually makes the calculating easier: 36″ is a yard; 100 cm. is a meter. In the example, 26″ is the long dimension of the frame loom.

26″		65	cm.
+12″	tie-up	+30	cm.
38″	length of each warp	95	cm.

Then divide the length of the thread by 36″ or by 100 cm. to find out the yards or meters length of each warp end.

38″	length of each warp	95	cm.
÷36″	per yard	÷100	
1 1/8	yds.	.95	m.

Rounding off the measurement to the higher figure, as in the metric example, is preferable, as well as using one meter length for each warp thread end.

YARDS		METERS	
54	ends	64	ends
× 1	yd.	× 1	m.
54	yds. of rug warp needed for each section	64	m. of rug warp needed for each section

Spools of rug warp often have 400–500 yds. or m. per spool. Buying extra rug warp has advantages: It can be used to make string heddles, to finish, and to mend broken warp threads.

A warp thread might break. But a new warp can be tied on at the top edge of the frame. A straight pin or tapestry needle can be inserted into the cloth and out again directly over the broken warp thread, about one finger length below the weaving area. The new warp, wound in a figure-eight around the ends of the pin protruding above the cloth, will keep the new warp end taut. After the weaving is finished and cut off the loom, the free ends of the broken and the new warps are cut; or they can be untwisted, pulled apart, and hidden in the cloth with a tapestry needle.

How to estimate weft or filling. Generally, if you use the same thickness of weft or filling rug yarn, approximately the same amount of rug yarn is used. When the rug weft is thicker, less yarn is used. There are approximately 300 yds. (275 m.) of heavy rug yarn to a pound.

Here's a handy technique. To see how many picks or rows of rug warp will fill 1″ (2.5 cm.), wrap the thread around a pencil or your little finger. Hold a ruler along the tightly wrapped warp. Count the number of turns and divide by two to allow for the overlap and thickness of the warp thread when weaving. The result is the number of thread ends, or pick ends, along a running inch (2.5 cm.) of fabric. The pick ends are multiplied by the length of the finished fabric. Then multiply this figure by the width of the cloth, and add an allowance for take-up.

Calculating weft is sometimes difficult because of the different textural qualities of the rug yarn. Softer yarns, more loosely twisted, pack down when beaten into place. The best rule is to buy about 20 percent more than you think you'll need. There are two ways to estimate. One is by weaving a small swatch of about 2″ (5 cm.) and then unravelling and measuring the yarn used. This is probably a more accurate way to estimate. Another way is to pre-measure about ten yards (meters) of weft. Using the measured strand, weave the beginning of the cloth. After completing one inch (1 cm.) of fabric, calculate the amount used by subtracting the yarn remaining from the total amount measured. This amount is how much yarn you need for every inch (cm.) in your cloth. Total up the inches (cm.) left for you to weave. Multiply the distance left to weave by the total amount of yarn used and you will know how many yards (m.) of weft to buy.

If you weighed the weft before you wove the beginning inch, you could multiply by weight instead. Round the calculated amount of weft off to the higher number. You can easily estimate the ounces and pounds (or grams and kilos) of rug yarn to buy. The total amount of thread to buy includes the linen or cotton warp thread and the various amounts of colored weft yarns.

Keep a creative log or record book with the name of the yarn, fiber content, dye lot, place of purchase, cost. Keep a record of the weight in ounces or grams of the yarn used for later reference. Double over the top edge of each page and punch holes through it. Loop a small length of yarn through the holes. With this record you can match color and know your costs. Date every entry in your log. A photo of the rug, with its measurements, provides a record for your homeowner's insurance policy and for future reference.

Using the Tools The parallel warp threads are stretched lengthwise away from the weaver on a holding device (see Figure 3-26). This frame or loom may be as simple as the backstrap style loom, an inkle loom, a card-weaving loom, a rectangular wooden frame or a door frame loom; or it may be as complex as an eight-harness floor loom or an industrial weaving machine with a laser beam to propel the shuttle across the opening between the alternate threads.

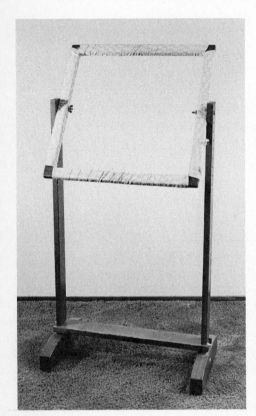

FIGURE 3-26a   Rug frame designed by Frank DeMouthe. Wing nuts make this easy to take apart or carry with you. Rug backing canvas or needlepoint canvas can be pinned or sewn to the cloth strips for loop rugs. Finishing nails placed on opposite sides will make this frame into a loom.

FIGURE 3-26b   Weaving on a frame loom. The dowel rods are tension devices to be removed as the cloth tightens. The shed stick on the edge creates an opening. The shuttle is pulled through the shed.

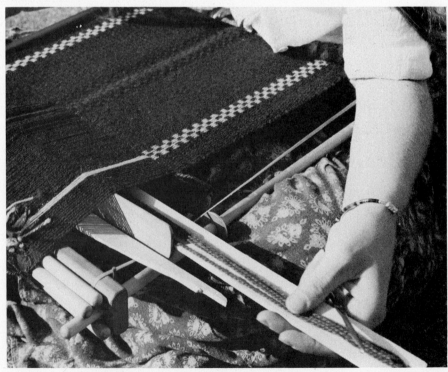

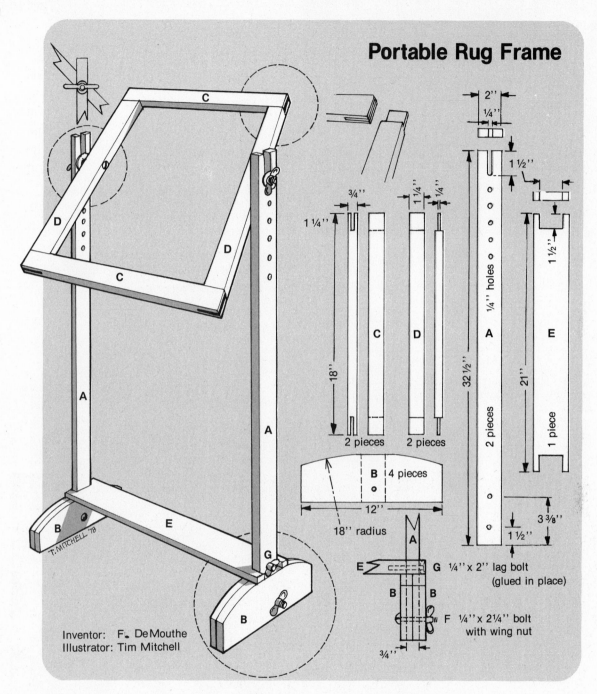

Portable Rug Frame

C

D

D

C

A

A

B

E

G

B

Inventor: F. DeMouthe
Illustrator: Tim Mitchell

T. MITCHELL '78

3/4''

1 1/4''

C

18''

2 pieces

1 1/4'' 1/4''

D

2 pieces

B 4 pieces

12''

18'' radius

2''

1/4''

1 1/2''

1/4'' holes

A

32 1/2''

2 pieces

1 1/2''

1 1/2''

1 1/2''

E

21''

1 piece

3 3/8''

A

E

G 1/4'' x 2'' lag bolt
(glued in place)

B B

F 1/4'' x 2 1/4'' bolt
with wing nut

3/4''

FIGURE 3-26c   Diagram for building the portable rug frame (illustration by Tim
Mitchell).

73

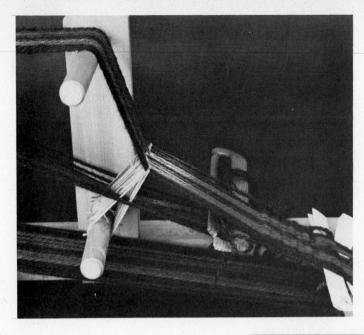

FIGURE 3-26d   Inkle loom. When the lower set of warp behind the heddles is pressed down, an opening is made in front of the heddles for inserting the weft. The next motion is to lift up the lower set or warp and continue weaving.

FIGURE 3-26e   Cardboard carton inkle loom. The white cord indicates two warps. One is attached by a string heddle loop to the heddle support rod. The rubber bands are a tension device, which are removed when the weaving becomes tight, photograph courtesy of the author.

FIGURE 3-26f   Weaving on a cardboard inkle loom, photograph courtesy of the author..

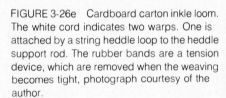

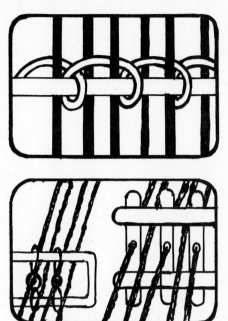

String heddles can be used to pick up alternate warps. You can make one continuous strand or use a single heddle loop for every other warp thread, as in the inkle loom shown in Figure 3-27. However, both finger weaving or using a shed stick and a shuttle are easy and fast techniques.

Making simple frames to hold the parallel warp threads securely is easy. An old picture frame can be used as a loom frame. Or four pieces of pine lumber, 1 1/2″ × 1 1/2″, can be glued and screwed together. A small lightweight frame can be made from 1/4″ × 1″ × 10″ (6 mm. × 2.5 cm. × 25 cm.) fir lathing strips that have been cut, glued, and stapled together.

The smaller frame looms are easy to carry, hang up, and store. A large rug design, however, has to be made in sections, then laced together. Rugmakers with limited space can warp around a door.

Several problems encountered when working with frame looms are

1 keeping the warp evenly spaced,

2 maintaining the correct tension in the warp threads, and

3 the beginner's mistake of using yarn that is too thin and breaks from the weight of the filling. Either double thin cotton seine twine warp to make it thicker, or warp with a heavier wool rug yarn.

FIGURE 3-27 Putting weft through shed on inkle loom with string heddles, photograph courtesy of the author.

FIGURE 3-28 When marking the frame for placement of nails, dots must be exactly opposite each other. Nails have been hammered into some of the dots along the edge of the frame. Mistakes can be taped over.

To control the spacing of the warps, measure and mark along a pencil line drawn on the frame exactly where the long finishing nails will be hammered to hold the warp. To avoid splitting the wood, place the nails at 1″ (2.5 cm.) intervals. Stagger the line of nails in zigzag fashion, so you have two lines of nails 1/2″ apart. Mark the top bar of the frame first, from left to right; then mark the lower bar in the same way, so that all the nails are directly opposite one another.

If the frame is not square at the corners, measure from the side that is most perpendicular on both top and bottom. Check that the nail marks are in a straight line opposite each other by holding a steel edge ruler from one side to the other. If you made a mistake when marking, place the tape over the edge and measure again.

Warping **Warping a nailed frame.** Plain or tabby weave involves weaving a fill strand over every other warp strand. Using two colors for the warp makes the alternating pickup easy. With one color, warp from the outside nails of the upper row to the inside nails of the bottom row; then switch across to the next nail and return to the top—and so on (Figure 3-29). With the other color, warp from the inside nails on the top to the outside nails at the bottom row. Each warp 1/2″ (2 cm) apart is the same color, making alternating the pickup easy. (Weaving with thick soft yarn covers these warps.)

76

FIGURE 3-29 Warping a frame loom. Finishing nails are alternated to prevent splitting the frame. Two colors are used to make it easy to locate the alternating warps. The large thread at bottom is the heading, which is later removed. Vertical columns are formed when two "butterfly" shuttles of different-color yarn are used alternately. The fill weft is packed tightly together with a comb or beaten down with a ruler.

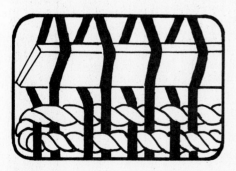

Warping a frame loom with a continuous strand. You can warp around a frame or any rigid set of bars, eliminating the need for hammer and nails. Just warp figure eights around the bars (Figure 3-30). Notice, in the photo, that the ruler on edge has picked up alternating strands to show an *opening* or *shed* between the top strands and the bottom strands. The cross formed by warping this method keeps the strands from tangling and getting disorganized. Insert one ruler or flat stick into the opening, or shed, formed by the crossing warp;

77

insert another in between the alternate warp threads. These sticks, taking up some of the slack, are removed when weaving progresses to help control the tension.

FIGURE 3-30a   Warping a frame loom using a continuous strand and looping around the frame in figure-eights.

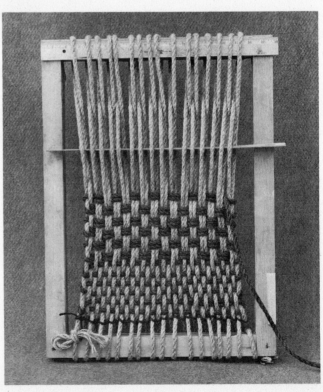

FIGURE 3-30b   The ruler on the edge has picked up alternating warps to open a shed for the next shot of weft. The twining at the bottom keeps the warps separated. The plain weave at the bottom contrasts with the basketweave style of alternating a double strand of weft over pairs of warp. As the fabric tightens, the rulers are removed.

Warping a door. Tape two dowel rods or sticks to the top of the door. These rods assist in adjusting the tension of the warp. Later they can be taken off, inserted into the two alternate sheds, and pushed to the top of the frame (see Figure 3-31). The warping, wrapped around the door, is pushed along the top and bottom towards the hinge side as it is looped over the top. One rug may therefore be woven on one side, a second rug on the other. If the strips are narrow, they may later be sewn together.

FIGURE 3-31　Continuous warp around a door. The rods at the top act as a tension device and are withdrawn when the fabric tightens.

Keeping the warp evenly spaced is a problem when using any frame loom. Spacing is controlled by twining two strands of weft yarns around the warp top and bottom. The strands of the weft or fill yarn are easier to see if they are either of two colors or of alternating light and dark shades. Make sure each strand is four times the width of the weaving. Join them with an overhand knot.

Loop the center of the twining strand around the first warp yarn, then bring both strands to the surface of the cloth and twist. Twine the other strand around the next warp and twist again, proceeding in this way across the whole warp. The twists between each warp are made in the same direction across the row. Knot the two strands at the end. Later these ends may be worked into the weaving with a needle or a crochet hook or hidden in the finishing fringe, braid, or binding. You can also make an additional row of twining. This edge gives a professional finish at each end of the rug. If you think you want to have a knotted fringe along two edges, you can weave spacers or heading strips of rags or rulers for five or six inches, before the two rows of twining, then remove the heading material. The warps can be knotted for a fringe.

Inserting the fill or weft. The two tension sticks are on the side of the loom opposite where you are sitting and working. Turn the nearer stick on its edge and an opening or shed is made between the threads that hold the alternate warps up. The shuttle stick that carries the weft passes easily through the shed. Turn the shed stick flat.

The next row of fill or weft is put through the opposite alternate warps, which are picked up either on a free shed stick or with your fingers. As you work away from your body, beat the weft firmly toward you. If you beat it down with a fork, the warp thread can be hidden.

Uneven selvedge. Often the fabric pulls in at the center. As a result, the edges become crooked, curving inward like a bow. This problem can be controlled in several ways. Either inserting the shuttle through the warp at an angle or leaving a line of filling that looks like a loose M shape should beat down into a firm line of weft that isn't too tight. Beating down the weft with a fork or beater sword will not stretch the wool, but allows it to fill in evenly. Since the warp yarns are dimensionally round, the weft must intertwine with them, not lie flat across in a line. If you want to completely cover the warp, you can beat the weft down so it's tightly packed, use a fill yarn that's thick and fluffy, or use double strands of thinner weft yarn.

Another way to control the pulling-in problem is to work your design from both top and bottom. When the middle is reached, your weft yarn may have to be threaded through with a blunt-tipped tapestry needle.

Naturalistic and Geometric Designs

Tapestry weave, a flat weave, is a variation of plain weave and is used to make areas of colored shapes in various directions across the warp. Naturalistic and geometric designs are often made this way. As shown in Figure 1-5 and the color insert, a motif of stylized birds and trees was woven into a wall tapestry by an Egyptian child while he sat before his frame loom. He followed the tradition of many weavers, picking up sections of warps to inlay areas of different colors, making flower shapes and landscape details.

This contemporary Egyptian tapestry, woven by a child of Harrania, near Cairo, is the result of a fascinating experiment begun in the 1950s by the late Ramses Wissa-Wassef, a French-educated Egyptian architect who founded a tapestry workshop based on the principle that the potential to create exists in everyone. He took totally untutored children from a small village and gave them some rudimentary technical education on how to operate a loom, provided them with colorful and naturally dyed yarn, and let them go to work. At his workshop he allowed no interference with or criticism of the children's work, no formal instruction, and as little contact with the outside world as possible. Unlike weavings done elsewhere, this tapestry was woven freehand, without sketches or "cartoons," with no repetitive designs, and without reference to textbooks or instructions. The child's imagination was transformed directly into a one-of-a-kind woven scene.*

Inlay patterns. Using plain weave in an area to create a shape like a bird or an angular line creates a problem. What do you do with one color end when you want to change to another color? An obvious solution is to cut the end and let the warp hang loose behind the surface. Another solution is to

*W.R.B. Forman and Ramses Wissa-Wassef, *Tapestries from Egypt Woven by the Children of Harrania* (Prague: Artia, 1961). Reprinted: Feltham, Middlesex: Hamlyn Publishing Group Ltd., Hamlyn House, The Centre, 1968. Also: Forman, *Woven by Hand.* (Feltham, Middlesex: Hamlyn Publishing Group Ltd., Hamlyn House, The Centre, 1972).

carry a loose thread along the back until the color is needed again.

When the yarn is woven back and forth over an area, turning on the warp thread at the edge of the shape, a slit appears in the cloth, especially when the edge is a vertical line (Figure 3-32). To avoid slits in the tapestry when weaving a rug, the two color yarns may share the same warp end. This results in a slight thickening of the edge of the area and also a sawtooth edge around the shape (Figure 3-33). Another way of joining two areas of color is to intertwine the two colors between the warps at the edge of the color areas. This method also results in a slight thickening of the outline of the shapes. Whichever method of joining color areas is used, it should be used consistently throughout the rug.

FIGURE 3-32 Tapestry weave; insert weft colors into shed using adjacent warp threads to turn back to their area of design. If threads meet in regular progression, diagonal slits will be produced. These can be moved to the right or left. Illustrations by Kathy Puccio show variations.

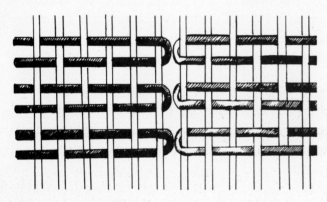

FIGURE 3-32a Straight slits.

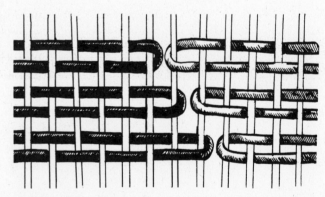

FIGURE 3-32b Diagonal slits.

FIGURE 3-32c Small slits.

FIGURE 3-32d   Dovetailing and Hatching.

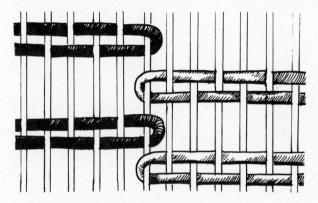

FIGURE 3-32e   Interlocking over common warp.

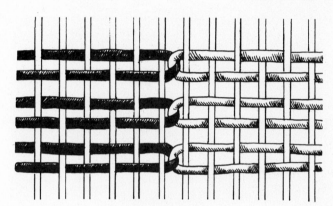

FIGURE 3-32f   Interlocking weft.

FIGURE 3-33a   Sawtooth edge of a tapestry weave.

FIGURE 3-33b   Slits in tapestry weave are more noticeable when wall panel is hung against the light.

Regional Designs   The Navajo began weaving in the eighteenth century using cultivated cotton. The eclectic Navajo prospered from their contact with the Spanish who had brought sheep, horses, and Christianity to the Southwest Indian lands in the 1500s. However, in 1863, the weaving industry of the Navajos almost collapsed completely when they were incarcerated at the Bosque Ridondo reservation. By 1885, the Navajos had begun to recover, boosted by the 30,000 sheep paid them for their hardship by the U.S. Government. Free at last, their designs became bolder, enlarging tiny zigzags into a bolder Z-form on the blanket.

Traders from the Fred Harvey company bought up all the blankets they could find in Indian territory during the 1880s. They sold the blankets to soldiers and shipped them back to the Eastern markets, where they were used as rugs.

A great many blankets at the end of the nineteenth century were hastily made of analine-dyed, imported yarn and controlled and designed by the traders, rather than by the weavers. They were therefore of poor quality.

Rugs made in this century are of higher quality.

Navajo rugs are flatly woven. The changes of color or weft are made over shared warps and the design carried in the weaver's head. Usually the border pattern matches, but not always. Such handmade rugs age gracefully. Even the fading of the colors enriches the design because the dark and light pattern still leads your eye to see the design. (See Figure 3-34 for two beautiful examples and Plate 14 in the color insert.)

FIGURE 3-34a Navajo Granada red rug, handspun brown, natural, grey, black, and Germantown red dyed wool, 63″ x 39″ (161 cm. x 100 cm.), c. 1907, author's collection.

FIGURE 3-34b Navajo rug, gold wool dyed with cedar bark, natural grey, black, brown, and analine dyed blue, 56″ x 37″ (140 cm. x 92 cm.), c. 1949, author's collection.

The Navajo Indian women of New Mexico and Arizona weave a beautiful geometric design without a cartoon, or drawing to size, on a vertical loom. Their handwoven rugs and blankets, like the Oriental carpets of the Middle East, are taken seriously by collectors. The men of Oaxaca, Mexico, are also renowned for their woven blankets and rugs. These craftspeople use tapestry techniques: dovetail, interlocked, and stepped weft weaves.

FIGURE 3-35   Mexican tapestry weaving.

Each of other American regions has its own characteristic designs and motifs. For instance, in the northwest corner of New Mexico, stylized animals and birds predominate in the pictorial designs. These Yeis and Yeibechais-style rugs are finely woven of naturally white, grey, brown, black, and vegetable-dyed wool. The "Two Grey Hills" weaving region produces exceptionally fine, tightly woven rugs and blankets with distinctive black borders on most of them. A 120-thread count per inch is usual—approximately the thread count of bed sheets!

Known today for their geometric patterns, weavers in the southwest part of Arizona produce rugs and blankets known as the Granada reds and Klagetos. In the Western Reservation area of Arizona, the popular "Storm" patterns are indigenous; the lightning symbol is a heavy zigzag construction emanating from a central storm core.

Of course, each weaver adds his or her own interpretation to the weaving. Customarily, an Indian woman owns her own flock of sheep, supervises the shearing, spins and dyes the wool, warps the frame loom her husband has made, and keeps calm and beautiful thoughts in mind while she sits at the loom.

Pile Rugs
The origin of making long pile, a method of knotted weaving, is lost in antiquity. There is evidence that nomadic tribes in the Persian Empire of more than 2,500 years ago were weaving hand-knotted rugs for saddle blankets, tent flaps, and ground covers for their tents. The amazingly well-preserved *Pazyrk* carpet, dating back to about 500 BC, is on exhibit at the Hermitage Museum in Leningrad. The first hand-knotted

FIGURE 3-36 Iranian Meskin rug, right-hand Persian Knot, dark blue, black, burnt orange, grey, green-brown, bright blue, pink, and green on cotton warp, 59″ x 41″ (150 cm. x 104 cm.), c. 1950, author's collection (see detail in color insert, Plate 17).

Oriental rugs were brought to Europe by Italian merchants; such rugs can be seen in the paintings of the fourteenth and fifteenth centuries. The tradition was brought to America by settlers from the Scandinavian countries.

Oriental rugs are known by many names, which usually indicate from which city or region they originate. They provide a general guide to the character of the style, as native weavers in each locale tend to favor certain traditional motifs, symbols, and colors. Like paintings, the hand-knotted Persian and Turkish rugs have become long-term investments as well as works of art.

Weaving the Pile

A pile texture can be made by two basic methods. One way is a loop method. Our terry bath towels look like the finely woven ancient cloth. The ancient Egyptians, Greeks, and Peruvians made the loops by hand-weaving the weft thread through a shed, up to the face of the cloth, around a small rod, and then back under the next weft, and so forth. Weaving pile in this way requires that you put in two rows of tabby to hold these loops in place.

You can also make a pile shag by knotting strands around the warps and tying the wool pile to the backing mesh through a pair of warps. The two basic knots are the *Persian Knot* and the *Turkish Knot*.* The Persian Knot, an S-shaped knot, is sometimes called the *Sehna Knot* after the Persian town of that name; it is a variation of the Turkish or *Ghiordes Knot*, a T-shaped knot or clove hitch, also known as *rya* by the Scandinavians.

Another method often used for making pile is to tie the rya knot on pre-woven linen or cotton backing. This requires no loom, and the rug can be finished more quickly than a woven rya rug. Chapter Four tells how a group of students used this method to make the rug in Plate 15, color insert.

A large, blunt tapestry needle or wooden needle, a pile gauge, scissors, and yarns of your chosen colors are needed to get started weaving the pile. A shuttle will hold narrow-gauge yarn, but for thicker fill, tie the yarn into a butterfly.

Leave two to four warp ends along each edge to be woven in plain weave; this edge becomes the selvedge, protecting the knots from wear.

After weaving in your heading, make a couple of tabby rows before knotting. If you're right-handed, work from left to right, and if left-handed, work from right to left.

*The type of knot used is important in determining the Oriental rug's origin.

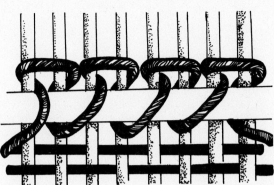

FIGURE 3-37a & b Tabby and Rya knots. Use 1/2″–3/4″ tabby between rows; close shed; use butterflies to wrap yarn around stick as shown across the warp; wave a few rows of tabby (a); cut along top of stick with knife and remove stick (illustration by Kathy Puccio).

Pile yarns are tied around two warp threads. The needle is inserted between the two warp threads, then pulled around the left thread, across the two warps to the right, then inserted into the back and brought up through the center of the same two warps. Pull the ends of the yarn to knot the loop.

A cardboard or wooden gauge, of whatever height you wish the loop, is placed against the fabric below the row you are working. Using the needle, bring yarn down under the gauge and back again to advance to the next pair of warps to make the knot.

Cutting the Pile   When the weft runs out, cut the end to the height of the loops. You may leave loops, cut them against the gauge, or have areas of both. Cut the loop with sharp scissors inserted between the yarn and the gauge. On large carpets, sheep shears are used to cut the pile after the weaving is finished.

Weave two, four, or six rows of tabby in between each row of knots. When a dense pile has been made, the next row of knots may start above this row. This next row can be knotted on the same pairs of warp. Or, the first warp can be skipped and pairs started with the second warp, resulting in rows of knots alternating with the usual rows of tabby between. The dense, thick yarns fluff out and cover the warp (Figure 3-38).

Ending the rows of knots requires a slightly different tying pattern. About four rows of knots from the end of the rug, work every fourth knot upside down and pull the ends so they fall away from you. In the third row, knot every third

FIGURE 3-38   Rya pile knotted carpet overlapping the back to show light-color woven tabby between rows of knots. Collection of Terence M. Campbell.

and fourth knot upside down. In the next-to-last row, make every second, third, and fourth knot fall upwards and away. Insert all the knots in the last row from the top. This process hides the final row of knots, so the rug appears to have neither a top nor a bottom. The knots radiate toward the outside edges, and the rug lies flat on the floor.

Patterns flow with uneven outlines for changes of color because the pile is 2″ (5 cm.) to 5″ (12 cm.) long. Rich, glowing color combinations result when you group several related colors of yarn in the weft strand. For subtle, shadowy areas, group several strands of darker colors together.

Finishing the Rug   Sometimes the rug is made like a Navajo rug, so that when the rug is taken from the loom it is complete with twined finished edges. In other cases, finishing methods may be required.

Stitching the edges.   Before the rug is cut off the loom, both ends can be stitched with one of several stitches to hold the weft together and prevent it from slipping off the warp. A

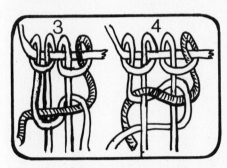

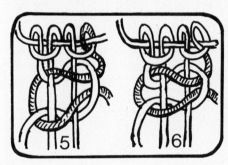

back stitch or a blanket stitch can be used, or the edge can be crocheted. You can use thin cotton to blend with the color of the edge that it overlaps or thicker woolen yarn for a decorative element.

Finishing the warp ends. The warp ends are easily worked into one of several finishes when they are cut off, a few at a time. If the ends are left long enough, they can be threaded individually on a tapestry needle (a wide-eyed, blunt-tipped steel needle) and worked back into the cloth. Carefully, cut the loose end close to the tabby woven end. Then tie the warp ends in groups with an overhand knot. You give the edge additional strength by using one end from the first group in the second set.

Long warp ends, four to seven times the length of the macramé lace pattern, can be knotted into beautiful designs. Repeating only one knot—such as the overhand knot, half hitch, or the square knot—on alternating strands in different rows is quickly done. Braiding the ends is another method. Add more strands of the same or contrasting color yarns, using a clove hitch, lark's head knot, or a rya knot, to make a thicker edge. You can group the ends together and wrap them with left-over bits of colored yarn, adding sparkle to a colorful rug with this random element. (See Figure 3-39 for illustrations of these techniques.)

FIGURE 3-39a The overhand knot.

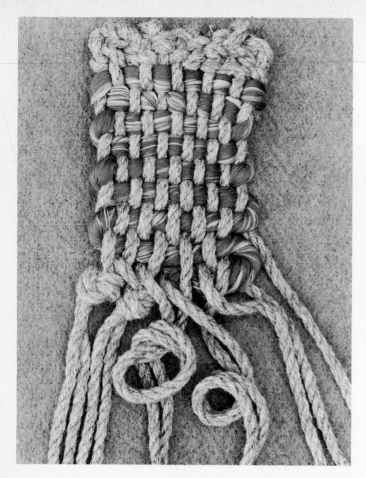

FIGURE 39b   One way of using the overhand knot. The first and third warps are knotted; the second warp is carried over to knot with the fifth warp; the fourth warp goes in to knot with the seventh. This knot holds weft securely in place.

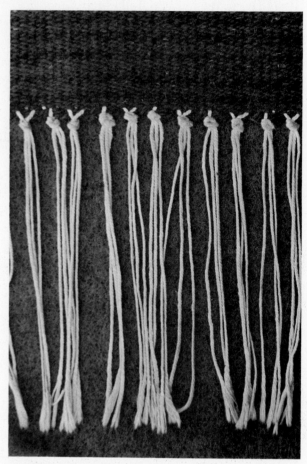

FIGURE 3-39c   The overhand knot is used to tie the warp threads together on a weaving; the weft threads do not slip.

FIGURE 3-39d   The clove hitch, lark's head knot, or reverse double half stitch. Note its similarity to a rya knot.

FIGURE 39e The half hitch is looped around another cord held taut; it may be looped around a vertical or horizontal cord.

FIGURE 3-39f The square knot. Four ends are used, with the center two held taut. It may be looped around a vertical or horizontal cord.

FIGURE 3-39g Wrapping technique that hides the knot. Start at the bottom and read up; double the wrapping cord and place the loop on the left; take one of the ends and wrap tightly toward the loop; insert the end through the loop; pull both ends. The loop becomes a knot inside the wrapped area. The top shows the ends trimmed.

Decide your finishing technique before you cut the warp ends to remove the rug or rug unit from the loom. When stitching small units together to make a larger unit, think about the finishing of that piece also. Will it be stitched by machine or by hand to rug binding? Will it be crocheted together? If both ends are fringed, how will the selvedge edges be joined to the other pieces? Invisibly with fine stitches? Or, will the joining be a linear element of dark or bright in the overall design of the rug?

Yes, even in the techniques for ending your weaving, there are opportunities for creative choices.

CROCHETED AND KNITTED RUGS

Crocheting and knitting are both looping techniques that use one strand of fiber looped on itself. Making a crocheted or knitted rug is a project that I call "rugmaking on the go" because you need one continuous strand of material and such easily carried tools as a crochet hook or two knitting needles, and you can work on a small section at a time.

During the Depression and Second World War, people used plastic bread wrappers to make mildew-proof door rugs or bathmats. In the folk-art tradition of America, rags were cut into strips and used.

It is not difficult to knit or crochet a rug. Rehabilitation programs at veterans hospitals teach these skills, and some hospitalized patients spend their time at this hobby, which can grow into a small business.

Planning the Rug There are several considerations to keep in mind when you decide to crochet or knit a rug. The location and purpose of the rug will help you decide its color, texture, fiber, size, and sturdiness. Where will it be used? Will it be an accent or decorative rug to call attention to a certain part of the room, such as a fireplace or coffee table? If your answer is yes, some liberties can be taken with the combination of natural and man-made fibers, as well as with the density and looseness of the rug. An accent rug need not necessarily be made of brightly colored yarn. Textural contrasts, in off-white fibers and rags, might accent wood floors or smooth, velvet-like wall-to-wall carpet. Where you want the rug will determine its overall shape and size as well. (A good way to determine whether the rug will fit the space you have in mind is to cut newspapers to size.)

Durability is perhaps the most important consideration when making a rug using crochet stitches or knit stitches. What are the differences in durability between these two techniques?

Usually the single crochet stitch (double crochet in the United Kingdom) is closer and more dense, making a durable fabric. Because the crochet's density differs so greatly from the elasticity of the garter stitch in knitting, you may think that no knit rug is durable. But a knit rug can be made less elastic by using the stockinette stitch or a combination of knit and purl stitches looped through the yarn on the backside of the loop being knitted. This technique adds an extra firmness because the stitch is tighter.

Of course, the type of fiber or rags you use as the working strand also influences wear. Yarns or fabric can be used. Wool rug yarn is more tightly spun than knitting yarn. Polypropylene and acrylic macramé cord are colorfast and stain resistant. Fabric such as denim or wool flannel is heavier than the medium-weight cotton sheeting. Ribbon may be used. Sisal and jute cord can be heavy and tightly spun. Cotton seine twine or braided cord will prove more durable than paper twine.

Generally, the denser stitches and the sturdier fibers and fabrics result in a solid enough surface.

Preparation Cords and twine made for knotting are tightly twisted and sturdy. However, some preparation is necessary before beginning. If a fabric strand is used, the cloth must be washed or pre-shrunk, then cut into strands and sewn together. Cut the fabric on the bias (the diagonal). Join the ends by cutting them diagonally and seaming together. Roll your material into balls. A wide strip, about 1 1/2″ (3.25 cm.) long, will crochet or knit up quickly. Recyclers can use unraveled sweaters. The kinks can be removed by dampening the wool or soaking in vinegar and water, winding it into a ball or skein, and then drying it.

Always begin by working a small test sample. Knit or crochet a swatch of fabric, 4″ × 4″ (10 cm. × 10 cm.), with a large needle and the fabric you are planning to use. This sample tells you several things. For one, you can calculate the number of stitches per inch and the number of rows to the inch. Then by comparing this scale or gauge to the size of the rug pattern, you can estimate the amount of material. The swatch can be weighed to find the grams or ounces used. Divide the total by four to find the ounces per square inch (or

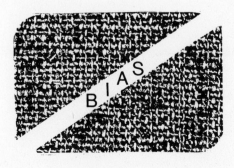

grams per fifty square centimeters). Pull skeins or balls of knitting worsted and crochet or macramé cord are marked with linear measure and weight. Rug wool is usually purchased by weight at a handweaver's store or from a distributor. Mill ends of rug wool or mixed yarns are an economical source for quantity.

The sample swatch also demonstrates the density of the planned rug. Decisions about whether to use two strands of fiber or thinner strips of rag can be made based on whether the sample gauge is too thin or too thick to provide a durable rug. In addition, by noting the time taken to make the sample, you can estimate how long the project will take.

Crochet gauges should also be made with the stitch pattern used. When a more intricate pattern than single crochet is used, a swatch is made to obtain the gauge. The swatches of the different stitches provide a visual example of how a variety of stitch patterns look together—the texture, the density, and the color.

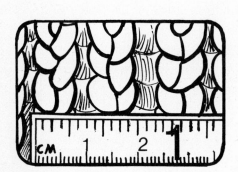

Choosing Your Yarn

There are some interchangeable yarns that make dense and bulky crochet or knit rugs. Every yarn can be knitted on several needle sizes and in many different pattern stitches, each of which changes the gauge measurement. These suggested yarns are based on the stockinette stitch before blocking or finishing.

Using a #10 needle, the following bulky-weight yarns work up to approximately 3 stitches per inch (7 per 2.5 centimeters):

- Reynolds Kirsit
- Ungers Les Bouquets
- Spinnerin Orlon Sayelle Tempo
- Brunswick Orlon Sayelle Bulky
- Reynolds Bi-Colore
- Spinnerin Orlon Sayelle
- Chunky Gleam
- Bowling Tweed.

When #13 or #15 needles are used, these yarns are interchangeable with the following, which work up to 2 1/2 stitches per inch:

- Nubby Fleece
- Bernat Scandia
- Homespun
- Gigantic Unger les Cariatides
- Spinnerin Toros
- Reynolds La Reine
- Irish Fisherman's Yarn
- double-stranded rug yarn.

If your swatch does not have the same gauge, perhaps you are working too loosely or too tightly. Use a larger needle if your sample gauge swatch has more stitches per inch. Using a smaller needle will tighten up your loose stitches.

The table that follows shows the relationship between sample yarns and cords and the approximate length of the strands of various fibers.

SAMPLE YARNS AND CORDS

YARN:	YARDS PER POUND	METERS PER KILOGRAM
Bulky wool knitting yarn	400–600	720–1,080
Heavyweight wool rug yarn (U.S. or Scandinavia)	320	576
Three-ply acrylic rug yarn	560	1,108
Four-ply acrylic rug yarn	440	798
CORD:		
Large diameter cotton seine cord	200	360
Small jute cord	250	490
Large jute cord	100	180

Estimating the Amount of Yarn

A pattern on graph paper scaled to size, four grids per inch, will help you estimate the amount of yarn to buy. Let's estimate yarn for a rectangle, 36″ × 36″ (90 square cm.). The total area is 1,296 sq.″ (8,100 cm²). Two colors of fibers, a dark-green tweed and a medium-green tweed, will be used in about the same amounts. Swatches will be made measuring 4″ × 4″ (10 cm. × 10 cm.), using the planned yarn, hook size, and stitch. The swatches determine the stitch count, the density of the rug, and the amount of yarn used in the 16 sq." (107 square cm.).

Weigh the swatch to find the grams or ounces needed for the sample. Divide the total area of each color used in the rug by the area of the sample size. Round off any fraction to the next highest number; multiply the weight by this number to obtain the amount of yarn needed.

FIGURE 3-40   To find out how much yarn is needed, determine the amount of yarn in inches or gram weight for a certain section using a swatch of crochet mesh, then multiply this amount by the total area of the final piece.

Weighing the sample, however, when the crochet stitch is worked over fabric strip filling gives a false amount. So another way to estimate length is to pull out the yarn from the sample and measure it by the yard or meter. Use the linear measure instead of the weight to multiply. For accuracy, pull out the swatch sample and make a linear measure or weigh it without filling. A general rule of thumb: the fabric strip needed either to fill a round rug or to work the crochet strand is 2 yds. (2 m.) of fabric for every square foot (30 square cm.) of rug.

Planning the Design Any graphed pattern can be translated into crochet or knit design by allowing each block of the graph to become one stitch. For example, a drawing notation for crochet used by the Japanese can help you plan the rug visually. This diagramming technique for crochet patterns appears in Mon Tricot *Knitting Dictionary Stitches and Patterns.** The diagram uses such symbols as an oval for chain stitch, a curve for slip stitch and a vertical line for single crochet. Examples of U.S. abbreviations are:

- *ch* = chain
- *ss* = slip stitch
- *sc* = single crochet
- *dc* = double crochet
- *hdc* = half double crochet
- *tr* = triple crochet
- *yoh* = yarn over hook
- *st., sts.* = stitch, stitches
- *inc* = increase
- *dec* = decrease
- *isr* = international size range.

If you emphasize color in all its tones, tints, and values and combine different textures of yarn, you will find that using the easiest, basic stitches allows concentration on the pattern. You can insert small areas of bright color accents, or you can contrast small areas of warm or cool colors as you work. A graphed cartoon or pattern may not be needed because the stitches are basic and easily executed. Again, swatches to determine stitch count and density should be made to determine the amount of material.

Using the Basic Stitches and Movements The six basic stitches of crochet are the *chain stitch, slip stitch, single crochet, double crochet, cluster stitch*, and *looped crochet*. The three movements of knitting are *casting on loops*, the *knit stitch*, and the *purl stitch*.

A fabric with horizontal ridges is produced when you knit every row. This is called a *garter stitch*. A fabric with a smooth side of vertical rows and a reverse side of ridges is made by alternating the knit stitch and the purl stitch every

*Mon Tricot, *Knitting Dictionary Stitches and Patterns; Mon Tricot Workbook 0 D14.* (Paris: 44 Blvd. des Capucines, 75002), p. 146.

other row. This combination is called the *jersey* or *stockinette stitch*. (Fishermen's wives on the Isle of Jersey have knitted sweaters using this stitch for their husbands for a long time.) Knit patterns are combinations of repeated areas of raised ridges and smooth surfaces. (See Figures 3-53 and 3-55.)

Though variations of stitch patterns can be found in any dictionary of crochet or knit stitches, the need for a dense and durable structure for a rug limits the choices of pattern. Lacy or fish-net fabric can be filled with a strand of wool, fabric, or leather. The weight of a large knit rug means that most knitters work with modular units of strips or blocks. In this way, knitting can be done on the go!

Making the Initial Loop

Both crochet and knit stitches begin with an initial loop (see Figure 3-41). Holding the end of the crochet thread in the left hand, twist the ball of thread with the right hand in a clockwise direction around and over the left strand. The ball of thread will be in back of the loop. Insert the hook under this ball of thread and draw the strand through the looped thread. You will then have a looped stitch on the hook. Pull the end of the thread to tighten the knot below the stitch. The loop on the hook is the beginning of the foundation chain stitch. This

FIGURE 3-41a   Begin loop sequence using 3/15-ply acrylic cord, making an initial loop clockwise over the end.

FIGURE 3-41b Draw the cord under the circle.

FIGURE 3-41c Insert the crochet hook under the central cord; pick up the loop.

FIGURE 3-41d Draw the loop through onto the crochet hook. Tug the end to tighten the loop.

FIGURE 3-41e   To cast on loops or slip stitch, hook around the yarn held in the left hand over the forefinger. The yarn goes over the hook.

FIGURE 3-41f   Hold the chain or crochet fabric with the left hand. Draw the slip stitch through the loop on the crochet needle.

same loop can be made by using the knitting needle to pull the thread through the loop. Tighten the loose end to form the slip knot and then, using two needles, begin the casting-on stitch to make the foundation edge of the knit rug.

THE CROCHETED RUG

Crochet is a technique that can be done by young and old. It can be picked up and worked on in small bits of time. It can be used in combination with other techniques.

In rugmaking, a large hook and thick thread help the beginner learn this technique. They make it easy to see what is happening as the work proceeds. Each stitch can be practiced until all the stitches are of a uniform size and the hook slips easily through the loops.

Using the crochet stitch without chaining in between creates a more solid surface. Some of the stitches used in crochet rugs are the shell stitch, popcorn stitch, cluster stitch, moss stitch, back stitch, and single crochet. Figure 3-42 shows a cluster stitch worked from a center chain; the bulky surface makes a thick rug, but it takes a great deal of yarn.

FIGURE 3-42 Cluster stich worked from a center chain.

Making a Hexagonal Crocheted Rug

An easy way to start crocheting rugs is to use a hexagonal motif. Begin by assembling the following materials:

- crochet hook, U.S. Size "K" (ISR 7.00)
- scissors
- tote bag
- tape measure or ruler
- Aunt Lydia's Rug Yarn—75% rayon/25% cotton—2.25 oz. skeins, 70 yds. (65 m.)—total of 63 skeins or 4,410 yds. (4,095 m.)

To make a rug similar in overall appearance to that shown in Figure 3-43, you will be maintaining the relationship of five values in your colors. I shall be describing the color scheme in that particular rug, but if the colors don't appeal to you, you can use five shades of blue or red or green or brown instead. The emotional impact will be different because of the way warm colors and cool colors affect us. You can refer to the table, where I have listed the light to dark values next to the colors as a guide so you can choose your own favorite colors.

FIGURE 4-43 Hexagonal motif crocheted rug of rayon and cotton yarn using double crochet stitch in gold, light pink, pale avocado green, rush, dark brown, 52½" × 39" (134 cm. × 100 cm.), Amy Schaible, 1978.

The gauge of the single unit is 13″ (32.5 cm.). There are seven units of colors A, six units of colors B, six units of colors C, and three rows of single crochet in the darkest color for the border.

SKEINS	YARN AMTS.	COLOR (HUE)	VALUE (LIGHT TO DARK)
12	840 yds./780 m.	pink	lightest
13	910 yds./848 m.	medium gold	medium light
11	770 yds./715 m.	pale avocado green	medium
11	770 yds./715 m.	rust	medium dark
16	1,120 yds./1,040 m.	dark brown	dark

- 7 Motif A: First round with gold (m.l.); second round with pink (l.); third round with avocado (m.); fourth round with brown (d.).

- 6 Motif B: first round with brown (d.); second round with gold (m.l.); third round with pink (l.); fourth round with rust (m.d.).

- 6 Motif C: first rond with pink (l.); second round with rust (m.d.); third round with gold (m.l.); fourth round with avocado (m.).

- * Border: three rows of single crochet in brown (d.).

Designing the Rug The hexagonal motif starts as any "granny square" with a center worked of five chains joined with a slip stitch to form a ring.

Work seven motifs using A set of colors. At the join of the ring, chain three to make the height of the design row. Double crochet in the ring twice. A double crochet is made as follows: yarn over hook and two loops are on needle. Push needle through center of ring, which is held in the left hand; pick up yarn over hook and pull loop through. There are three loops on hook. Yarn over hook and pull through two loops. Two loops are on hook. Yarn over hook and pull through two loops. One loop remains on hook. Repeat.

The pattern abbreviation as far as completed reads: ch 5, join in ring with sl st. Round 1—ch 3, 2 dc in ring*. The asterisk indicates that the stitches which follow are repeated. The next sequence is * ch 1, 3 dc in ring, repeat from * four times. There are five groups of stitches. Each is separated by a chain stitch. You will have arrived around ring at the first ch. 3. Ch 1 and join in top of ch 3 with a slip stitch; cut yarn. Each round is a different color and value. Join in a chain space with a knot that is to be hidden by the crochet stitches as you work. The complete directions for making the hexagon motif are as follows:

- Center Ring—Ch 5, join with sl st. to form ring.
- Round 1—Ch 3, 2 dc in ring* ch 1, 3 dc in ring, repeat from* 4 times, ch 1, join in top of ch 3, cut yarn.
- Round 2—Join in any ch 1 space, ch 3, 2 dc, ch 1, 3 dc in same space, * ch 1, 3 dc, ch 1, 3 dc in next ch 1 space, repeat from *4 times, ch 1, join in top of ch 3, cut yarn.
- Round 3—Join in any corner space, ch 3, 2 dc, ch 1, 3 dc in same space, ch 1, 3 dc in next space, * ch 1, 3 dc in next corner space, ch 1, 3 dc in next space, repeat from * 4 times, ch 1, join in top of ch 3, cut yarn.
- Round 4—Join in any corner space, ch 3, 2 dc, ch 1, 3 dc in same space, ch 1, 3 dc in next space * ch 1, 3 dc, ch 1, 3 dc, ch 1, 3 dc in next corner space, ch 1, 3 dc in next space, repeat from * 4 times, ch 1, join in top of ch 3, cut yarn and tie.

Make seven units, six units and six units following the color patterns. Finishing requires working on a large table or on the floor. Lay out the units with the dark motif in the center. Sew with double strands of yarn. Make sure the corners meet. The edging is done in single crochet. Increase one stitch at the corners by working twice into the same hole. Skip one stitch at the seams.

Making a Circular Crocheted Rug

Thinking through the process of making a circular rug using rags and rug wool with a J-size needle (I.S.R. 6.00) will give you a foundation for planning your own rug. An overview of the process includes knowing about materials and their preparation, tension problems, joining threads, working the circular pattern in single crochet stitches, and the finishing techniques, including blocking.

The circular rag and crochet rug I made for my kitchen is 39″ in diameter (1 m.). Two old velour housecoats, one a forest green and the other a kelly green, were washed, cut open at the seams, and cut into 2″ wide (5 cm.) strips lengthwise. These strips were joined together, seamed on the diagonal, and trimmed to a 1/4″ (6 mm.) seam edge. I rolled each strip of color into balls. Mill end rug warp was used as the crochet strand. I chose a medium value, two-ply woolen yarn of variegated greens, natural, and a little red-orange to be worked over the dark green and a thinner, two-ply dark green with rust flecks for the other crochet thread. The two strands were combined to provide a thicker yarn. The dark green contrasted with the bright green fabric fill strip.

Starting the Center   There are three ways to begin the center of the circle. Two variations start with a loop and a chain for the foundation. The third way starts with a rag strip center for a crochet rag rug.* The 3/4″ fabric is folded into figure-eights four times. It is stitched through the center and knotted. The loops are then

*Lorna B. Silver, *Rugs from Rags* (New York: Drake Publishers, Inc., 1976), pp. 37, 41.

FIGURE 3-44a   Starting a center. *Top:* Single crochet stitches are made over a filling and center and joined until a sturdy ring is formed. *Bottom right:* Single crochet stitches are made over a central ring made from a chain stitch. The second row is made over a fill strip of cut fabric tapered at the start. *Bottom left:* The fabric strip was looped on itself, with crochet stitches made in loops (because it wasn't sewn tightly, the thread broke and the center became loose).

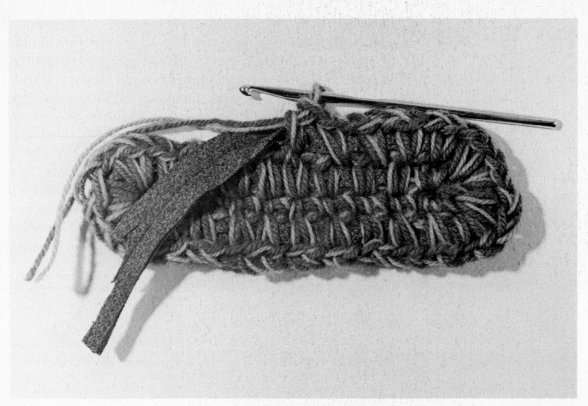

FIGURE 3-44b The oval center for a crocheted rug uses the same idea as the proportions for making the center of an oval braided rug. The desired width subtracted from the desired length equals the length of the oval's center strip. Turning the corners requires several single crochet stitches in the same loop. Using three values of the same hue adds textural interest to the loops.

crocheted into, using the single crochet in each loop. Naturally, I tried this method in my sampler when testing the color combinations and my yarns. I didn't like the result because I didn't stitch the center firmly enough or tie my knot together. The center lost the flower-like petal shape and was loose. The usual start for a circular rug is a ring center, so that was my beginning.

Stitching the Center of the Rug   I put the ball of bright kelly green filling and pull skeins of dark-green rug yarn in a basket near my chair. Using the yarn, I chain stitched a small cord of six stitches to form a foundation chain. Then I joined the last loop on the hook to the first by looping through it, and this slip stitch pulled the crochet chain into a circle.

I did the single crochet stitch over the fabric strip filling. The fill strip was folded with the velour side out as the rug was worked, keeping the raw edges tucked inside. (It takes about 9 yds. [9 m.] of fabric to make a 3′ × 4′ [90 cm. × 120 cm.] rug.) If you are a beginner, you need to know how to hold

108

the crochet hook. I find it is more comfortable when working with larger, thicker materials to hold the hook at the flattened part of the shaft with the hook facing in toward the body. My little finger helps turn the shaft, as does my wrist. The left hand controls the yarn and fabric strip and holds the area taut where the hook is inserted. The yarn is pulled up from the ball at the left. It goes between the fourth finger and little finger, crossing the first finger at the second knuckle and extending into the fabric. The tip of the thumb and the fourth finger hold the work in place (see Figures 3-41 and 3-45).

FIGURE 3-45 Holding the crochet fabric with the yarn feeding over the extended first finger enables you to have the hook ready to move over and catch another loop to finish the single crochet stitch.

Left-handed people hold the hook in the left hand between the thumb and the forefinger. Place the yarn at your right side. The fingers of the right hand guide the yarn and fabric. The strand, manipulated by the right hand, runs between the fourth and little fingers across the back of the hand and over the first finger to the crochet row. By bending the first finger, you can exert some control of the tension.

When you do the first part of a single crochet stitch, the extended yarn is taut over the forefinger. Pass the hook under and over the extended yarn above the fabric. Draw the overlapped thread through both loops. (The two parts of a single crochet stitch may be the reason the British use the terminology "double crochet stitch.") See Figure 3-46 for the sequence of this stitch.

Continue twelve single crochet stitches, pushing the yarn along the chain to make a compact center. You are now at the first stitch to spiral out from the center to continue the circular shape.

FIGURE 3-46a   Begin the single crochet stitch by pushing the hook through both loops on the chain of the preceding row. Hook over the yarn to draw the loops through both cords.

FIGURE 3-46b   Leave two loops on the hook. Push the hook over to reach the working yarn stretched from your extended forefinger.

FIGURE 3-46c   Hook over the yarn and draw the loop through both loops on the crochet hook.

FIGURE 3-46d   Draw the new loop through both loops on the crochet hook; now only loop on the hook.

FIGURE 3-46e   Detail of texture, single crochet fabric. Loop through both loops on the edge of the working row.

FIGURE 3-46f Detail of double crochet fabric. The open areas can be woven with yarn, ribbon, fur, or leather.

FIGURE 3-46g Single crochet looped through one thread at the edge of the working row makes a ridge across the fabric. (Note the mistake in one row—there is no ridge.) You can draw the new loop through only one loop on the working row to make the ridge.

Expanding the Rug The hook is inserted into both horizontal loops of the first stitch, passed over the fill, and then hooked over the extended thread. The overlapped thread is drawn through, making two loops on the hook. The hook is passed under and over the extended thread and drawn through both loops. At each horizontal loop making two single crochet stitches allows the circle to lie flat.

A rectangular rug will lie flat because the shape is established by the number of stitches in the foundation chain. The rectangle is kept even because the hook is inserted into the stitch nearest the turning chain stitch.

A circular rug and the curved ends on an oval rug are shaped by increasing the number of stitches on the foundation chain. To increase the number of stitches, a rule of thumb is to multiply the stitches by pi to increase the diameter of the rug. As it usually works out, make one increase stitch in the second round in every chain. In the third round, crochet one single crochet stitch in every stitch. On the fourth round, increase every other stitch. In the fifth round, increase every third stitch.

To make an oval expand in a regular pattern, mark where the increase stitches are made with pins. Placing the rug on a table or on the floor shows how flat it is. Ruffles are the result of too many increase stitches.

Cupping or pulling at the edges indicates not enough increase stitches. Increasing stitches is easy: Single-crochet another stitch through the same double strand of the stitch just completed.

Joining the Yarn

You have several ways to join threads together—knotting, hiding the new strand along the top of the crochet stitch, or plying the new yarns. All of these should result in hidden joins to add to the overall look of regular pattern.

Knotting. Because I was working over a filling, I chose to join the threads by knotting. I knotted the new ends using a slip knot and hid the ends inside the fill. If I had been using yarn alone, I would have laid the end or new color along the top of the row and worked the new end along for three stitches. Then I would have dropped the old thread behind, picked up the new thread and continued. Later, using a wide-eyed needle, I would have sewn the loose end into the stitches.

Hiding the stitch. An invisible join can be made by unravelling the ending tail about 3″ (7.5 cm.) Unravel the new yarn starting tail into two parts. For the next three crochet stitches, use one of the ending tail strands and one of the new starting yarn strands. Drop the ending strand and add the new strand. Later, clip the hanging threads.

Plying. Another way to join, using woolen yarn only, is to pull the end of the wool, stretching it thinner into a taper for about 1′ (30 cm.). Taper the starting strand of wool; holding both tapered strands together, twist them into a thicker strand.

Tapering the End of the Rug

How can the end of the circular rug be made to look neat? I finished the end of the fabric strip just as I would have when braiding. The strip was tapered for about 20″ (or 50 cm.), enabling the single crochet stitch to become smaller and closer around the edge. The last stitch was chained and then a knot tied when the last overlapped thread was pulled through.

Blocking and Finishing the Rug

Because this rug was made of synthetic fabric and yarns, little stretching and shrinking will occur. I blocked it by immersing it in a sink full of water and rolling it in a large turkish towel. I dried it like a handwashed sweater, laying it out flat.

If you are using wool or any cord that might shrink, before you wet the rug trace a pattern on brown wrapping paper with a pencil or indelible felt-tipped pen. Gather together steel T-pins or rustproof carpet tacks and a cellotex board larger than the rug. Place the damp rug on the pattern, which is taped to the baseboard. Starting at one edge, place pins every inch along the edges of the rug. For a rectangular rug, place pins along one edge. Then pin from the center outward along the opposite edge, stretching the material to fit the outline.

After several days, when the rug is completely dry, apply Scotchguard to make the rug more soil resistant. A mat a little smaller than the rug can be used underneath to prevent wear and slipping on a wood floor. To clean the rug, shake it outside or vacuum and turn it over. The crochet rug is reversible, a feature that gives it double life.

Variations

Other stitches. Single crochet makes a dense, firm foundation. If a double or triple crochet stitch is used and separated by two chain stitches, a looser fabric with open spaces can be made. Fabric, leather, or several strands of yarn can be woven vertically over and under the two chain bars separating the treble or double crochet. Figure 3-47 shows an example of a crochet accent rug. From the center out, the colors are rust, yellow orange, lemon yellow, pale avocado, yellow orange and rust. The rug, 75 percent rayon and 25 percent cotton, was made by working two strands in triple crochet separated by two chains. Having worked the background, two strands were worked over the leg of the grid. The undulating effect was achieved by omitting the usual two turning chain stitches for double crochet.

FIGURE 3-47a   Crochet accent rug, 20″ x 20″
(50 cm. x 50 cm.), Amy Schaible, author's
collection.

FIGURE 3-47b   Reverse side of crochet
accent rug.

115

Other materials. The circular mat can be made of fabric, rather than yarn, single crocheted over a filling. Fabric cut on the bias or in a spiral has more elasticity. I tried cutting a fabric in a spiral, cutting from the outside edge and working around and into the center. Crocheting with a strip about 1/2″-wide (1.3 cm.), the fabric twists on itself, making a cord. The wider 1 1/2″ (3.75 cm.) strip is harder to use, because it has to be rolled as it's crocheted.

For the larger strip, I tried a wedge-shaped "Le Sure" braid aid. The strip was folded in on itself as it was pulled out of the braid aid. For me it works well, perhaps because I am used to using these for braiding.

Other shapes. Crochet rugs can be rectangular, square, or oval. If these shapes are larger than a kitchen table, they are cumbersome to work because they are heavy and bulky. A rug frame or an old table can be used as support. This isn't rugmaking on the go!

So what can be done with a rug to make it portable? Make smaller units of the pattern—like granny squares, long rectangles, triangles or hexagons. These units can be joined together by chain-stitching or sewing.

Interesting variations to this basic building-blocks idea for design are endless. Different sizes of the basic unit or motif can be crocheted together using a contrasting or darker color of the dominant hue in the unit.

This weaving can become a plaid if the colors are planned ahead. A loop or pile can be crocheted into the backing while making the single crochet (see Figure 3-48). If the loop is

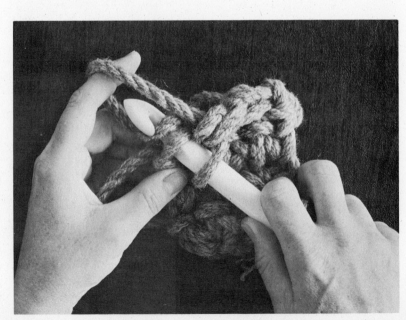

FIGURE 3-48a   Making a crochet looped pile texture using a single crochet on one row and alternating with a loop on the second working row with a single crochet hook.

FIGURE 3-48b   Continue the single crochet. Draw the yarn through the loop. Two remain on the hook and the pile loop falls away on the underside.

FIGURE 3-48c   Finish with a slip stitch.

FIGURE 3-48d   The pile twists on itself. Now make a row of single crochet. The pile row alternates with the single crochet row.

FIGURE 3-48e A tapering technique for thick yarn. The ply can be separated by twisting the strand in the opposite direction of its twist. The smaller strands can be pulled out of crochet loops at intervals and cut.

made on every other row of the single crochet, it will fall on the same face of the fabric. The hook is inserted under the double strands of the stitch, then passed over the back part of the extended thread. This overlapped yarn is drawn through the stitch, keeping the extended yarn taut over the finger. Pass the hook under and over the extended yarn and draw the overlapped thread through both loops on the hook. Drop the yarn loop off the finger and bring the yarn up over the extended forefinger, ready for the next stitch.

Combination with other techniques. Crochet can be combined with other techniques to make a sturdy rug. Knitted sections in cable stitch can be joined with single crochet using handspun Irish yarn. Another variation combines hand-dyed fleece, which was felted, cut, dyed, and then crocheted together to make a beautiful rug. You can use rags or even strips of fur. The small rugs can be fun and full of color—even a family project. Large crochet hooks and thick yarn can make a sturdy, usable rug. Jute, sisal, macramé cord, string, twine—any kind of single thread can be used. When mixing types of fibers, make sure you check their shrinking, matting, and bleeding properties before starting. If the strands are of

118

different thicknesses, several may be used together. Thus, an area of jute could be combined with an area formed of two strands of cord. Tweedy areas of color can be made easily by using two different values of one color, such as dark green and medium avocado, or two different colors like pewter grey and burnt orange. The double strands of different colors and values give the tweed effect in the rug in Figure 3-49. Although one color strand from the center area is used in the next area to make a visual transition, the eye jumps back into the large, dark central area. Different widths of stripes would have made a more unified pattern.

FIGURE 3-49   Tweed rug of double-strand colors, 22″ (55 cm.) diameter, Amy Schaible, author's collection.

THE KNITTED RUG

While walking through one of the crowded rooms of the Textile Study Collection in the Victoria and Albert Museum in London, I noticed the large quilt-size, framed textile shown in Figure 3-50. It was made of a fine, almost fingerling weight wool. The burnt orange, teal blue-green, golden green, medium tan, pink, and dark brown colors glowed in the light amid the exhibit of crewel-stitched bed covers.

FIGURE 3-50 Knitted woolen carpet, Alsace (Strasbourg), 1781. In the center is a depiction of Jacob's Dream. The inscription around the border may be translated, "God will continue to send help in despite mine enemies." Crown copyright, Victoria and Albert Museum, London, England.

Imagine my surprise as I paused and looked at the date worked into this fabric—1781! And it was a knit rug! This woolen carpet was knitted according to the specifications of the Strasbourg Guild of Knitters, a surviving "masterpiece" that an apprentice produced within a limited period of time. Regulations for achieving "Master" status and the right to have one's own shop and apprentices were modeled after those of Prague. In a given period of time, the apprentice had to knit a bonnet, a pair of gloves with fingers, a woolen jacket, and a carpet of a certain size defined by regulations dating back to 1605.

Fabrics disintegrate with age and with the vicissitudes of climate and use. The history of knitting can be traced only to the Bronze Age. Few early examples of textiles exist. One, a Coptic sock from the sixth century BC, appears to be worked with the angled stitch of knitting; but other twining techniques from Peru, for example, have a similar stitch.

Although it is known that William Lee invented a knitting machine in 1589, no one is sure when we first used needles to make the repetitive loops. There is evidence that the Aran knitted motifs or patterns were knitted by Irish monks of Bainin wool.*

The fishermen in the remote Aran Islands of Galway Bay knitted their own weatherproof sweaters up into the nineteenth century—for weren't they accustomed to looping and knotting their nets? The women spun the unrefined sheep's wool and waited for their men to return from the sea. Drowned men were identified by the beautiful, intricate pattern motifs which each family knit into unique designs passed down in the family from as far back as 500 or 600 AD. Knitting is an easy and economical way to make a cover. Two long, straight, pointed rods are used, one in each hand, and the technique is based on one strand of yarn looped on itself. There are two basic stitches used, the knit stitch and the purl stitch, on which all the motifs and designs are based. By increasing and decreasing loops and picking up loops on the edges, the fabric can be shaped into rectangles, triangles, free forms, and cut or bonnet-like forms. Variety is given to the fabric by your choices of texture, thickness, color of yarn, and combination of several yarns.

You may choose to knit in blocks or strips so you can carry your project around with you easily. The investment in equipment is minimal—two oversize needles, yarn or fabric strips, a measuring tape, a wide-eyed tapestry needle, scissors, and a bag for carrying the materials. Knitting needles are versatile and light enough even for those with physically impaired hands. In fact, knitting can be taken up to loosen joints stiffened by arthritis or to strengthen weak muscles.

*See Heinz Edgar Kiewe, *The Sacred History of Knitting* (Oxford: England Art Needlework Industries, Ltd., 2nd Ed., 1971). This is a fascinating history of knitting and other nonwoven needlework with ancient examples of knitted fabrics and garments. My personal opinion is that Kiewe's speculation as to the linking techniques needs further research by a craftsperson who knows many looping techniques. His romantic account is interesting.

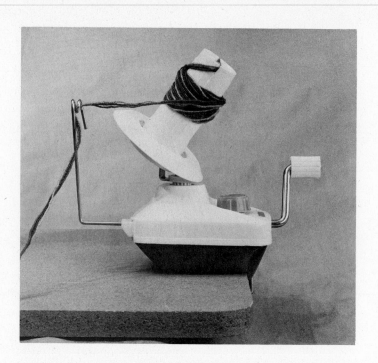

FIGURE 3-51 A plastic winding device for making a pull skein ball.

You will find that using longer needles will help you balance the weight of the fabric and that a pull skein of yarn is easiest to use because the yarn draws from the center and does not tangle.

Casting on Loops All knitting begins with a foundation row of stitches. There are two ways to cast on loops. The easiest is with the knit stitch, casting on the loops using heavy four-ply yarn and thicker-sized aluminum or wooden needles, sizes 8–14.

Everyone can hold the tools the same way, whether left- or right-handed. To knit on the loops, make a slip knot of yarn on a needle held in the left hand, between the forefinger and the thumb and with the needle slanted inside the palm. Take the other needle in your right hand like a pencil, the needle resting on the third finger with forefinger along the shaft, grasped between thumb and forefinger. Keep the pull skein ball of yarn near you on the floor or chair. To control tension, wind the yarn over and under the fingers above the middle joint. Work with your hands close together. Insert the right-hand needle through the loop stitch on the left-hand needle from the back. Draw the wound thread through the loop stitch with the point of the right-hand needle. Now transfer this loop stitch on the right needle by inserting the left-hand needle through the front of the new stitch and lifting this from the right- to the left-hand needle. (See Figure 3-52 which illustrates the casting on and knitting sequence.)

FIGURE 3-52a   Push the right-hand needle behind the left-hand needle and through the loop.

FIGURE 3-52b   Catch the yarn over the right-hand needle with the extended right forefinger.

FIGURE 3-52c   Slide the right-hand needle forward, pulling the yarn onto the right-hand needle.

FIGURE 3-52d   Pull the loop out onto the right-hand needle. (When knitting the garter stitch, the yarn remaining on the left needle is slid off, becoming a horizontal ridge on the reverse side.)

FIGURE 3-52e   For casting on and increasing stitches, slip the loop off from the right-hand needle to the left-hand needle.

FIGURE 3-52f   Slipping the loop off the right-hand needle has increased the number of stitches on the left-hand needle by one. Continue adding stitches by knitting through the last stitch on the left-hand needle, slipping the increase stitch from right to left.

Working with your ball of yarn behind the needles, continue casting on stitches by inserting the right-hand needle between the two stitches through to the back. Wind the yarn under and over the right-hand needle. Draw the yarn through the center of the previous stitches with the point of the right-hand needle, thereby forming a loop stitch. Continue in this way until the foundation row is as wide as you wish.

Knitting the Stitches   Insert the needle from left to right to the back of the first stitch. Steady the right needle tip against the forefinger of the left hand. Then bring the yarn on the right forefinger under and over the point of the right-hand needle. Draw the wound loop through the stitch with the point of the right-hand needle. Slip the stitch off the left-hand needle onto the right-hand needle. Continue across the row, knitting each stitch. Now change the needle with the knit stitches to the left hand with the continuous thread on the right side and continue knitting. The other side of the work shows the knitted stitches forming a ridge.

The second and succeeding rows are knitted in the same way until you wish to change colors, increase stitches to change the shape, or decrease stitches to narrow the shape. Such an area of knitted ridges is called the *garter stitch* (shown in Figure 3-53). It is elastic, especially sidewards. If

FIGURE 3-53   The garter stitch—horizontal rows of plain knitting.

you wish to make a tighter stitch, insert the needle between the loop from the front to the back and catch the loop around the rear part of the loop.

Purling the Ridges of the Stitches

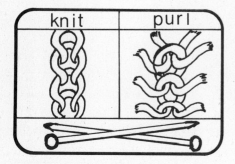

There are two differences from the knit stitch when making the purl stitch. First, you must keep the thread at the front of the work. Second, put the right-hand needle through the stitch from right to left and wind the thread under and over the point of the needle. Draw the wound thread through the center of the stitches with the point of the right-hand needle making a loop stitch on the right-hand needle. Drop the stitch you have purled into from the left-hand needle. (See Figure 3-54 for the purl sequence.) The *stockinette* or *Jersey stitch*, as it is called, is produced by knitting one row and purling the other. All ridges show on the back side.

FIGURE 3-54a   Begin the purl sequence by slipping the tip of the right-hand needle in front of the left-hand needle and through the loop.

FIGURE 3-54b   Bring the yarn up in front of the fabric and around behind the right-hand needle.

FIGURE 3-54c   With the right-hand needle, push the new loop back and through the space onto the needle.

FIGURE 3-54d   Push the loop that remains on the left tip off the needle to form a ridge. The yarn end should be on the face of the fabric toward the knitter.

FIGURE 3-55   The smooth vertical of the stockinette stitch combined with the bumpy horizontal of the garter stitch (see Figure 3-53) create decorative knit patterns. Note the characteristic vertical chevron on the reverse side of the fabric.

Adding and Dropping Stitches

To make another stitch, work twice into the same stitch. After knitting the first stitch in the usual way and placing the new loop on the right-hand needle, don't slip off the stitch on the left-hand needle. Put the right-hand needle through the back of the same stitch, knit another, and *then* slip off the stitch. Two loops are thus cast on the right-hand needle. A slight bump appears on the surface where stitches are added.

To lose a stitch or cast off is simple. Knit through two stitches on the left-hand needle and slip both off when pulling the new loop onto the right-hand needle.

Ending the Stitches

Knit stitches onto the right-hand needle. Put the point of the left-hand needle through the first stitch. Lift the first stitch over the second stitch and off the needle. It then lies as a ridge below the second stitch.

Knit another off from the left. Insert into the first, loop over and drop. At the last loop, cut a length of yarn. Pull it through the loop. With a wide-eyed tapestry needle, sew the end back into the edge and cut off the excess yarn.

You can also add new yarn, as well as motifs or patterns. New yarn can be knotted at the edge of a row. This knot will be hidden later on in the joins or by the finishing stitch on the edge of the rug. Motifs and patterns are variations of knit and purl stitches grouped in areas to give the contrast of the ridges of knit and the flatness of stockinette stitch. Figure 1-4 shows a splendid example of a crocheted and knitted rug with the wonderful possibilities that can be achieved by mixing techniques. You may be inspired to try. However, start with simple stitches and variations of yarn twists, textures, and colors. Walk before you run!

Making a Knit Throw Rug

You can make a quick ridged edge and smooth center throw rug, approximately 25″ × 36″ (63 cm. × 85 cm.) before fringe, with the following materials:

- acrylic rug yarn—8 skeins of 180 yds. each, 4 dark, 4 medium-dark (suggestions: chocolate-brown and blue, maroon and blue, rust-brown and black)

- size 17 knitting needles

- scissors

- crochet hook, U.S. size "J" (I.S.H. #6.00)

Three strands of yarn are used throughout. Your rug will have a total of about 2 stitches per inch (2.5 cm.). Make two pull skeins of three strands in the dark color for the edges. Make one pull skein of three strands in the medium-dark color for the central area. Carry the colors on the back.

Cast on 10 stitches of dark, 20 stitches of medium dark, 10 stitches of dark. The knots at the first loop of each color are worked into fringe.

- Row One—with dark, knit 10. This is a knit row. Drop dark and pick up next color from *under* the last color. This twists the two strands and prevents a hole at the change of color. Knit 20 of medium dark. Pick up dark from under last color. Knit 10 dark.

- Row Two—With dark, knit 3, purl 7. With medium dark, purl 20. With dark, purl 7, knit 3. This is basically a purl row.

Continue alternating this pattern for 74 additional rows of the above basically stockinette stitch, with the slight variation of the first and last three stitches of every purl row being knit. Bind off. Pull the loop next to the tip over the first loop and continue across. The dropped edge looks like a crochet chain.

Finishing detail. To make fringes, cut 12″ lengths. Take three strands, double them in half. Insert the hook from the top into the stitch; pull the loop through. Then pull the ends through the loop. Work a fringe in every stitch across. Then, trim the fringe evenly.

Block the rug on a large flat surface out of direct sunlight, where it may be left to dry completely.

Other
Types of Rugs

You've probably seen and admired the colorful, lush Scandinavian rugs displayed in furniture showrooms or in quiet interiors—often hung on the walls. Such luxurious pile carpets are made by using three techniques, *needle rya knotting*, *latch hooking*, and *mechanical looping*. (We've already discussed rya knotting in Chapter Three, under "Pile Rugs" in the section on "Woven and Coiled Rugs"; here we shall expand on that information.) The other type of rug discussed in this chapter, the *stitched needlepoint rug*, is known for its beautifully colored flat surface.

These four methods of rugmaking usually require more time and sometimes more equipment and more expensive materials. A frame or a table are generally used to support the mesh background or cloth background on which these techniques are worked. A table permits you to keep the large rug lying flat and also allows you to see the pattern of long shag as it is worked. A frame for needlepoint canvas prevents the stitches from distorting the perpendicular weave of the mesh backing. When using a table or frame for a large rug, the craftsperson usually sets aside a permanent work area. Of course, if space and time are limited, such large rugs can be worked in small units, which are later taped, sewn, or laced together.

RYA RUGS

Nine students in a rugmaking class at De Anza Community College, California, visited the Fine Arts Division Office. They were immediately aware of how stark and "businesslike" their surroundings were—the uncarpeted floor, two brown leather couches forming a right angle to a bookcase and file cabinet, a large executive desk dominating the other side of the room. They discussed the need for texture and color accent to make the couch area a more relaxing place for conferences and decided that as a group they would make a rya rug. Each student worked on a section, and each section took from forty to sixty hours to knot. The rug was laced together and finished in six hours. During the course of making their rug, they shared all choices and decisions—and problems. The beautiful result can be seen in Plate 15 in the color insert.

Making a Rya Rug   The first decision was size. In order to determine the best size, they arranged pieces of newspaper on the floor to see what worked best in the room. They agreed to try two different sizes, and they went home to sketch some ideas and to think about color.

Planning the Design   It is interesting to see the different approaches the students used in deciding on the design. All are perfectly good options. For example, one student made a collage of cut-and-pasted areas of cloth and paper.

For their needs, they decided that the finished rug should be 9′ × 7′ (2.7 m. × 2.1 m.) and they chose a color scheme of bone, dull gold, bright red, medium grey, walnut brown, wine red, and black. The lighter colors and the red added some contrast to the room, while the brown, dark red, and black related to the dark furniture.

Selecting the Materials   The students selected needle rya knots (refer back to Chapter Three) as the technique for the pile. The linen and wool rya backing, with plain woven bands between the open double warp threads to which the knots are attached, was very expensive—twelve dollars a running foot, and they couldn't locate cotton backing; they could have used three-ply, heavy-duty burlap if sets of warp threads were to be pulled

FIGURE 4-1 An example of needle rya. The strands of yarn can be different values of one hue or contrasting hues for a tweed effect. The traditional rya rug backing has tabby weave between the open row.

out at regular intervals. However, their choice for the backing was scrim or cotton leno canvas. A large-eyed, #13 steel tapestry needle was used to sew the knots. Machine-washable antron rug yarn in pull skeins of 2 1/2 oz. (45 gm.) and 100 yds. (91 m.) per skein was purchased. The dye lot number of each of the twelve skeins of every color was checked to be sure that all the colors would be of the same dye lot, since minute variations in color of different dye lot numbers may show as a stripe or shadow in the finished rug.

Estimating the Canvas   Mesh rug canvas comes in various widths and with different numbers of openings per inch (or centimeter). The twisted double threads of the weave form the sturdy scrim. The starched scrim makes work easier because you can roll the finished end under as the knotting progresses. Four openings per inch (4 per 2.5 cm.) was a good size mesh for this project. The needle, threaded with one or two strands of rug yarn, could easily pass into the center of the hole.

But choosing the mesh size was only part of the decision. Since the widest mesh canvas available was 54″ (1.4 m.) and the planned size of the rug was 9′ × 7′ (2.7 m. × 2.1 m.), 9 yds. were purchased. The extra material was cut into 4″ (9 cm.) squares for samplers.

Estimating the Amount of Yarn

Swatches or samples of knot patterns were made to evaluate the density or closeness of the pile, as well as to decide on the height of the pile. A single strand of knotted rug yarn seemed to cover the backing and, when looped over two fingers, had a good pile height. A double strand, the samples showed, made a harsh dense surface. The decision was made therefore to use a single strand.

There are two ways to check the quantity of yarn worked in 1 sq." (2.5 cm.²). One way uses the fact that there are 8 knots and 4 half-knots in a square inch, since rya knots are made between and over two warps. You can unravel the yarn and discover how much is used. Then multiply the length by the number of square inches (square cm.) in the total rug. Another way is to weigh the swatch, using a baby scale, and multiply the weight by the square inches (square cm.) in the rug. Of course, if you are fortunate enough to live near a weaving or rugmaking supply store you can use the charts of yarn quantities that are often posted in the store.

Designing the Cartoon

The undulating wave design was sketched on wrapping paper that had been taped together and cut to the desired rug size. The stripes were numbered from one to seven to indicate the progression in the waves from dark (one) to light (seven).

The cartoon was cut into nine parts so each person could work on a section. Each received rug backing 1" wider and longer than the cartoon size. Immediately, the cartoon was placed under the long strip of backing. With a waterproof felt-tipped pen, the rug was marked at the division of each wave stripe. Each student numbered the cartoon from one (dark) to seven (light). Some wrote in the color sequence on the cartoon to be sure to remember the proper order: black, wine red, walnut brown, medium grey, bright red, dull gold, off-white.

The mesh was turned back along both long sides. As the knots were made, the hem was tied into the surface. The folded edges made a strong area to be joined by a facing stitch, or blanket stitch.

Making the Knot

The stitching of the rya knot begins at one edge. The long strip is rolled up at the top and pinned together. As the work progresses, the closest edge is rolled under and pinned. Starting at the left the knotting rhythm is worked in pairs of warp; the needle with the single strand goes into the center, to the left around the warp, up and across two warps, down on the right side of the warp, around and up and out between the

133

two. Then, before entering the center of the next pair of warps, it travels over the pile gauge of two fingers or a ruler. Working with the darker colors first keeps the light colors cleaner from dust and fuzz from the dark colors.

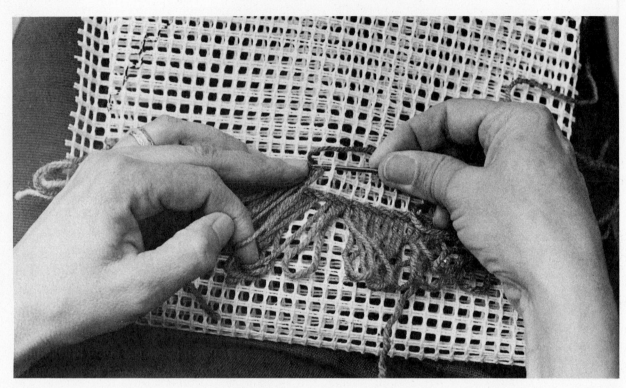

FIGURE 4-2 The rya knot is made between and over two warps, using the fingers as a gauge.

Allowing for the color transitions. The knots are worked in rows. When ending, cut the tail to the height of the pile. When beginning a new strand, no knot is necessary. To avoid an abrupt change of colors, allow about two inches for a transition between the two colors. At about 1″ away from the pattern mark for the curve, start the alternation of the next color for five rows.

Joining the Units   Since a few of the people had been unable to finish their pieces, the finished pieces were laid on the floor to see if the missing pieces would distort the waves in a peculiar way. One strip that could not be pulled or turned—or even partially reworked—without a tremendous amount of time and effort became a permanent sample for the studio. The rest of the pieces were marked on the back with tape and a number so they would be in the proper order when they were sewn. A lacing, or figure-eight, was used to stitch them together.

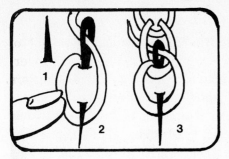

The edges of the rug were all turned over and worked together while knotting. The pile was long and covered the edges.

Thanks to group planning and decision making, a task which would have taken an individual approximately 400 hours to complete was accomplished in six weeks. And the completed rug makes a beautiful area accent.

Variations Using the modular idea, you can mix different techniques: for example, weaving with needle rya or latch hook with needle rya and chaining stitch. Constance Chase used rya knots, latch hook, and the chaining stitch to make the wall hanging in Figure 4-3. If Connie had not cut it into several sections, it would have been more cumbersome and heavy to handle while working. This design was inspired by an aerial photograph of land, and the pattern of linear shapes in the design may remind you of farmland or irrigation ditches. The tones of grey and brown wool are looped together with shiny off-white, 2-ply acrylic and wool yarn to achieve the exciting color and textural effects. The pile height varies. The chaining stitch used to cover the flat lower areas saved yarn. Rug binding tape was sewn to the cotton muslin cloth backing, turned and

FIGURE 4-3a   Wall hanging using rya knots, latch hook and chaining stitch, 60″ x 48″ (150 cm. x 120 cm.), Constance Chase, 1978.
FIGURE 4-3b   Detail. The combination of techniques adds dramatic planes of texture and color.

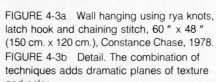

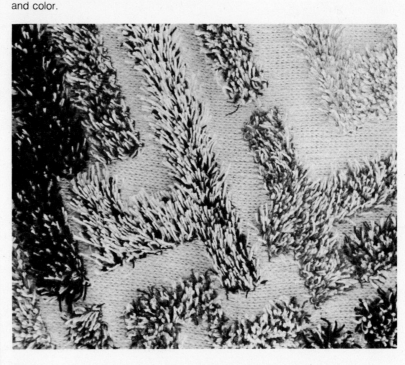

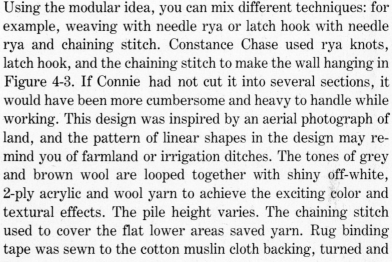

135

hemmed. (Refer back to Figure 3-11 for an illustration of this method.)

Another beautiful example of a needle rya knotting made by Anna Marie Lininger is shown in Figure 4-4. This rug is made of plied wool rug yarn (Nordiska brand), wool fleece, and wool and linen commercial rya backing. The colors range from the natural-color fleece cental area to red, orange, purple, brown, rust, and plum.

The rhythm of knotting on small sections is relaxing. You can listen to music, watch television, and carry it along wherever you go. Threading the needle requires a little dexterity and fingers do tire easily at first. However, give your hands a "shake–shake–shake" to loosen your muscles and you can work for hours when you have time.

FIGURE 4-4 Needle rya knotting, 199 ″ x 75 ″ (297.5 cm. x 187.5 cm.), Anna Marie Lininger, Lafayette, California, 1976; photograph courtesy of the artist.

LATCH HOOK RUGS

A latch hook rug is made of knotted tufts of yarn and has a shaggy texture that reflects light in a sculptural way when the pile length is varied. Most fabric and yarn departments in large commercial stores sell latch hook kits, stamped backing, and pre-cut yarns. Usually, the designs are pictorial in content and suitable for a wall decoration. Some of the larger and more expensive kits contain the stamped backing and yarn for making rugs. Often, making your own design and choosing your own colors make the rug less expensive. The growing market for latch hook materials has made the materials for a unique rug generally more available.

Planning the Design   All of us can cut and divide a rectangular piece of paper into three, five, or seven shapes of different sizes. All of us have a favorite color or two. Dreaming up these two important components of a design—shapes and colors—usually presents no problem, but tying these elements together visually can. There are some guidelines for unifying a design.

Think about a rug in your home that you like. Is there a texture change from smooth to looped? Does the shadow falling on the texture emphasize the repeat pattern? Are there more than two values (that is, great variation in the lights and darks or tones and shades) of the color? If there are two hues, are they used together in one strand to enrich the area? Or are the two hues placed to form a pattern that leads the eye around and across the flat shape? Is there a shape that is repeated and varied, such as a flower or half-circle? Is the shape varied by changing the size? Or by the mixture of values of hues on the shape? Or by the hue itself?

The guidelines for planning your design are:

- Establish a pattern of light and dark values,
- Repeat them with variations of shape and hue,
- Use some contrast to make centers of interest.

Decide on an overall geometric emphasis or on a realistic image as the unit motif and the pattern on the rug. A checkerboard design is the obvious way to achieve repetition. Just as the bright red checker starts on the black or dark square and the dark or black checker starts on the red or brighter square, you can use this plan for organizing a design. Basically, the checkerboard pattern is the repetition of a bright and a dark color alternately across the surface. The checkers form a reverse pattern.

Another geometric pattern that you already know is the brick repeat. Look at a brick fireplace or wall. In the first row the rectangles touch and march with narrow end to narrow end across the row. Half a brick starts the second row. End to end, the brick continues across. This is often called a *half-drop repeat pattern*. Old brick is pleasing to look at because the red color has been altered from a single red color to a softer pink, red, and darkish red. The grout line between the brick pattern is a grid that holds together the pattern visually and the bricks physically.

Another idea can be gotten from a stained glass window, which has a grid of lead cams that strengthens the glass and forms a dark pattern. Fifteenth-century church windows told stories in glass with the realistic images of people and flower forms.

Selecting the Materials   Although a crochet hook can be used, a latch hook is easier and will increase your working speed. A latch hook looks like a crochet hook with a hinged gate on the side opposite the shank of the crook (Figure 4-5). This tool speeds up the pulling-through of the loop when yarn is inserted into the interlocked mesh of the rug canvas.

One kind of rug canvas is a mesh that has interlocked warp threads. There are three-and-a-half to five holes per inch (2.5 cm.). The other kind of rug backing is penelope canvas, in which the threads of the mesh are woven in pairs.

FIGURE 4-5   A latch hook rug in progress. The edges are turned back and two layers of mesh are knotted together. Using two different lengths of pre-cut yarn results in pile of different heights.

Canvas is sold in widths of 28″ (70 cm.), 36″ (90 cm.), and 40″ (100 cm.). Two widths can be overlapped, the mesh pattern matched over each other, and then hooked as one. The widths may be hooked separately, then butted and laced together in matching mesh.

Pre-cut latch-hook rug yarn is made of wool or acrylic. Wool is more resilient, has richer tones, and comes in two lengths: 2 1/2″ (6.25 cm.) and 3 1/2″ (8.75 cm.). The acrylic yarn length is 2 1/2″ (6.25 cm.). Both are packaged in 320 to 350 thread ends per ounce. Usually the colors have at least four values of each hue. The limitation of pre-cut yarn is the length—two standard heights, 2″ (5 cm.) and 4″ (10 cm.), make tufts of 3/4″ (1.8 cm.) and 1 1/2″ (3.75 cm.). To hook contrasting areas into a rug, you may want longer lengths of yarn. Wrapping yarn around a box cover or around a board is a good way of measuring longer lengths; they can be tied together and then cut into strands. Binding tape is used on the edges of oval, circular, and irregularly shaped rugs. These shapes are cut out of the rectangular shape after the loops have been hooked. A blunt and wide-eyed tapestry needle can be used in joining the sections and in finishing the rug with the overcasting stitch. A small sewing needle and buttonhole thread are used to secure the rug binding. A rug frame is not necessary.

Transferring the Design to Canvas

If you prefer having an exact plan for the rug rather than letting the dark and light patterns evolve as you work, make a drawing on wrapping paper to the size of your rug. This cartoon may be colored with cut-and-pasted bits of colored photos taken from magazines. Color can also be indicated with crayon, ink, paint, or by using the symbol of black to mean dark, cross-hatching areas to mean medium, and so on.

There are many ways to apply the design. You can place the cartoon under the canvas mesh and outline the areas of color with an indelible pen. The cartoon will guide the placement of colors later. Acrylic paint or dye transfer crayons may be used to color the areas of mesh. Or you can count the mesh, sketching the original idea on a graph paper grid and coloring it. By counting the grid openings and the rug mesh, each knot can be made to follow the design.

You can make a unit design by dividing a square into a simple shape. A repeat pattern can then be planned by making several square units to manipulate in different ways. Repeat them in straight rows, turn them upside down, or reverse them. The darkest band or area of color in one unit that touches the dark in the other unit may create new shapes or

FIGURE 4-6 Latch hook rug design drawn with indelible pen on **Penelope** rug canvas.

areas. Draw this unit design with an indelible pen onto the rug canvas, purchased at the same time to insure a matching weave of the mesh.

Knotting The usual way to make the latch-hook knot is to work the separate strands row by row, pulling the knot in the same direction until it is 5″ from the opposite end. If you are using the modular method of making a larger rug, you may have to knot the pattern on some units in a different direction. The joins between sections that reverse the pattern cannot be easily seen, and the pile on all pieces lies in the same direction. Before ending the knots on the side opposite the direction of the lie of the pile, reverse knots must be knotted.

140

Plate 1 (above)   Detail of tapestry from Harrania (handspun wool), 33″ x 24″ (83.8 cm. x 61 cm.), Egyptian youth, 1970; author's collection; photograph courtesy of Terence M. Campbell.

Plate 2 (right)   Detail of needle-point rug (bargello stitch, double or smyrna cross stitch, #4 mono canvas), 48″ x 36″ (121.9 cm. x 91.4 cm.), Joyce A. Hupp, 1978; photograph courtesy of Shirley I. Fisher.

Plate 3 (above)   Detail of "Inuzik" (tapestry, wool, pneumatic rug punch), 66″ x 16½″ (167.6 cm. x 41.9 cm.), Lynden Keith Johnson, 1971; photograph courtesy of Terence M. Campbell.

Plate 4 (right)   Detail of "Full Moon after Portugal Bay", 39″ (99 cm.) square, Lynden Keith Johnson, 1976; photograph courtesy of the author.

Plate 5 (below)   Detail of crochet rug over velour fill strip, 72″ (182.9 cm.) diameter, Lillian Mary Quirke, 1977; photograph courtesy of Terence M. Campbell.

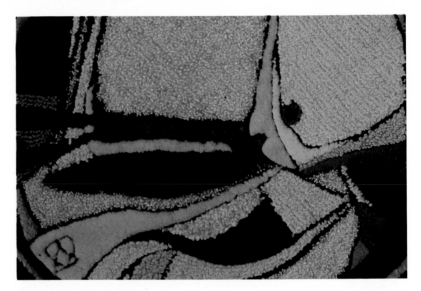

Plate 6 (above) Detail of Hamadah rug (Turkish Knot, wool, natural dye), 76″ x 40″ (193 cm. x 101.6 cm.), author's collection, c. 1905; photograph courtesy of Terence M. Campbell.

Plate 7 (left) "Persian Prayer Garden" (electric rug punch, wool rug yarn), 72″ x 48½″ (182.9 cm. x 123.1 cm.), Patti Henry; photograph courtesy of the artist.

Plate 8 (left)   Detail of Early American style hooked rug (wool), 36″ x 21″ (91.4 cm. x 53.3 cm.), Peninsula Rug Guild, 1973; photograph courtesy of George M. Craven.

Plate 9 (below)   Detail of Iranian Kelim rug (handsewn edge of tapestry weave), 81″ x 50″ (205.7 cm. x 127 cm.), author's collection, 1925; photograph courtesy of Shirley I. Fisher.

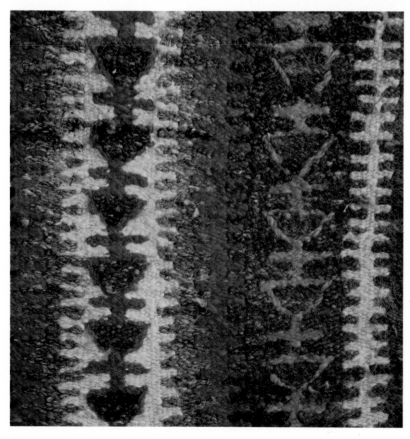

Plate 10 (right)   Detail of braided rug (wool fabric strips, variegated warm colors), 36″ x 72″ (91.4 cm. x 182.9 cm.), Berkeley Cooper, c. 1971; author's collection; photograph courtesy of Terence M. Campbell.

Plate 11 (lower right)   Detail of "Tide Pools" (shuttle hook and latch hook wool rug), 84″ x 72″ (213.4 cm. x 182.9 cm.), Howard Milton Warner, c. 1965; photograph courtesy of Terence M. Campbell.

Plate 12 (below)   Detail of area carpet (glued pieces of carpet scraps), 120″ x 84″ (304.8 cm. x 213.4 cm.), Judy Miller Johnson, 1976; photograph courtesy of the author.

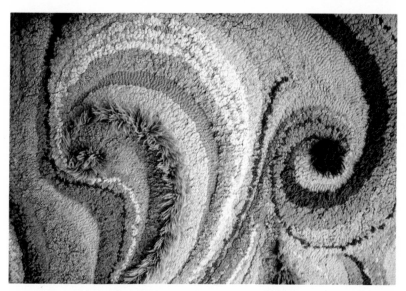

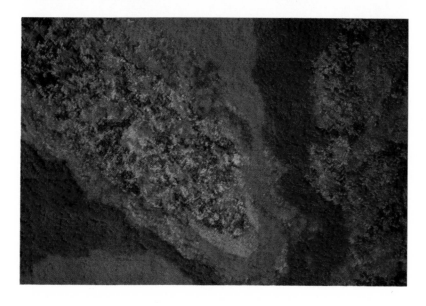

Plate 13 (above left)   Numdah felted rug (wool, couching and chain stitch embellishment), 69″ x 43″ (175.2 cm. x 109.2 cm.), author's collection, c. 1928; photograph courtesy of Terence M. Campbell.

Plate 14 (above)   Navajo rug (handspun, cedar bark dye and natural color), 56″ x 37″ (142.2 cm. x 94 cm.), author's collection, 1950; photograph courtesy of George M. Craven.

Plate 15 (left)   Group needle rya rug, 60″ x 84″ (152.4 cm. x 213.4 cm.), De Anza Community College students, 1977; photograph courtesy of George M. Craven.

Plate 16 (right) "Flowers Wired All Over the World" (wool felted tapestry), 108″ x 88″ (274.3 cm. x 223.5 cm.), Robert Freimark, 1976; photograph courtesy of the artist.

Plate 17 (below) Detail of Iranian Meskin rug (right-hand Persian Knot), 59″ x 41″ (149.9 cm. x 104.1 cm.), author's collection, c. 1950; photograph courtesy of Terence M. Campbell.

Plate 18 (left)   Hooked rug, 156″ x 132″ (396.2 cm. x 335.2 cm.), Annie Bird Plumb, 1959-1961; designed by Mortimer F. Quirke; photograph courtesy of Jack McConnell.

Plate 19 (below left)   Rya technique (plied wool rug yarn, wool fleece, commercial rya backing of wool and linen, cut pile 2″ [5 cm.] long), 199″ x 75″ (505.4 cm. x 190.5 cm.), Anna Marie Lininger, Lafayette, California, 1976; photograph courtesy of the artist.

Plate 20 (below)   "Bedroom, Circa 1900" (electric rug punch, wool), 65″ x 60″ (165.1 cm. x 152.4 cm.), Patti Henry; photograph courtesy of the artist.

Beginning five rows before the edge, every fourth knot is looped to fall in reverse. On the fourth row, the third and fourth knots are reversed. On the third row, the second, third, and fourth are reversed; on the second row, the first through the fourth are knotted in reverse; on the ending row all are knotted in reverse. The pile will lie flat all around the rug.

Be advised that latch hooking is slow. You can estimate the time involved by knotting a sampler of one square inch and timing yourself. There are 16 knots per square inch in #4 rug canvas, and 25 knots per square inch in #5 rug canvas. Multiply this figure by the number of square inches (square cm.) and you can estimate total time. Figure that approximately 4 1/2 hours are required to hook 1 square foot (10 square cm.).

FIGURE 4-7   Detail of latch hook rug made of modular units, 36 ″ x 24 ″ (90 cm. x 60 cm.), Patti Jauch, 1976. (The joint can be seen in the light areas where knots weren't reversed.)

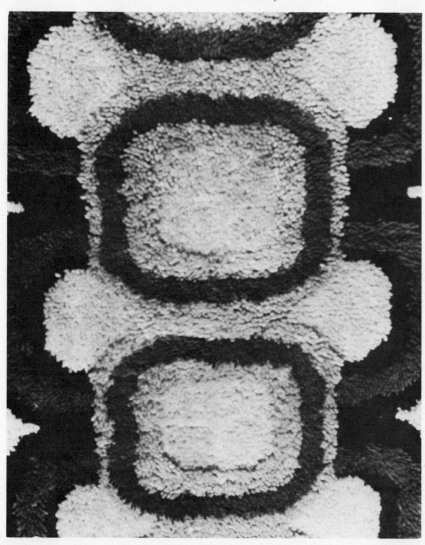

Finishing the Rug   A rug made in a rectangular shape needs no finish because, at the beginning, the rug mesh is folded over on the top at the fifth or sixth row. The knots are worked through both layers. The cut end of the warps are covered by the ends of the knot. The selvedge edges may be turned under and treated as binding tape. However, it is better to remove that edge and fold to the top, working through the double thickness. The completed rug has a level back side. The mesh ends are hidden by the pile.

Irregularly shaped rugs are trimmed, leaving a border of canvas the width of the rug binding tape after all the knots are made. Sew the rug binding tape securely onto the mesh at the edge of the design. Turn, miter the corners or pleat the curved ends, and stitch the other edge of the binding tape securely to the mesh. Use small stitches and heavy-duty cotton sewing thread.

There may be loose fibers. Acrylic yarn, for example, sheds and pills. Give the finished rug a slight shake and brush the rug in the direction of the pile. With scissors, you can even off the pile. Use a rug pad or rubber under the carpet for longer wear. Scotchguard it before using—spots can be more easily sponged off the surface. Do not wash in hot water or dry in an automatic dryer. Wool shrinks, and the size or stiffening in the mesh washes away.

Variations   Latch hook can therefore be combined nicely with other rug-making techniques. Felted areas, as thick as the short pile, can be stitched to the rug canvas before the knots are made.

FIGURE 4-8   Hexagonal latch hook rug, folded torn-paper design, 30 ″ x 66 ″ (75 cm. x 155 cm.), Laura Dahlke, 1978; photograph courtesy of the author.

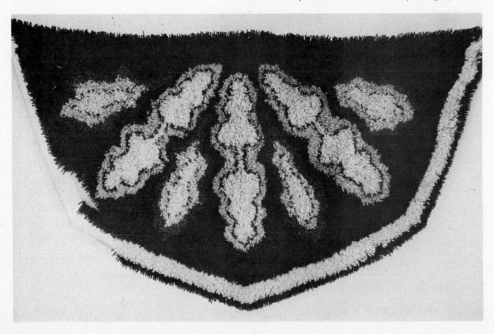

Needlepoint stitches make colored patterns of flat texture between tufts of short, medium, and long strands (Figure 4-9). Two or more strands of different hues or textures can be used together. Why limit yourself to a kit? You can make a beautiful, richly colored, textured rug—a rug that expresses your interests, your colors, and your unique decisions.

FIGURE 4-9 Face and underside of rug sampler combining latch hook and bargello stitch in diamond shape, Stephanie Thomas.

Making a Latch Hook Rug

To make a 25″ × H. 30″ (63 cm. × 75 cm.) rug, use

- interlocked rug canvas, 30″ wide × 36″ high (75 cm. × 80 cm.), 16 openings per square inch (2.5 cm.) [note that twisted strands run vertically]

- 26 1 oz. packages of pre-cut rug yarn, 4-ply, wool or acrylan if allergic to wool, 350 ends per package; 3″ length (7.5 cm.).

- tapestry needle and 8 yards (8 m.) of blending dark hue (used to overcast stitch the edge)

- your work time should be approximately 43 hours; if you gauge 16 knots per square inch, figure the rug will be 1 1/2″ high.

Cut a dramatic shape out of dark paper and explode the shape. Plan the design to scale on graph paper, 4 grids per inch. Indicate your colors, grouping all dark value hues in the dark area of the original cut-paper design. Use medium light values and bright hues in the light areas.

Transfer your design by the count grid method. Mark the outlines of the color areas with fabric marking felt pen, or cut large shapes from newspaper and trace.

Work the knots row by row across from the bottom to six rows from top, when every fourth knot is looped in reverse direction. Gradually change the direction by alternating loops until the ply of the final row faces in the opposite direction.

PUNCH HOOK PILE RUGS

Making a punch hook pile rug is an ideal project for those people who have busy schedules. Once they have mastered using mechanical looping and tufting tools, the actual working process for such a rug is very quick.

A beginner can usually complete one square foot (30 square cm.). in an hour, two at most, with a punch hook, a rug tufting tool, or an electric tufting needle. A rug measuring 21″ × 36″ (52 cm. × 92 cm.) can be made in forty to eighty hours; eight to fifteen hours (about 20 percent) of the time would be spent sketching ideas or cutting paper designs, buying the rug backing and yarns, setting up the frame, and transferring the design onto the backing. After tufting the rug, another 20 percent of the time would be spent finishing the rug— shearing the pile, applying latex, and turning hems. With practice, a person acquires speed, and once the basic tools and equipment have been acquired a considerable amount of time can be saved when the next rug is made.

Making a Punch Hook Pile Rug

The basic kit of materials to have available can be assembled quickly:

- a sharp pair of scissors to cut material
- a sewing needle and cotton thread #50, or a sewing machine to join the material
- a piece of chalk to mark a pattern
- a tape measure
- a ruler and paper, or Dietzen ruled vellum graph paper, 4 grids per inch (2.5 cm.).

To make a rug frame you will need:

- pine or fir lumber, about 24 board feet of 1″ × 2″
- oval-headed wood screws
- a screwdriver and drill or nails
- a hammer.

You'll also need C-clamps or rope to tie the frame onto a chair or saw horse; 5 yds. of sturdy burlap or cotton-dacron woven sailcloth to make a rug backing, or polyethylene woven rug backing; a punch needle set, an eggbeater-style punch hook; a two-handed up-and-down shuttle hook; a rugcrafter looper; and rug yarn (cotton, wool, or acrylic).

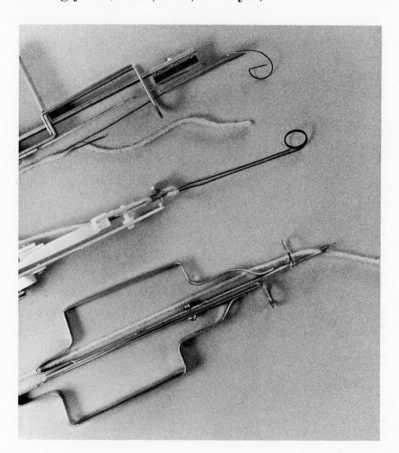

FIGURE 4-10 Automatic rug tufting tools. *Top:* Punch hook. *Middle:* Eggbeater-style punch hook. *Bottom:* Shuttle-style punch hook.

Keep in mind that a rug of wool yarns on linen or cotton backing is more durable than one made with burlap and acrylic yarns. Though both fade in direct sunlight, the commercial dye industry now has the fading factor up to eight. In sun and dampness, warp and weft threads of the burlap fabric rot more easily than linen or cotton.

Thinner yarns can be combined. Using several different values or a range of five to eight values of darks and medium-lights of the same hue make a lovely textured pile that is more imaginative in color than commercial carpets are. If dark colors predominate, use a greyed color for the lightest rather than bright white. Another way to achieve a contrast that enriches the texture is to use cotton floss, shiny and silk-like in appearance, in the same loop with wool.

To finish the rug, you'll be using:

- liquid latex (1 quart covers 9 square feet [1 square m.])
- rug binding adhesive
- strong buttonhole thread
- wide-eyed needle
- cardboard squeegees or spatula applicator
- scissors

Be sure to work in a well-ventilated area. Protect your working surfaces with newspaper or butcher paper and your hands with gloves when you work with the liquid latex. And, when you finish, mark your name permanently on the rug and list its height and width, fiber content, and washing instructions.

Estimating the Amount of Yarn

The salesperson at a craft shop that carries the equipment can help you estimate the amount of rug yarn to buy. Be sure to buy more than you need. As we've seen before, a valuable way to find out how much you will need is to make a sampler and weigh the swatch (most yarn is marked in ounces and grams). Find the area covered with yarn by multiplying length times width. Do this for each sample of pile height. Once you decide the total size of the rug, you can divide by the swatch size and multiply by the total number of swatches it takes to make the rug. A handy reference table follows.

YARN COUNT FOR PUNCH NEEDLE

SIZE— SMALL TO LARGE	YARDS TO COVER 1 FT.	100 YDS 2-PLY SYNTHETIC
1	200 yd. (183 m.)	75 square in. (875 square cm.)
2	230 yd. (209 m.)	60 square in. (150 square cm.)
3	300 yd. (273 m.)	50 square in. (125 square cm.)
4	310 yd. (283 m.)	48 square in. (120 square cm.)
5	320 yd. (291 m.)	45 square in. (112 square cm.)

Calculating yarn for the rug tufting tool. An outline of the rug design is made on graph paper to size. Each unit of the grid represents one square inch (or one square centimeter). When a curved line of a shape cuts a square, count the grid as one. This will provide a little extra yarn. The total square inches of yarn needed for each color area can easily be calculated. If the pile height of an area is different, it also can be planned by counting. The following yarn chart shows how Dorothy P. Cutler calculated her yarn need as one pound, five ounces (figures were rounded off).

YARN COUNT FOR RUG TUFTING TOOL

COLOR AREA— LIGHTEST TO DARKEST	PILE SIZE	AREA— 1 SQUARE IN. (2.5 SQUARE CM.)	MILL END 2-, 3-, 4-PLY RUG YARN OUNCES	YARDS/METERS	
1	1	20	1	50	46
1	3	20	1	50	46
2	1	15	1	50	46
2	3	15	1	50	46
3	1	35	1½	75	69
4	1	46	2	100	91
5	5	80	2½	120	110
6	5	35	2½	120	110
7	1	137	5	250	229
8	1	137	5	250	229

Using the Tools Using the mechanical looping machine, punch hook, punch needle or electric rug punch is the fastest way to make a rug. Figures 4-11–4-16 show what the tools look like and how to use them.

Working with a punch needle requires a continuous length of yarn with a long loose loop on the work area (2 yds. or 2 m.) feeding from a pull skein or ball of yarn twirling freely in a can or container. The punch hook can be adjusted with a coin or screwdriver to make longer loops (directions usually come with the tool). The long loops add a shadow pattern to the rug. Place the loops with care, and use a rug with drastic combinations of pile heights where people won't trip. A sharp contrast between the area rug and the surface on which it lies not only accents the pattern but also clues the people walking in the room where to walk.

You might ask: How portable are these tools? Or, how

FIGURE 4-11a When using the rug-tufting tool, the shuttle tips forward and the needle pierces the fabric to leave a loop on the reverse side.

FIGURE 4-11b The reverse and underside of the burlap backing shows the tip of the tufting tool in the process of leaving the loop.

FIGURE 4-11c To end a stroke, the tip is drawn up above the surface of the rug backing.

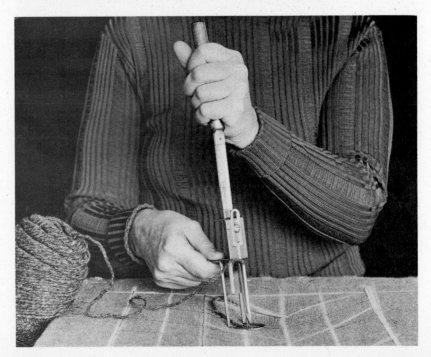

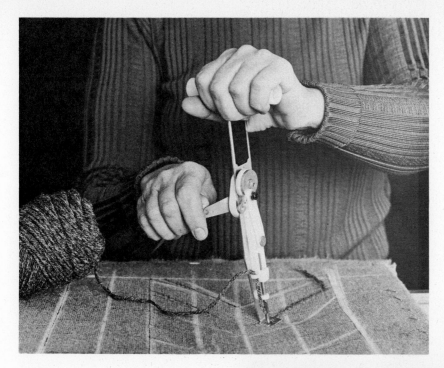

FIGURE 4-12 The eggbeater-style hand punch is held against the stretched burlap in a perpendicular position. The yarn must be kept loose to feed the punch.

FIGURE 4-13 Shuttle-style punch hook with adjustable needle. The foot must be tilted slightly backward to pick up the needle tip and travel toward.

much strength is needed to use them? They are to be used with a rug frame to support the rug backing. Look at it this way: You can spend those rainy and snowy stay-at-home days at the rug frame, which can be made at home, purchased at a rug crafters shop, or ordered through the mail from rug suppliers. (See Sources of Supplies.)

As for strength, most of the mechanical rug loopers require two hands. The electric rug punch is heavy and used with one hand. The industrial pneumatic rug tufting machine also weighs a lot; working with this machine especially requires excellent coordination and good health. (One person found that it was easier to control the speed and the heights of the pile when using a rug punching tool manipulated by hand rather than electricity.)

Learning to use new tools like the electric needle may require practicing with scrap materials. Mistakes may be pulled out easily. The pile then is punched perpendicular to the used area. Tears can sometimes result, but they can be patched by basting another piece of cloth, slightly larger in area than the tear, over the holes. A long running stitch is made in parallel lines, then crossed with stitches, like a grid.

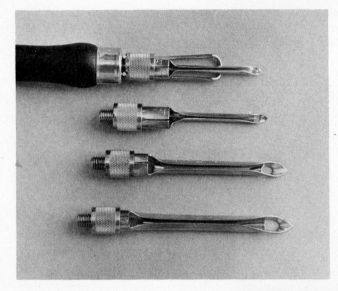

FIGURE 4-14 Punch needle set. Different-size tips are used with thicker yarn or several strands of yarn.

FIGURE 4-15 The electric tufting gun is adjustable to five different heights and is worked on the reverse side. It should be held upright with the foot flat against the rug backing, which is tightly stretched and stapled to the frame. The frame should be raised above the work surface so loops can be formed, and the yarn from the pull skein must be kept loose.

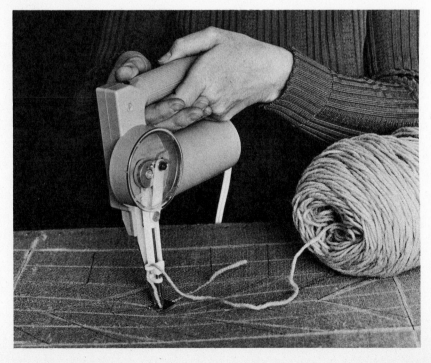

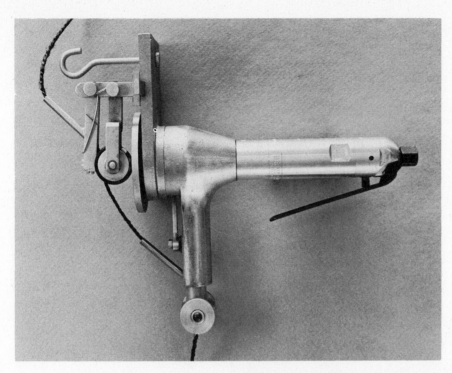

FIGURE 4-16 Professional mechanical tufting machine. The tip of the needle barely shows from beneath the circular wheel that rolls across the fabric, synchronized with the up-and-down thrust of the tip.

Working with the
Rug Backing and Frame

No matter what the shape of your rug, you should decide the dimensions before you buy the backing. It's economical to plan ahead. And, whatever size you choose, allow a minimum of 4″ (10 cm.) or larger to become the unworked border surrounding the rug. To make a larger circular rug, 5 yards of sturdy burlap, natural or medium brown, will be cut in half. The two pieces, 40″ × 2 1/2 yds. (100 cm. × 2.5 m.) long, are joined along the selvedge edge, sewing by hand or machine after the rug is hooked. A large upright frame could be used with the wider material. Circular rugs are cut and finished after working the rectangular cloth on the frame. Since punching is done from the back side, stretch the rug backing tightly and test it by bouncing a coin. Be sure to mark the center drawing line from side to side.

Punch hooking the loops with one of the mechanical tufting tools requires stretching the rug backing over a frame. The loops, which form the varied heights of pile, are formed on the underside of the working surface. The distance between loops and the direction of the rows of pile are controlled more easily from the tautly stretched top side. A mirror placed below the frame will reflect the pile and how the density, height, and colors look.

151

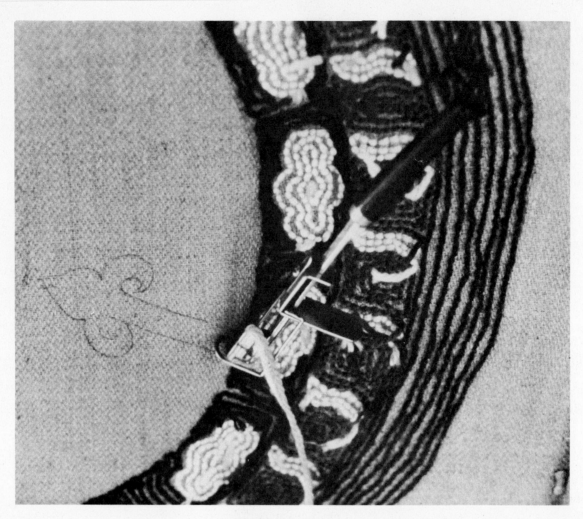

FIGURE 4-17 Working on the reverse side of a rug. The outline was made with an indelible pen on the backing. The loops made by the mechanical tufting tool follow the contour of the shape.

To make a frame, nail or screw together two 1″ × 2″ × 4′ and two 1″ × 2″ × 8′ lengths of common pine, using an overlapping joint. If you're using finishing nails, place them at one-inch intervals around the frame. Using wing nuts will allow you to disassemble the frame quickly into four sides, which can be tied and stored standing up behind a door. Fir and red pine are soft woods with a large grain pattern. Burlap, cotton, or polyethylene rug backing can be easily tacked or stapled to the soft wood frame. The frame should be 4″ wider than the final rug size on all sides—or allow for seaming and matching the pattern afterwards.

Drawing the Pattern You can draw your own patterns and transfer them to the canvas by using a grid of squares around the picture you want to copy. Enlarge the grid on the burlap backing.

152

Once you have sketched out your outline, you can use acrylic water paints to mark out color family areas. Don't waste time painting the burlap the true color. Red on the backing, for instance, can indicate that three of four shades of red are to be used. Of course, if you make a good enough color sketch to work from, you can merely outline where the color families will go.

Variations   Some of the geometric rugs in the illustrations were designed and executed by beginners. If you prefer images as well as rich color, large areas can be filled with realistic flower forms or child's drawing. Textural variations other than high and low loops are options you have. Some looped areas may be sheared; other areas may remain looped. Yarn seen from the top cut edge looks darker than when viewed from the side. The use of cut and looped pile adds a subtle color change in values. There is also a textural contrast between the soft cut yarn and the tighter loop.

There is no reason tufted rugs cannot be made in combination with other techniques. Gluing commercial carpet scraps into areas of looped colors shows a contrast of thick, velvety areas with textured areas. This use of scrap material may also save money for the craftsperson.

FIGURE 4-18   Skirt for Christmas tree with primitive holly leaf and berry design worked with tufting tool, 38" (95 cm.) diameter, Judy Chargin, 1978.

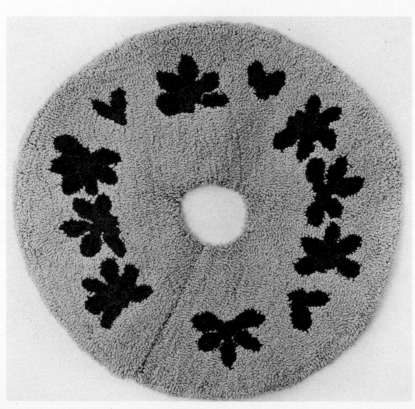

Josephine Lee made a rug with a diamond motif and pattern of angular lines (see Figure 4-19). The design is a striking pattern of dark, medium-dark, medium-light and light values. A sparkle in the central area of light value is achieved by randomly hooking the pale pink and pale lemon yellow in the diamond motifs. The black and white photo does not do this justice, unfortunately, since the simultaneous use of different close shades of colors in the diamonds photographs as one tone. Thirty-five working hours after the sudden inspiration for the design, the rug was finished. It is not being used as a rug but as a wall hanging to add color and texture to the room!

FIGURE 4-19   Speed tufted wall hanging, 30 ″ x 45 ″ (75 cm. x 112.5 cm.), Josephine Lee, 1978.

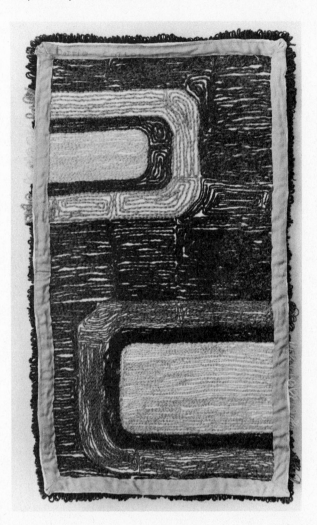

FIGURE 4-20a   Looped rug worked with both electric rug tufting needle and manual tufting tool, 36 3/4 ″ x 21 ″ (91 cm. x 52.5 cm.), Dorothy P. Cutler, 1978.

FIGURE 4-20b   Reverse side of looped rug. The thicker yarn and the highest pile were punched into the area with more backing exposed between rows. A rug binding machine stitched on the face, folded over and whip stitched down the back.

Using several values of the same color yarn adds richness and variety to an analogous color scheme, like the rug made by Dorothy P. Cutler (shown in Figure 4-20). Using the cut paper method of designing she cut out parts of rectangles from a piece of black paper. Separated and expanded, they made new patterns on a paper background. The simplicity of the design inspired the use of various height loops. The dark and medium-dark values of the avocado green, the medium and light values of sage green, and the pale value of the lime yarns mix well with the dark brown accent color. Looking at the black and white illustration, you cannot see that the field behind is made of a double strand of yarn. One strand is brown, the other is dark avocado. A rich and subtle color effect has been achieved like pine needles in the shade of a tree.

155

FIGURE 4-21a   Detail of a formal robe for a Chinese civil official of the second rank, dark blue silk with Mandarine Square; embroidery and coral beads; length of robe is 123.2 cm. (Gift of Colonel and Mrs. John Young, Stanford University Museum of Art, Stanford, California 94305).

NEEDLEPOINT RUGS

From the simple binding of edges using a sharp thorn for a needle and a fiber strand from the leaf of a cactus plant, people have progressed to making elaborate, decorative, and beautiful fabrics. Cloth can be embellished with a linear pattern characterized by the directions of these colorful threads. Needlepoint is one specific style of decorative embroidery.

FIGURE 4-21b *Dragon Robe*, China, Tao Kuang Period (c. 1821-1850). Silk tapestry *(Ko᾽ ssu)* woven in gold, silver, and colors, the ground is maroon. Length: 56″ (140 cm.) (Gift of Colonel and Mrs. John Young, Stanford University Museum of Art, Stanford, California 94305)

Needlework has become a big business. Erica Wilson, for example, produces needlework kits, a newspaper column, and a TV lecture series, as well as running retail shops and needlework cruises and writing a dozen books.* Many references are out there somewhere for you to discover, along with places for you to exhibit your work. County fairs offer opportunities for competing and for showing your needlepoint, the categories often broken down by age and skill. National competitions also divide the exhibits by skill ranging from work made from pre-packaged kits to using designer-printed canvases to planning and executing one's original work.

Making a Needlepoint Rug

In needlepoint, the entire surface is covered with stitches. No fabric shows through the beautiful patterns of threads. Technically, needlepoint means that threads are stitched on a loosely woven fabric with specific straight and diagonal stitches to make a pattern.

By sizing with a starch or glue, the grid-like mesh background is made stiff enough to work more easily. While stitching the design, this canvas may be carried with you. By winding the canvas around a simple dowel or circular pole or by pinning, stitching, or stapling it to a lightweight frame, you can work anywhere. Needlework of any type is a way of relaxing from tension-filled days: The rhythm of the stitches seems to calm the nerves. Seeing the design grow in its colorful array pleases us as we work.

Selecting the Tools and Materials

To make a needlepoint rug, you will need to be aware of some information about canvas, needles, and yarn—information that I shall discuss in more detail. You will also need:

- 2 pairs of scissors—one with a sharp point to snip off ends of threads that have been worked through the yarn on the reverse side of the design, another larger and stronger to cut the rug backing

- one-inch (2.5 cm.) masking tape or cloth tape for binding the cut edges of the canvas

- measuring tape and a ruler

- an indelible needlepoint marker, which comes in colors that do not run when wet

- graph paper with the grid pattern the same number of spaces as the mesh count per inch (cm.).

*Rita Reif, "While Everybody Does It (Men Too), Erica Wilson Sews Up Needlework," *People Weekly* (Dec. 12, 1977), Vol. 8, No. 24, pp. 68–74.

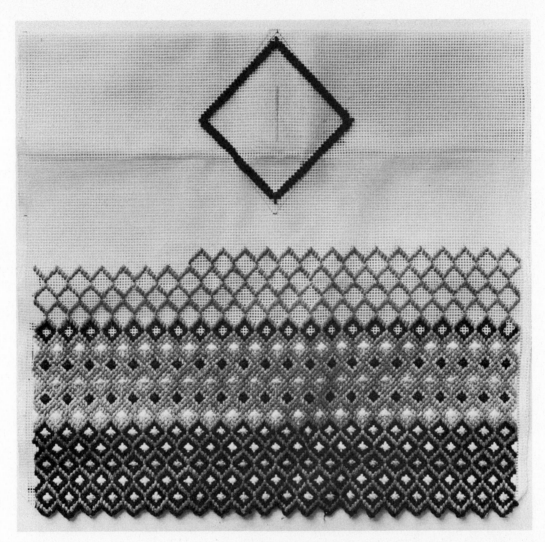

FIGURE 4-22 Needlepoint rug in progress, bargello stitch for diamonds, double or Smyrna cross stitch centers on # 4 mono canvas, finished size 48 ″ x 36 ″ (120 cm. x 90 cm.), Joyce A. Hupp, 1977–1978.

Your blocking materials should include:

- brown paper
- white vinegar and water to set yarn colors and to dampen the finished piece for stretching into shape
- sponge
- steel T-pins or staples and staple gun
- rabbit-skin glue for backing
- spatula spreader
- draftsman's triangle or right angle
- an old flat wood or plywood for stretching and blocking the finished rug.

To finish the edges you'll need:

- rug binding tape
- heavy buttonhole thread
- needle and pins.

For keeping all your yarns and things together, use an old purse, a sports tote bag, or a basket. You'll be able to carry your supplies with you and ready to work on your needlepoint during those hurry-up-and-wait moments we all have during the day.

Canvas. In needlepoint, stitches are made on the canvas over the crossed threads, called a *mesh*. The way we measure canvas is by the number of mesh per inch. This count varies from 3 1/2 per inch to 22 per inch, and even finer. Although canvas of 3 1/2 and 5 mesh per inch may be executed faster, rugmakers can make a fairly intricate gradation of tones on canvas with 10 mesh per inch.

Canvas is sold in different widths, fibers, and colors. A few canvasses also have a design woven with a light contrasting color into the structure. One of these designs marks the canvas off with a blue thread into blocks of 10 mesh per inch, by which a repeat pattern is easily counted. Canvas is made in white, yellow, and medium-brown cotton, linen, and polyester. If you use cotton, keep in mind that the mesh may shrink a little when blocked or stretched into shape. All mesh is stiffened with a *size* or starch-like coating that washes off during cleaning and blocking.

Does one type of mesh canvas make a better background for a rug than another? The answer is yes. Let's look at the three structural types: mono, leno, and penelope.

Mono canvas is a non-interlocking mesh. The single vertical (warp) threads and the single horizontal (weft) threads are woven over and under each other in a regular grid. This canvas mesh has a tendency to slip when worked too tightly. You may also find that the canvas distorts easily as you work.

Leno canvas is also known as *interlock canvas*. At the mesh intersections, two vertical (warp) threads are twisted together around the horizontal (weft) threads. This structural difference from mono canvas prevents the mesh from slipping at the crossing of the warp and weft.

Penelope canvas is made of four threads at the mesh intersections. A twisted pair of vertical (warp) threads is more closely set than the paired horizontal (weft) threads.

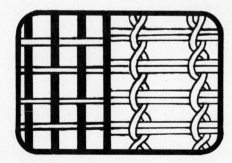

This canvas mesh is strong because the interlocking prevents slipping. The paired mesh also make the canvas versatile because the threads can be separated and smaller stitches worked into a detailed pattern, using a thinner strand of yarn and a narrower needle. Penelope canvas is measured by the number of *paired* mesh per inch.

Choose the width that is two or three inches larger than your rug will be. The selvedges make sturdy edges that keep the weave straight. The edges outside the working area can be used for stapling or pinning during the blocking process. They provide a turn-back edge for the binding stitch and the hem.

Needles. A rule of thumb, when choosing the blunt-tipped and wide-eyed tapestry needles you are going to use, is that the threaded needle must drop easily through the opening in the mesh. The large eye of the needle is made smooth and long for easy threading of the one, two, or even three strands of yarn used to cover the backing. The blunt tip won't stab you when working with both hands or split the strands of the mesh or yarn. A needle case and an emery pin cushion will keep your needles ready to use.

Yarn. Don't skimp on the amount or the quality of this material when you are investing hundreds of hours—several months—of your time. Wool yarn is moth-proof and comes in about four hundred colors. Different manufacturers have slightly different dyes and choices of color ranges. Go to a needlepoint shop to see the colors, or write to a manufacturer for swatches and information. Several types of yarn may be used.

Persian-type yarn, one of the best for needlepoint, is spun of long fibers and twisted loosely of three strands of smooth two-ply thread. The yarn fluffs out to cover the mesh. It may take two yarn strands or more to cover a wide mesh. Another advantage is that this yarn is easily separated to work small mesh and details. The separated strand can be added to another darker colored yarn for a subtle sparkle.

While no one is certain of the origin of the term "penelope" for the mesh, the origin of Persian yarn is known. This yarn of many hues was developed for use when repairing Persian carpets. It is usually 33″ (73 cm.) long and sells by the ounce or gram. An 8-oz. skein (226 gm.) contains about 320 yds. (291 m.).

French tapestry is twisted more lightly than Persian-type yarns. The single strand four-ply needlepoint yarn gives a smooth finish to a canvas done in the appropriate size. The choices of colors in this wool fiber are rich and jewel-like—great range of value and chroma choices.

Rug yarn is thicker, tightly twisted, and comes in cotton, acrylic, wool, and sometimes a mixture of fibers. The acrylic rug yarn has a glossy, slick look, and it pills or throws off excess fiber in little dust-like balls. Cotton rug yarn presses down and mats more easily than other fibers, but it has a flat and sometimes dull look after a few weeks' use. Wool rug yarn is the most versatile and very resilient. The fiber, which looks something like barbed wire when magnified, refracts the light. This broken reflected light gives a glow and richness to the color, even with darker colors. *Rya yarn*, a Scandinavian woolen rug yarn, is an excellent choice. The range of colors is extensive and, like the Persian-type yarn, well worth the added expense.

Knitting yarns should *not* be used. They are not twisted as tightly as tapestry wools and rug yarn. Also the elastic quality of yarns for sweaters and the like is not the kind of flexibility and sag you want in a rug. By combining wool yarn with a single strand of rayon, linen, cotton, or silk, you often achieve a richness of sheen, color, or texture without sacrificing durability.

Other fibers might be used on the larger mesh canvas, such as satin-covered rat-tail, tight seine cord, sisal, and jute. The fiber should cover the canvas completely. The wide mesh may need two or three strands to cover.

Be experimental. Mix the textures and colors. Buy an extra amount of canvas to try out your ideas.

Estimating the Amount of Yarn

You can estimate how much yarn you need by making a swatch 1″ (2.5 cm.) square. Draw a square on the penelope, interlocked, or mono canvas with an indelible needlepoint pen. Thread the needle of the appropriate size for the canvas mesh opening with a pre-measured strand of yarn. Record the yarn measurement. Use the straight stitch or the diagonal stitch to cover the mesh with the pattern you are planning.

Now total the amount of yarn you have used in this sampler. Multiply the total number of square inches of your canvas area to be covered with the stitch by the amount of yarn used in the sampler. This total can be divided by 36″ or 100 cm. to obtain the number of yards or meters needed.

Skeins of yarn are usually sold by ounces or grams with the yardage listed. Always buy a little more yarn than you have estimated. The surplus can be used to adjust tension changes or permit you to change your mind about color accents. Dye colors are not always exact matches, so keep a record of the dye lot number, the dye name, and the manufacturer for your own reference.

The Stitches

Stitches are divided into three categories according to the number of stitches per inch (per 2.5 cm.) on the canvas on which they are worked: quick point, gros point, and petit point. *Quick point* is the term used for 3 1/2 to 7 stitches per inch. *Gros* (pronounced grow) *point* includes 8–14 stitches per inch. *Petit* (pronounced petty) *point* is a fine, small stitch of 16 to 40 or more stitches per inch; this stitch is not practical for rugmaking.

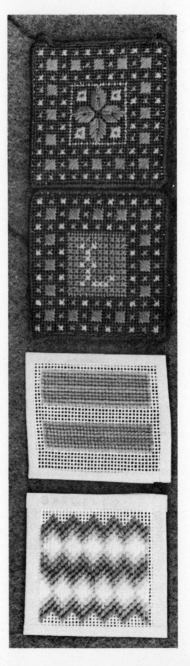

FIGURE 4-23 Samples of needlepoint stitches that can be used with large mesh (samples a-g done by Joyce Hupp).

FIGURE 4-23a Needle case: Scotch, fern, double cross, diagonal, Hungarian, and squared daisy stitches, Mark Daly, 1977.

FIGURE 4-23b Half cross (diagonal) and continental (diagonal).

FIGURE 4-23c Bargello diamonds (straight).

FIGURE 4-23d   Rice stitch (diagonal).

FIGURE 4-23e   Woven basket stitch (straight).

FIGURE 4-23f   Double cross or Smyrna cross.

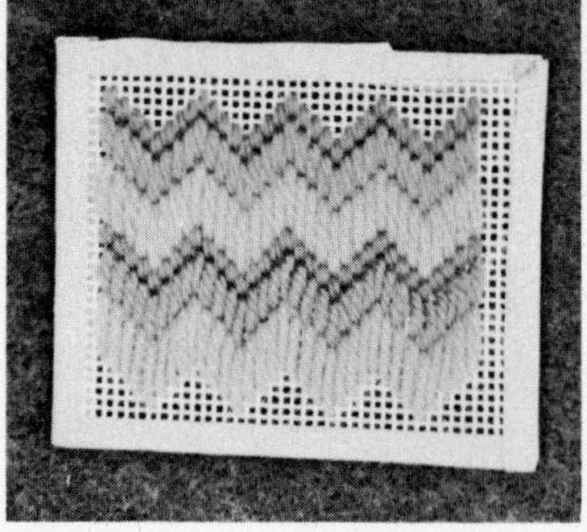

FIGURE 4-23g   Bargello (straight).

FIGURE 4-23h   Pockets embroidered in cross
stitch on cotton cloth, Huichol Indians
of Mexico. The strong light and
dark patterns are inspirations for rugs.

Do various stitches make a rug more or less durable? The answer to this question is yes. When making rugs, a *flat stitch* is usually the most practical for durability. The flat stitches are further classified into *straight stitches* and *diagonal stitches*.

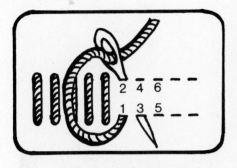

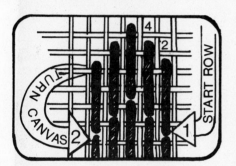

Straight stitches. Straight stitches are worked horizontally or vertically. They do not distort the canvas as much as diagonal stitches. One stitch which grew out of an embroidery stitch, the *satin stitch*, has many variations: Florentine stitch, Hungarian point, flame stitch, Irish stitch, gobelin, and bargello. This type of stitch is based on counting the threads or the meshes to establish the striated repeat pattern. The satin stitch may cover one mesh (gobelin) or many meshes (bargello).

The *gobelin stitch* is a straight stitch worked vertically over one mesh in rows or horizontally in rows by turning the canvas. The *brick stitch* is a vertical stitch worked alternately bottom mesh to top mesh starting at the right. The half drop repeat pattern reminds one of bricks. The cloth is turned 180 degrees at each row, or upside down, to continue.

The *bargello stitch* is a quickly executed straight stitch that, if not used with long floats, is very sturdy, with a good backing that makes a well-defined geometric pattern. This stitch lends itself to rhythmic patterns, patterns that often look like flames, waves, and snowflakes because of the rhythmic repetition of the counted units. It also lends itself to shading colors, from light to dark or bright to dull.

Understanding how the bargello stitch is executed helps a person in planning a bargello pattern. This stitch is vertically a straight stitch that looks diagonal on the underside. Starting at the top of the area to be covered, the first row establishes the rippling stripe or horizontal band pattern. Colors are used with four or five values of light to dark. Each row of stitches changes in value and the length of the stitch. (A caution for rugmaking is that the longer stitch [over 7 mesh openings] catches easily—beware of, for example, cats.) For an alternate pattern, locate the center of the canvas by measuring, folding, or counting. Mark both the vertical center and the horizontal center with an indelible needlepoint marker or a basting thread of contrasting color. Turn the canvas as you work each quarter section to rotate the pattern of flowing stripes around the background.

Use a grid paper and colored pencils to plan out the design. Try various groupings of straight strokes repeated

FIGURE 4-24 Bargello stitch.

across the top. The needle comes up from underneath at the top of the stitch and enters two or more mesh openings below in the same column. The back of the work has diagonal lines to indicate where the needle moved over one column to the next row for starting the next stitch. Right-handed people work from left to right; left-handed people, from right to left.

By rolling up the finished canvas at both ends and pinning it with large safety pins, you make the canvas portable and distort it less. Steam pressing and pulling any distortion square after every day's work may eliminate blocking at the end. As the rug progresses, you may need a table to support the weight of the rug while you work.

Diagonal stitches. The three basic diagonal or tent stitches—the half cross stitch, the continental stitch, and the basketweave stitch—are worked on the diagonal over the intersecting warp and weft threads. The *half cross stitch* distorts the canvas and has poor coverage on the back; it's not a good stitch for rugmaking. The *continental tent stitch* begins at the right side of the canvas. The needle comes up from the

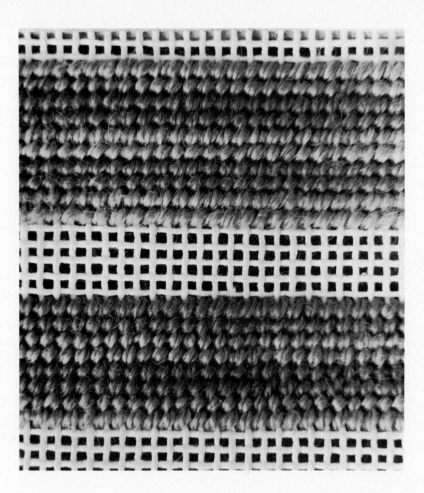

FIGURE 4-25   Half cross stitch *(top)* and continental stitch *(bottom)*.

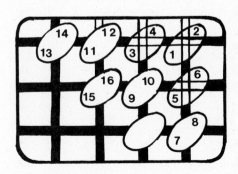

underside to the left, crosses the diagonal of the mesh, and is inserted on the right. After completing the row, the usual method is to turn the canvas 180 degrees. The underside stitch makes a diagonal ridge. This stitch doesn't distort the canvas as the half cross does. It's good for small areas and as a background stitch because it is snag-proof and flat textured. Both of these stitches require blocking.

The best stitch to use when you're working a large area and don't want distortion is the *basketweave stitch*. Like the continental tent stitch, it makes a good, flat-textured, snag-proof background. It is worked from the top right across to the left and diagonally downward in alternate rows without turning the canvas at the end of a row. When the stitch is executed correctly, the bottom side of the canvas looks like a wicker basket. The woven structure of this stitch adds firmness and makes for a long-wearing surface.

Some hints for making the stitch are: hold the needle in a vertical position when you are working down the diagonal line and passing the needle over a vertical warp of the mesh intersection over one thread from left to right and under two

FIGURE 4-26a Basketweave stitch.

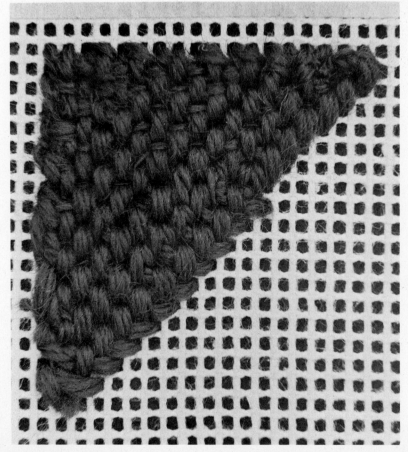

FIGURE 4-26b Reverse side of basketweave stitch.

threads on the way to the next stitch; hold the needle in a horizontal position to begin the stitch when you are working up the row and the needle is passing over a horizontal warp of the mesh intersection.

Decorative stitches. Decorative stitches combine straight and diagonal and sometimes looped stitches. Usually, they are not flat stitches. Each of them has a special name and can be found in any needlepoint book. For example, Figure 4-22 shows the double or smyrna cross stitch, a durable and decorative combination of straight and diagonal stitches.

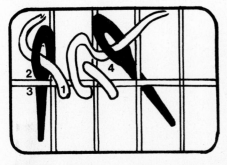
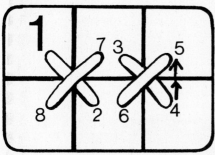

FIGURE 4-27 Double or Smyrna cross stitch.

Figure 4-23 shows a needle case using the continental stitch and diagonal Hungarian stitch blocks for the small squares and the Scotch stitch for the larger squares. The initial was made with the double or smyrna cross stitch. The fern stitch and squared daisy stitch were also used.

In another such combination the padded cross stitch with tramé yarn sewn through the double horizontal mesh of the penelope canvas, is easily worked. The tramé yarn peeps out

FIGURE 4-28a   Needle case. The small squares are done in continental stitch and diagonal Hungarian stitch blocks, the larger squares in Scotch stitch, the initial "L" in double or Smyrna cross stich.

FIGURE 4-28b   Detail of back of needle case, showing fern stitch and squared daisy stitch.

from between the cross stitch and produces a speckled or tweed effect. Complementary contrasts of hues, which complete the color sensation and contrast with each other, create an illusion of a third color along the edges of the pattern. You can discover how to create an illusion of a third color along the edge pattern by placing a piece of brightly colored paper or cloth on a larger white piece of paper or cloth and focusing on it for 40 to 60 seconds, then focusing on the white background; you will see a faint color—the opposite of the brightly colored paper or cloth. Skiers who use colored skis may have already discovered this when they look away from their red skis to see "greenish" snow!

For additional visual impact, the contrasting color cord you underlay can be very thick or furry; you can also use strands of braid or strips of rags. Think big and adapt the slanting stitches and straight stitches to make beautiful color patterns.

Decorative stitches may be too complex to work successfully for an entire rug. They snag easily, and often, they do not cover the underside of the rug, so they are less durable. If you do decide to use decorative stitches, apply latex to the backing to hold them and make the rug last longer. You may want to use decorative stitches for small areas, such as a border.

Now that we've discussed mesh, needles, yarns, and stitches in detail, the table that follows will give you a good summary of which goes with which.

GUIDELINE FOR CANVAS, NEEDLE, STITCH AND YARN

NUMBER OF MESHES PER INCH	SIZE OF TAPESTRY NEEDLE	NEEDLEPOINT STITCH	AMOUNT OF YARN PER SQUARE CM.)	PERSIAN TYPE YARN
5	13	Basketweave Diagonal Tent	21 in.	two full threads
5	13	Cross	1 yd.	two full threads
10	18	Basketweave Diagonal Tent	46 in.	one thread
10	18	Cross	2 yds.	one thread
NUMBER OF MESHES PER CENTIMETER	SIZE OF TAPESTRY NEEDLE	NEEDLEPOINT STITCH	AMOUNT OF YARN PER SQUARE INCH	PERSIAN TYPE YARN
2	13	Basketweave Diagonal Tent	53 cm.	two full threads
2	13	Cross	90 cm.	two full threads
4	18	Basketweave Diagonal Tent	115 cm.	one thread
4	18	Cross	180 cm.	one thread

Planning the Design   A good design for a rug is a repetitive pattern with many variations and values of one hue. The darker shades, medium and light values, vivid and dull tones of a single color are soothing and interesting. Using a graph helps you count out the repeat pattern. Another way of designing is to use a unit motif. Be sure that your rug canvas is two or three inches (5 to 7.5 cm.) longer and wider than your rug design.

A translucent grid paper, with the same number of openings per inch (2.5 cm.) as your rug canvas backing, aids you in visualizing your design. The graphed design is worked by counting. Using graph paper with a darker grid at the 1″ mark makes the counting easier. You could put your drawing underneath the canvas. The outline will show up between the mesh and can be drawn in with an indelible needlepoint pen. Color can be painted on the mesh with thinned acrylic paint, which is permanent and will not run later during the cleaning and finishing. If you don't have any color on your graph or on your drawing, you can use dots, lines, and crosses to indicate the color. You can also paste a thread of color in the area as a visual aid.

Stitches made of straight or diagonal lines can be drawn on the graph paper with short strokes of a colored pen or sharp crayon. You can immediately see how the flipped or rotated pattern of the linear bargello pattern looks, how the rose with the saw-tooth edge looks. The shading of highlights to dark shadows can be planned, as well as the blocks of decorative stitches that are repeated often.

A word of caution: If you enlarge a picture or another needlepoint design, the larger scale of the mesh and the rug tends to simplify the image you copy. Changes have to be made. A spot of red as big as your fingernail looks bright and makes an accent. Now, imagine that bright red as large as your hand. Wow! That area of red becomes a bold, shouting shape. You must use yarns of the same hue in a gradation of values to integrate such a large shape into the rug. Designing the rug to the final size with cut paper and with areas of dark and light helps you see the scale.

Other problems arise with the wider mesh which dictates a bolder edge to the lines, shapes, and border. These edges may be softened by using different color yarns with the same brightness or dullness next to each other.

Piecing. If the projected size of your rug is larger than the widest mesh you can buy (60″ or 150 cm.), you can piece together two widths of canvas. Always buy both sections at the same time and from the same bolt so the weave of the mesh matches. When you use the overlap method, cut off the selvedge edge of the overlapped pieces. Stitch the canvas together or carefully glue it together with liquid latex applied with a toothpick. The canvas remains flexible. Another way of joining is made after both sides have been worked and before blocking. Bend back the penelope canvas on both edges to one line of mesh. Overcast both edges with strong sewing cotton thread. Cover the joint with a diagonal tent stitch in the color of the background.

Preparation Cut brown paper the same size and shape as your rug canvas. Mark this paper and save it to use as your blocking pattern. Any distortion of the canvas caused by stitching can be stretched out when you finish the rug.

Bind the outside edge of the canvas with tape to prevent raveled threads, and mark the design area with an indelible needlepoint pen. Mark both the vertical and horizontal center lines by measuring or folding the canvas in half and then in quarters.

Threading the needle can be done in a number of ways, and you can use any way that works for you. You can use a stainless steel needle threader. If you don't have one, wrap a piece of paper, slightly smaller than the eye of the needle, around several strands of thread; then pull the ends of the paper through the eye—and the yarn follows. Another way is to fold the last 2″ (5 cm.) of the yarn in half over the needle and pull it tight which creases the yarn, hold the loop of yarn, barely exposed, between the thumb and first finger, holding the needle in the other hand, place the eye of the needle over the loop and push it onto the yarn.

Stitching Starting and finishing your stitches without a knot is advisable to prevent a lumpy background. Hold a 1″ (2.5 cm.) tail end of the thread underneath when you start. Stitch over it when coming through to the next hole. End the stitch either by sewing the end through the yarn on the back or by sewing, loosely, between the backing and the stitch in a horizontal or vertical direction. A very slight raised bump appears on the top side when stitches are ended.

Change colors by sewing the new yarn underneath the stitches already made at the back. In this manner, the color changes at the edges of shapes, both colors share the same mesh, and no canvas is exposed. Also, your stitches always go in the same direction.

If the strand of yarn becomes twisted, dangle the needle and thread from the canvas back. The thread spins itself straight. Another problem to avoid is crumpling the canvas. Roll the excess canvas out of your way over a paper tube. If the canvas is distorting on the diagonal, you may be pulling the thread too tightly.

Finishing the Rug   Blocking, or squaring the mesh canvas, is done by wetting the canvas and stretching it back into shape. The brown paper pattern that you have cut to match your rug is taped to a board. Draw lines down the center, both horizontally and vertically, with your indelible marking pen. This sketch will be your guide.

After dampening the rug and rolling it in a towel to absorb the excess moisture, lay it on the paper guide. Make sure the center of the rug matches the center of the pattern. Use either rust-proof T-pins or rust-proof staples to tack the rug to the board. Start with one side, working from the center outward to the corner of the rug, tacking every 1/4″ (6 mm.). Do the opposite side in the same manner; then repeat the process for the other sides. Make sure the rug is squared to the pattern.

Leave the rug for several days to thoroughly dry. Don't try to hurry the drying process by putting it in the direct sunlight or heat, you could distort it or hurt the fibers. If, after you remove the rug from the frame, it still appears distorted, repeat the blocking process again.

After blocking your rug, spread a thin coat of rabbit skin glue on the backing, mixed according to the directions on the container. This application helps the rug retain its shape and adds strength.

When the dry rug is removed from the board, turn the edges back, leaving one free thread of mesh. Miter the corners and stitch the mesh into place. Overcast a whip stitch with a double strand of yarn around the edges of the rug over the remaining mesh strand. Then sew binding tape over the mesh border, after removing the masking tape. A lining of sailcloth or duck canvas may be sewn to the back for added protection. Tapes fixed at the angle of each corner can anchor any rug padding placed under the needlepoint rug.

Now that the rug is complete, fluff up the yarn on the topside by running a steam iron just above the wool. Scotch-guarding the rug when it's dry, spraying two or three applications in different directions, makes the rug soil-resistant.

Variations   The rug canvas for needlepoint is often used for backing rya pile rugs and latch hook rugs. A pleasing combination of the sewn loop, latch hooked loop, and decorative stitches might be worked as a sampler. The sampler helps you not only to see how the colors and textures work together and how to estimate the amounts of yarn, but if finished with knots or fringe can become a decorative wall hanging.

Changing a needlepoint design from a #10 monocanvas into a #5 quickpoint canvas expands the design four times. A 54″ (135 cm.) wide rug stitched on a 60″ (150 cm.) wide #10 Monocanvas has 510 stitches across one row. A 54″ wide rug stitched on a 60″ wide quickpoint penelope canvas has 270 stitches across one row. The 60″ wide canvas allows 3″ (7.5 cm.) of extra canvas at each side for a hem.

Combining stitched units with crochet joins offers new possibilities. Rya loops can add textural emphasis to a needlepoint pattern. You might want to experiment with chicken wire or hog wire mesh and jute cord as a variation. You could make a good rug for the outdoors this way. How about a wall hanging or a divider screen?

Meet Some Fiber Artists

Understanding the inventive process and construction methods that an artist uses can help you weigh the cost of buying a handmade rug against the cost of a mass-produced, commercially loomed, tufted, or needlepunched carpet. You may be surprised to know that a commercially made rug with a thick and dense pile can cost as much as—and sometimes more than—a hand made one.

This chapter introduces you to some of the many craftspeople who make rugs or who use rugmaking techniques for making tapestries. Some of these artists work spontaneously and others work from pre-sketched and exact cartoons. You may gain an insight into the creative process while reading about these people.

CROCHET RUGS

Nancy Koren Nancy Koren knows what she likes and believes in doing things as well as she can. Born in Cincinnati and having graduated from Cincinnati Art Academy as a painting major,

Nancy came to the Santa Clara Valley with her husband a few years ago. She has an exhibition record in painting and silk-screen prints, and she currently teaches creative crochet.

The excitement of learning to dye fleece and to spin yarn influenced her to translate her mastery of color nuances into tactile form. Her beautiful crochet rug is shown in Figure 5-1. She used about 3 lbs. (1.5 kg.) of fleece, Cibalan dyed. Nancy dyed parts of the fleece in various shades of the warm colors—reds, oranges, golds, and mustard yellows. She dyed another amount of fleece with the cooler colors—blue, blue-green, and green. She teased and layered the fleece into two rectangular bats: one, all warm colors, the other, predominantly cool colors with some reds.

After felting, these became compact and soft masses, which she cut into strips about one finger-width wide. Turning the strips on the side exposed the vivid layers of colors, and these strips were used as the core.

FIGURE 5-1   Crochet rug over handmade felt, Cibalan dyed, 60 ″ (.150 cm.) diameter, Nancy Koren, 1977; photograph courtesy of Norman Koren.

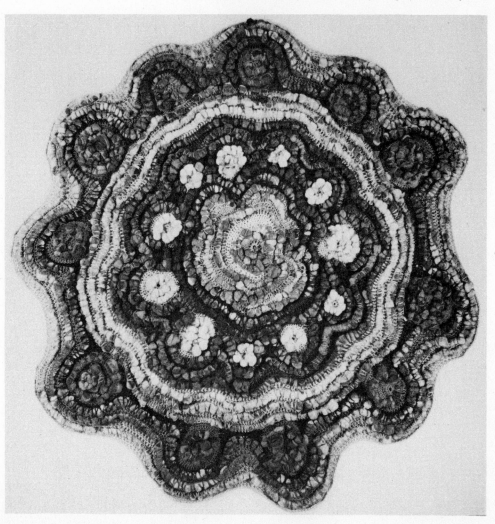

"When beginning to crochet a circular rug, you should first decide whether you want to make the circles concentric or have them spiral out," she advises. "Spiralling outward from the center requires no marking. You simply chain an extra stitch, then single crochet into the second loop. For a concentric circle, you have to know where to begin and end. Nancy began the center crocheting in the round, using gold *Cum* woolen rug yarn. Since this kind of imported yarn comes in a large selection of colors, Nancy could almost match the hue of the yarn to her fleece. (We have already discussed the circular format and some choices.)

This rug was looped in a free and spontaneous manner. Often, when a circle was to be joined to another, clusters of stitches were used to prevent large open spaces at the joins—single crochet, double crochet, triple crochet, any stitch that would fill in the area (see Figure 5-2).

FIGURE 5-2 Detail of crochet rug showing fill-in stitches.

"I joined these with a tapestry needle. When I felt that I needed a change from my central circle, I crocheted thirteen gold circles, placed the rug on the floor to plan where each would fit, and laced one end of each circle to touch the last row of stitches of the yellow center."

I asked Nancy to tell me how she made a tight center.

"When I want the circle as tight as possible," she said, "I chain two loops and then single crochet seven, eight, or nine stitches back into the first chain.

"Pulling the tail tightens it up. As I crochet around the circles to make an even circular shape, I decrease stitches in the valleys, or in what I think of as negative areas."

Nancy single-crocheted backwards to end the rug (sometimes called the *shrimp stitch*), giving the rug a nice cord-like border.

Two weeks of hard work were required to complete the rug. Four full days were spent on felting; seven days in making the rug. First, Nancy worked it on her lap, then on the floor. "When it grew too large to hold, I used a table to keep it flat," she said. Cupping and rippling could be easily seen and corrected.

Working the crochet over the core of felt was a new way of working for Nancy. The result is soft and colorful.

"I'm excited about the effect," she said.

SHUTTLE HOOK AND LATCH HOOK RUGS

Howard Milton Warner

Most of us are content to be skillful and create in one area of art, like drawing, painting, ceramics, or rugmaking. Few of us can say that we are competent in all four areas, but Howard Milton Warner is. He has an M.A. from Long Beach State University in California. His latest colored pencil drawings, which were exhibited in Huntington Beach, California, have realistic content. He jogs along the beach everyday, in sun and fog, absorbing the look, feel, and sound of the waves, their textures and rhythms. His beach scenes with swimmers, surfboards, and wetsuits create areas and patterns of shape and color. Our eyes enjoy the shape of the surfboard, the action lines of the figures, and the hot colors of sand in contrast with the cool colors of sky and water. In the past, his high-fire stoneware ceramic containers, jewelry, and looped pile rugs have been accepted in juried art exhibits. Why did he begin making rugs?

"I looked over all the crafts shows in Southern California and it seemed to me something was missing in those days [during the early 1960s]. It had to do with scale. Most fiber and crafts projects were small, so I thought I'd try making something large. I came by unlimited amounts of various colored wool yarns, a punch hook, and some burlap—and just started making rugs."

Howard Warner's first rug was a sun face image of yarns the colors of bronze gold, sandalwood beige, spice brown, aqua blue, and hot pink. He made larger area rugs later, and he never used an image twice.

"It just seemed to me that there were great colors and textures in the yarn itself and that I'd need a spontaneous doodle-like line to begin. I took off from there!"

One of his rugs, called "Tide Pools," was started in just that way. The colors were related to the greens, aquas, blues, greys, purples, and yellows of the undulating eddies of the tide pools with the anemone, starfish, and shells. (Figure 5-3 shows this rug in its environment, and Plate 11 shows the wonderful colors.)

The pattern for "Tide Pools" was started by drawing a few lines in chalk at the center of the backing. (Chalk dusts off easily when a mistake is made.) Then the curves were repeated and the rug was punched using a shuttle hook (see Figure 4-13). High pile textured areas added a sculptured surface to this rug. The very long strands of rug yarns were inserted from the looped side of the rug after the rest of the design had been completed. The latch hook easily knotted these various lengths of yarn. Because these areas are three-dimensional, the light falls at different angles on each single thread of the group of strands in the knot. As the colors change from dark to light, depending on the source of light, the rug appears to have great depth and rich, jewel-like colors.

Another of his rugs was made in warm colors of orange, hot pink, golds, bronzes, bright red purples, and purple, with greyed colors of the same warm emphasis. The doodle pattern looks like a seed pod repeated in a regular pattern across the rug. These rugs took about thirty to forty hours to make, from stapling the backing on the frame to applying latex to the back and turning over the hem.

Asked why he doesn't make rugs now, Howard said, "I haven't any more floor space to keep them in. I proved to myself I could do something in fibers when nothing much was being done and I made a few shows. Anyway, I'm into something else now."

FIGURE 5-3 "Tide Pools," shuttle hook and latch hook wool rug, 84 " x 72 " (213 cm. x 183 cm.), Howard Milton Warner, c. 1965.

ELECTRIC SPEED TUFTED RUGS AND TAPESTRIES

Patti Henry

Patti Henry has been making one-of-a-kind pile tapestries and rugs since 1970, when she quit teaching design and crafts at the high school level to complete a master's degree in fibers and related media. She works with galleries from Tokyo to San Francisco to Oklahoma City and the East, and her work has been commissioned by private and corporate clients. Her largest creation is 20 feet long. The largest total footage for a single commission is 375 square feet.

As I walked into her studio, an entire wall of windows cast daylight on two very large frames constructed of two-by-fours and bolted to the ceiling. Along the frames were nails every 3″ or 4″, onto which woven polypropylene rug backing had been tightly stretched, with major shapes marked onto the back. An apprentice was working with an electric rug punch, from the underneath or back side. From every other wall, hundreds of pounds of every possible color and texture of yarn overflowed from huge wooden bins.

Using an electrically powered tufting tool (see Figure 4-15), the entire piece can be worked at once like a painting, and the yarn can be removed and repunched easily, affording spontaneity. Though the electric tool speeds the tufting process considerably, each square foot can take anywhere from one to three hours to complete, using approximately one-half to three-quarters of a pound of yarn. (A 10′ × 10′ piece would take between 100 and 200 hours to complete, with thirty-five to seventy-five tufts per square inch!)

The tufting tool makes loops of five different heights. Besides just filling in a solid color area, Patti has used striped and cross-hatching techniques. One color can be punched loosely 1″ high. Going at right angles to this row, another color can be punched across the row, creating a feeling that goes beyond the rendering. Because of the constant joy of these endless discoveries, Patti prefers to do as much of the tufting as possible herself.

Even without the continuous decisions to be made—many the same as a painter encounters—it is really laborious. Apprentices can generally work for four hours or less in a day because of the fatigue factor. The limitations of human endurance and the fact that each piece is produced as a creative entity mean that Patti does not in any way expect to compete with wall hangings mass-produced for the general market. She can do no more than fifteen in an entire year.

Just how much time the technique takes was clearly

FIGURE 5-4 "Bedroom, Circa 1900," electric rug punch woolen tapestry, 65 ″ x 60 ″ (165 cm. x 152 cm.), Patti Henry.

shown in Patti's largest commission to date; three large pieces in the San Jose State University Student Union ballroom. Three immense brick pillars with geometrically patterned orange and brown drapes posed a special set of problems for her as she considered the space, with the added stress of a mere four days inwhich to complete the renderings. The pieces—two 10′ × 14′, the third, 12′ × 16′—took over six months for Patti and five apprentices to complete! Besides the shape of the arches and the texture of the fiber visually softening the square appearance of the hall, these elements have the added quality of improving the acoustics.

Patti works in two distinctly different styles—one abstract and the other representational. Her abstract style is inspired by the subtle patterns of antique Persian rugs and by painters such as the Austrian F. Hundertwasser, who, she says, gave her the courage to use exuberant color like a child. She does the large tapestries from small, intricate renderings, which are collages combining media ranging through watercolor, acrylics, colored pencils, and often layers of fabric scraps, lace, and tracing paper.

Patti photographs subject matter for her representational tapestries while travelling abroad and at home. She alters and combines these photos for the final piece. For example, see Figure 5-4 for her beautiful tapestry, "Bedroom, Circa 1900," whose dominant colors of off-white, greys, gold, dark blue, and brown can be seen in Plate 20 in the color insert.

The planning for "Persian Prayer Garden" (Plate 7 in the color insert) began with parts of former renderings and little fabric scraps. The middle layer, a precious translucent and shimmery silk remnant, alters the high-contrast underlayers. On top are transparent layers of tracing paper and acetate with notations of possible pile height changes.

Patti has found that anything works in mixing shapes and patterns in her renderings—a faded cuff from her husband's old pajamas, her son's discarded overalls, scraps of handmade lace, colored pencils, watercolor, torn-up pictures from newspaper ads. Much of the creativity comes from considering everything in your surroundings as media.

Lynden Keith Johnson

In 1966, practically nothing was being exhibited in tufted tapestries or rugs. The slow processes of latchet hook and needle rya looping discouraged production of original design rugs. But Lynden Keith Johnson had heard of an electric rug punch. He began to research rug tufting guns, and, in 1966, went to Germany where one was being made. Later, he found that an American inventor named Looper had invented an automatic tufting machine that was being used by large commercial carpet companies to mend looped rugs.* In 1968, after having graduated from San Jose State University with a Master of Arts degree, he went to Georgia, the only area in the United States where tufting guns were being used, machines

*There are about twelve to fourteen factories throughout the world—located in Switzerland, Ireland, Germany, Austria, and South America—which use rug tufting guns to make one-of-a-kind, commissioned pieces. All this has happened in the last ten years as a result of a tufting tool invented in the United States.

which had evolved from the smaller tufting guns used in producing chenille bedspreads.

After serving in the Army, Lynden returned to Europe and became a designer for a rug company that specialized in one-of-a-kind commissioned pieces for banks and special collections. In the course of his experience as a designer, he discovered other tufting guns, such as an air-driven gun that made a loop and then cut it as one worked, creating a velour or velvety surface (this was similar to a wool gun invented by Stanislaus V'Soske in the 1920s). While in Germany, Lynden made connections with a source of handspun wool, a spinner who imported Australian, Scottish, Afghan, and New Zealand fleece, dyed it to order, and spun colors to his specifications. Having gained some experience working in the rug industry, he went to Portugal, where he was licensed to import materials and start a small rugmaking industry. He set up his own shop, where he trained people in a small village to use the rug tufting gun to lay in his designs, teaching them new skills and a new trade to improve the rural economy.

After the revolution, when the Portuguese government began to seriously consider restructuring businesses, employee unions, and import and export taxes, it was difficult for a foreigner to continue in business. Lynden says, "In ten days I sold everything. I packed and shipped my rugs and personal possessions home because it was impossible for me to be creative and worry about maintaining a business with all the predictable hassles restructuring would bring." He settled in California in 1977.

Going to Lynden's home, which is also the Johnson studio, is an exciting experience. The studio part of his home is also a reconverted garage, which Lynden insulated himself and finished with storage racks, rolled up, moth-proofed carpets and rugs, rug yarns, and tools. I asked Lynden if he planned to continue making rugs and wall hangings in his garage studio. He said not this year, because he has too much inventory.

Lynden's house is hung with tapestries of all sorts and sizes. Some of them can be used as rugs because the design can be seen from all sides and the pile is even and regular. Others have pile cut high and low, shaped or rounded, to emphasize a curve in the pattern. His themes range from semi-abstract animals to the purely abstract, which set an aura of travelling around the universe. He feels strongly that the third industrial-cultural revolution will take place in outer space and communicates the feeling of grace and excitement of space environments through his work.

Lynden says he likes abstract design and prefers to work that way, even though he gives his pieces names that make you think of places or things—"Full Moon after Portugal Bay," for example, as shown in Figure 5-5 and Plate 4 in the color insert. It measures 99 square centimeters and weighs 5 kilograms (or almost 11 lbs.).

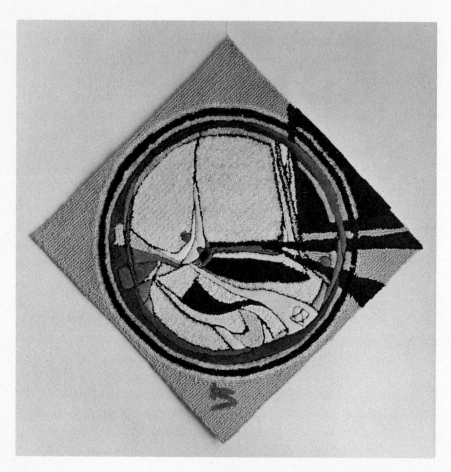

FIGURE 5-5 "Full Moon after Portugal Bay," 39 ″ (99 cm.) square, Lynden Keith Johnson, 1976.

I also asked Lynden why all his rugs were rectangular or had straight-line formats. Lynden answered that we're all used to looking at a straight format and rectangular shapes, so why introduce a shocking shape, especially if the rug is to be used on a floor in relation to the rectangular shape of the room. "Of course," he said, "I prefer designing to a rectangular format."

However, Lynden often incorporates circular or arch shapes into his wall hangings. In "Arciform" (Figure 5-6), a long, rectangular wall hanging, the arch shape is worked basically in greys and in tones of black and white. It is striking because of the variation in texture accentuated by long, thin grey tassles.

Lynden says he works from his imagination and sketches in color. Then, when he gets an idea, he makes a sketch or detailed drawing in color, one-fourth the size of the final piece. The sketch shows exactly the way the finished piece will turn out, including the color because, as he says, "I don't like to be surprised when I'm working. The reason I like everything exact is that while working spontaneously, some-

FIGURE 5-6 "Arciform," mechanically tufted tapestry with wrapped linear elements, Lynden Keith Johnson.

thing bad could happen just as easily as something good, and I'd have to pull out all that work. That's not the kind of surprise I'd like to happen."

Lynden transfers the outline of the color areas to the cotton canvas or synthetic fiber backing by tracing a cartoon made from the original, scale color drawing. He uses a waterproof marking pen that won't bleed into the pile. He also outlines the perimeter of the rug.

The backing material is stretched over a vertical frame with exposed nails. A 4″ (10 cm.) border is left around the rug. Later, this edge is turned back and latexed down to form a hem.

The rug tufting gun, driven by an air compressor (Figure 4-16), is threaded with a tightly twisted, handspun, and dyed rug yarn. The loop size is set; then the pattern is punched from the back of the rug. Running the machine in close horizontal rows results in a tightly packed surface. When cut with the velour tools, a velvety surface appears as the punching continues. While Lynden sometimes works in rows in large background areas, if he is leaving the pile looped he often follows the contour of the design. This adds a nice structure to the area because of the way light reflects off the surfaces of the loops.

One problem with hanging looped pile forms on a wall or with using them as rugs on the floor is, of course, the accumulation of dirt and dust. I asked Lynden about this and also about some of the finishing processes he uses. His pieces are worked on rug canvas—which is quite expensive and which is why the pieces cost from $200 to $2,200. To hold the loops in place, the rug is finished with two coats of liquid latex. The wool used is moth-proofed and dyed to color specifications by Lynden's yarn supplier in Germany, who sells to many of the rug factories on the European continent. The colors are permanent, fading only a little if the rug or tapestry is put in direct sunlight, as will all yarns unless left the natural wool color.

Lynden recommends using a mild, biodegradable soap, like Shaklee's Basic R, to clean rugs. He says simply clean them with a scrub brush, rinse, and lay the rugs flat to dry, and they'll be fine.

Lynden emphasizes his pile and looped rugs as art forms.

With his exhibition calendar planned, he will show many of his pieces during the next two years. He has participated in many competitive and individual exhibitions since 1968; and his work has appeared in "California Design" at the Pasadena

FIGURE 5-7 Lynden Keith Johnson in his living room with "Veridical" tapestry over the fireplace.

Art Museum; "Crafts Today," Museum West, San Francisco, California; and the *"Die Gute Form,"* Frankfurter Internationale Herbstmesse, Frankfurt-am-Main, West Germany. He also exhibits and sells his work through galleries.

His rugs are all over the house, covering both walls and floors. When discussing the different ways he uses rugs, Lynden made the comment that for centuries people have used rugs for a variety of purposes. Nomads have used them not only to cover earthen floors, but also to hang around tents for beauty and insulation: The thick pile absorbs sound. Other cultures have used pile rugs as covers for beds, sleighs, tables, and ceilings. So, why not use them for their beauty as well as their sound-proofing ability? As proof, see Figure 5-8.

189

Lynden Johnson believes you don't have to compromise your own esthetic taste. If an article is beautiful and well made, many people will buy it. His emphasis is on tapestries and rugs as an art form. He maintains a similar esthetic quality in his commercial freelance design work, his large silk screen panels, and his stoneware.

Being an overt optimist, Lynden's picture of the future is one meant to be seen in human environments, in the statement *no espirito do adiante*—in the onward spirit!

CHAPTER SIX

You're on Your Own

Rather than duplicating authentic artifacts or duplicating designs of other artists, you can produce your own product with design integrity. You can create a one-of-a-kind rug! This chapter is concerned with the creative process; with design, texture, and color; with finishing techniques, with caring for the rug; with law and the craftsperson; with general tips for photographing your rug; and with the resources to help you when you wonder about sources.

To know what makes the artist tick, ask an artist. You gleaned something about creativity as a process while reading the interviews with the artists. Each chose a different form of expression. Some were inspired by their environments, some used realistic patterns, others geometric. Texture and color were stressed. Although each person learned the technique after exposure to traditional forms, each expressed himself or herself in a unique way, a way that was new and original. Each had his/her way of looking at things and responding to them.

191

Design

The word *design* has two meanings. One is creative problem-solving, including the processes of gathering ideas, preparation, making the object, evaluation that each artist experiences—that is, imagining, making, and finishing a beautiful thing.

A more specific meaning of design is the concern with visual order, or the overall organized appearance of the rug. This perceived organization involves centers of interest, contrasts of texture and color relationships, and the patterns of dark and light with variations of details, creating the subtle enrichments that make us enjoy the rug every time we look at it. When the rug is used in a less functional way, on the wall or as a decorative object, more variation in combining techniques and in exaggerating the "look" is possible.

Sources for Images and Ideas

Geometry, nature, photographs, old cloth, anthropological exhibitions, and textile collections in museums are all sources for ideas. Look with wonder around you! Geometric shapes are excellent pattern motif units that relate well to anything constructed on a mesh or gridlike background. These shapes are found in nature, also with infinite variety. For example, an oval egg can be large, small, of different colors, speckled, plain, or whatever you want it to be. Natural forms might be inspirational, especially the brilliant plumage of a tropical bird or the iridescent feathers of a peacock. Other people's rugs may provide ideas for a technique or the use of value or color.

Become a collector. Keep a file of shapes, colors, textures, and patterns that you like. Leafing through a collection of pictures, shells, feathers, and the like often triggers an idea. Intuitively we respond to the organization in nature and things we see. But there has to be a reaching from within also, your own likes and dislikes. Variations of color, texture, and size relieve the mechanical regularity of the stitch. Enrichment of detail gives subtle pleasure to the eye.

Deborah Graham, director of an Instructional Media Center in the Long Beach Unified School District, California, was asked for some hints on researching techniques, materials, supplies, and the like. As a teacher, librarian, media specialist, and amateur rugmaker, Debbie feels that knowing your public library or local college library is an invaluable tool for your research. She strongly advocates that you become familiar with your library, its reference section, and the reference librarian.

In researching the craft of rugmaking, you naturally call to mind famous tapestries, as well as Oriental and Indian rugs. Even the small library can provide a wealth of illustrative material from manufacturer's booklets and picture files. Nor should you ignore volumes on primitive and early American life with their pictures of spinning wheels, looms, and handmade rugs. The card catalog has such subject headings as Arts and Crafts, Rugmaking, Weaving, Color, and Design—learn to use it.

Designs for floor coverings can come from many sources. Have you thought of following the history of design and historic patterns through modern design in wallpaper, textiles, and other items appearing in the advertising pages of magazines? How about pamphlets and materials put out by manufacturers? Or portfolios of color plates? These materials are usually available through the library's own files or through community art museums.

When you are looking for ideas, why not browse the library's art sections? Under the Dewey Decimal System, which many public libraries use, you would go to the 700s for Arts and Crafts—or more specifically 745.22 for Rugmaking. Under the Library of Congress system, used by many colleges and universities, you could go immediately to the area that houses Crafts—TT, Rugmaking TT850 or History of Rugs NK2775–2896.

One of the most valuable sources of current information is the *Reader's Guide to Periodical Information*. This tool is published semi-monthly from September through January and monthly in February, July, and August. A cumulative bound edition encompassing March to February is published yearly. The *Reader's Guide* contains magazine articles listed by subject—Arts and Crafts, Rugmaking, Design, and so forth. Get to know the Reference Librarian in your local library.

When asked about periodicals, Debbie said, "Why list the many publications available when there are several excellent directories available? The directories list all the needed information." She then gave the following list of her favorite "look-it-up" books:

1. *Artist's Market.* Kirk Polking, Ed. Cincinnati, Ohio, Writer's Digest, 1974. 479 pp.
   A directory listing the specific requirements of 2,123 buyers of fine art, photography, crafts, cartoons, and designs. Each entry gives the name of the person to contact,

rates of payment, and the type of work purchased. The section entitled "Craft Dealers" covers thirteen pages and lists fifty-four dealers.

2. *Contemporary Crafts Market Place 1977–1978.* Compiled and edited by the American Crafts Council, New York, R. R. Bowker Co., 2nd Edition 1977, 335 pp.
A comprehensive directory to craft materials, suppliers, organizations, reference publications, periodicals, audio-visual materials, craft courses, shops/galleries, annual craft events and fairs.

3. *Craft Sources.* Paul Colin and Deborah Lippman. New York, M. Evans and Co., 1975. 244 pp.
Everything you need to know about crafts books—which are the best, the least expensive, the easiest to follow. Where to find what you need to make whatever you want. Listed alphabetically by craft.

4. *Craft Supplies Supermarket.* Joseph Rosenbloom. California, Oliver Press, 1974. 214. pp.
Well-indexed, comprehensive directory of craft suppliers. Materials, kits, tools, and the like from over 450 companies are analyzed from catalogs. Covers companies nationwide.

5. *National Guide to Craft Supplies.* Judith Glassman. New York, Van Nostrand Reinhold Co., 1975, 224 pp.
The "Craft Yellow Pages." In addition to more than 600 suppliers (including some international sources), this directory lists crafts bookstores, places of instruction, galleries and museums, societies and organizations, fairs, and periodicals. It provides a bibliography of over 800 books.

6. *Selling Your Crafts and Art in Los Angeles.* Lila Weingarten and Kendall Taylor. Los Angeles, Wollstonecraft, 1974, 143 pp.
Information on galleries, licenses needed to sell, out-of-state information, monthly shows, tax information.

In addition, Debbie said you should not ignore the California Chamber of Commerce in Sacramento as a source of fairs and other goings-on in the state. The State Fair Commission has information on all fairs in the state. Many states have a Fair Commission and, of course, every state has its State Chamber of Commerce.

In summary, Debbie said, it is not what you know that counts, it's knowing where to find it.

Planning Your Design Size, technique, pattern, color, and texture are important things to consider when you make your rug.

Plan your rug design and size according to the technique

you will use and the purpose for which the rug is intended. A bold overall pattern is preferable to a small, spotty pattern, since you'll be viewing it from a distance. Patterns made of geometric or floral motifs are conventional treatments that are prevalent today. Symbolic motifs are often used in church and civic settings. The pattern motif can be an image. It can be complete in itself, or it can be repeated and varied. The pattern can be created by the material itself (for example, a braided rug with one dark strand, another in a middle value, and the third textured, depending on the fabric's weave, tweed, or plaid). Rugs for the floor should have a pattern that appears to lie flat and that may be viewed equally well from any direction. Dark borders often add a frame and unity to the central field.

The *motifs* (shapes) which make the pattern should be bold enough to be visible from a distance and rely on a contrast in tone rather than color. Rich, positive colors with light and dark accents are pleasant choices. Color looks darker on the actual rug than it does in the yarn. Avoid choosing a pure white for your light accent. Medium grey or beige blends in with the darker tone of colors. The muted colors of historical examples are difficult to match with modern commercial dye lots. Use two different strands of the same value and intensity; or use two strands of the same color that vary slightly in value to give an unexpected and pleasant effect. Definite color streaks are to be avoided unless they are used as a pattern of border stripes.

Texture   Texture is a consideration in choosing the materials and technique. The shag of a knotted pile rug softens the outline of motifs. The nubby texture of a looped rug results from using a punch hook or mechanical looper. Texture also relates to the soft, loosely spun yarn, the tighter twist of rug yarn, the weave of the wool or cotton fabric used for crochet, knit or braid. When you make your own rug you have a wider range of combinations. A small-size hand hooked rug can become a larger rectangle by adding a braided edge; the braid texture is a good contrast to the loops.

Pleasing textures can be obtained with 16 knots, stitches, or loops per square inch or square centimeter. Fifty units per square inch/cm. allow freely curving motifs and more details. Plan a motif and pattern that the scale of stitches, knots, or loops can interpret. When in doubt, make the detail large. The *TIME* it takes to make a rug depends on the number of

TIME CHART FOR BEGINNERS IN RUGMAKING

TECHNIQUE	HOURS/SQUARE FT. (30 CM²)		FIBER/FABRIC/SQ. FT.	EXTRA EQUIPMENT
Hand Hook	5	slow	1/2 lb. wool fabric	frame
Punch Needle	1 1/4	fast	1/2 lb. yarn	frame
Shuttle Hook	1	fast	1/2 lb.	frame
Electric Tufting Tool	1	fast	1/2 lb.	frame
Latch Hook	4 1/2	slow	1/2 lb.	
Needle Rya	4	slow	1/2 lb.	3 1/3", 4", 5" rug canvas backing
Braiding	3	medium	1/2 lb.	clamp, braid aids
Quickpoint	3	medium	1/3 lb./foot	rug canvas, #4, #5
Crochet	1	fast		
Knitted	1	fast		
Painted	1	fast	paint	dry between coats
Felted	3	medium	1/3 lb. per ft.	needle, muslin, hot and cold water

stitches, the number of knots, or the number of loops it contains, not on the actual size of the rug.

Designing Your Cartoon   Even if you can't draw, you *can* cut and paste. Gather scraps, imales, shapes, and texture and make a collage of them. Put tissue paper or lace or mesh over them to break up the space into areas of repeated colors and shapes. Establish a direction for your eye to follow by planning the darks throughout the area. Remember, most rug techniques do not permit small linear detail.

Then make a photocopy of your sketch. By removing the psychological effect of color, it will be easier for you to make an objective evaluation of the light-to-dark patterns. It's easier to see in black and white if the dark and light patterns are unified and balanced. You can see clearly the variety of textures you are using and can change focal points that dominate or seem to pop out like sore thumbs to make them more effective.

Enlarging the sketch to make the cartoon, or the exact-size drawing of the areas for the rug, can be accomplished several ways. One way is to cut up the sketch and bring the pieces to a local blueprinting service. An enlargement of the parts can be pasted back together, and the full-scale plan is ready. Another way is to use transparent blue-lined graph paper: Simply place it over the drawing, trace it, and enlarge it by placing a grid onto the final copy and sketching in each section free-hand.

Once you have your blown-up sketch, you can transfer it
to the canvas itself in any number of ways. Since the backing
for some rugs is an open mesh, you can trace the design after
it has been taped or pinned underneath the rug base, using an
indelible grey or yellow pen. A more closely woven material
requires that the design be traced onto it using one of several
techniques. You can stitch through a paper pattern with an
unthreaded needle in your sewing machine, leaving a record
of small holes. A pounce bag (filled with charcoal dust, fireplace ashes, or chalk dust) bounced up and down along the
holes leaves a dotted outline on your backing. A tracing wheel
can be used with special tracing paper that leaves an indelible
mark or a washable chalk-line mark, which in turn can be
outlined in stitches or with a waterproof pen. Often in needlepoint, when the design is a geometric one, such as flames
or blocks, the canvas is marked for the vertical center and the
horizontal center. Then a grid of lines, or running stitches
that are later removed, is made. The stitches are counted and
a rhythmic repeat is established. When you work directly
onto the canvas, as Howard Warner does, you may want to
draw in some large areas or shapes, or divide the rug into
sections to establish the contour direction for hooking. You
are in no way limited to one method of successfully drawing a
design on the rug backing.

A knowledge of your materials—as well as a wide diver-
sity of color tones, hues, and textures not usually used in
store-purchased rugs—permits you to alter the motifs or or-
namental areas as you work. Some people, spontaneous and
flexible, change their design slightly as they work. Other
people are more deliberate and plan well ahead to estimate
cost and time. Try both ways and decide which method you
feel most comfortable with.

Color   Even colorblind persons can choose colors and make beautiful
rugs, because they can create a pattern of dark, medium, and
light values. Often their mixtures of color hues in a rug are all
the more startling to someone who sees color normally.

The human eye can distinguish, with very little difficulty,
seven to eleven values of one color hue. The subtle variation
of one hue, in eight of its ranges from light to dark, provides
the richness in a handmade product—a richness that is often
missing from machine-made artifacts.

Color a kind of rainbow in your rug, one pleasing to yourself. It can shout and sing, or soothe and calm. You can also

make a monochromatic (single color) rug and vary the textures—soft and fine, like a Persian cat, or thick and coarse, like a bearskin. The repetition of the color in its values can be the subtle, diversifying element that evokes renewed interested in your rug each day.

Color is known by the company it keeps. Comparisons of one color with another begin with the perceptible differences in hue from red to blue to green to yellow, and so on. This comparative process becomes more and more subtle as we compare the lightness or darkness (the value) of the hue. The ultimate comparison is between the vividness and greyness of color (or chroma). The interaction of color on the three-dimensional fiber strand is also affected and changed by the source of light: natural, incandescent, or fluorescent.

Terence Campbell, an interior design consultant in color and lighting, shared his knowledge and thoughts about color with me.

On color: "I've found in reading many books about color that each author often uses different words to mean the same thing. Semantics get in the way of our understanding of color. The scientist often uses different terms to describe color than the graphic artist does. For example, he might use *chroma* to mean the amount of vividness or greyness; *frequency* to mean hue; and *value* to mean the relative lightness or darkness. It is important, when considering these elements, to know that color can be *additive*, *subtractive*, or most importantly with fabrics, *partitive*.

On additive color: "We usually think of this term as meaning adding to something else. In color, additive is related to separate beams of light. When they mix on a surface from separate sources, the resultant value is lighter than either of the light sources. You can see this effect with stage lights."

On subtractive color: "The resultant value is always darker than the values you begin with. This happens in paints and dyes. You find it when you mix physical pigments, or overprinting in lithography."

On partitive color: "The mix is always optical rather than physical. The fibers or paint spots in close proximity to each other mix optically. the resultant value is always a middle range between the lightest and darkest colors combined, as in an impressionistic painting. For instance, the color comics of the newspaper are printed with a dot matrix of yellow, magenta, cyan blue, and black.

"Fabrics constructed from smaller pieces, like rug loops or the interlacedwarp and weft of weaving, are never as bright or garish as the oiginal strand. One reason is the ability of the eye to mix colors. The other is the structure and three-dimensionality of the fiber strand, which casts a shadow that changes with the source of light."

Sources of Light   Lighting affects color. How often have you selected the "perfect" color under store ights, only to find when you arrived home that the color is not anywhere near the color you were matching? We have lived under fluorescent lighting since 1939. I discussed this problem with Terry. He said that natural light is the best light for all the colors of the rug, because it doesn't favor one end of the spectrum. The typical incandescent household lamp tends to dull or darken hues like blue or green while brightening and enhancing the warmer colors like red and yellow. An exception would be a commercial, high-intensity discharge lamp that balances out the spectrum.

"There is more choice of color ranges within fluorescent lamps," says Terry. "Consequently, light can be selected that enhances a broader range of colors in the rugs. Charts are available from the manufacturer that inform you about the color-enhancing effect of the lamp."

Terry advises that, when working on a commission, it is important to find out the lighting source and conditions under which your rug will be used. If you are working with an interior designer or architect, you may have the opportunity to help design the lighting that will enhance your rug. On the other hand, you may be working with existing lighting, and you could design your rug to be beautiful when viewed under that specific light.

Colors and Dyes   Many craftspeople who want to achieve beautiful soft colors and a wide range of gradation or value learn to dye their own rug yarn. For example, Nancy Koren dyed her fleece. Patti Henry often over-dyes her rug yarn. Lynden Johnson ordered his work dyed to specification.

The beginner often uses the dye full-strength and unmixed. Yet if the mordants, or fixative chemicals, and rinses are omitted, the garish colors fade or bleed onto adjacent grounds. The manufacturers of chemical dyes usually have printed information available to the consumer. Always read the dye package and follow directions.

Among the various classes of dyes, one colorant may be costlier than another. Some dyes made of natural materials are very expensive. But how do you get to know all this and the other technical information necessary for successful dyeing? Obviously, a need exists for a center of information.

Maggie Brosnan, craftsperson and member of the Bay Area Arts and Crafts Guild in San Francisco, California, received a research grant from De Anza College to develop a "Practical Color Selection Program for Acid Dyes." This project has produced instructional and resource material for acid dyes never before available to the student or layperson. From it the beginning of a textile dye resource center or library is emerging—a core research group willing and eager to continue additional investigation of synthetic and natural dyestuffs and to establish instructional aids for De Anza College and the community.* Maggie says, "My group of thirteen advanced student dyers learned that subtle and minute color change identifications are discernible only to the experienced and continuously practicing dyer. This art must be maintained by continual color mixing with basic stock colors. Actual color mixing in a controlled study situation is necessary to learn the dyer's art. The scope of the original idea is too sophisticated for general use but easily adaptable for existing textile design courses."

The original concept of the grant was to use dyed yarn samples as a color-sensitivity testing device for textile design students. In addition, the material was to be stored on the college computer and an accompanying manual developed for program use. It was ultimately decided to abandon the computer storage program in favor of a textile resources center or library because the handbooks are more portable and because of programming problems with data bank storage.

The program has produced thirty handbooks, each of which contains 800 Cibalan (Cibalan–Geigy Corporation) pre-metalized acid dye recipes with individual identifying swatches of colored yarns, organized as stock color charts.

*Special credit and appreciation must be given to the student dyers who have generously given their time, energy, and creative thinking to the success of this project. They are: Karen Cummings, Mark Daly, Julie Egbert, Hillary Farkas, Jean Heinz, Esther Hughes, Margaret Koph, Lois Lewis, Lorraine Rock, Bettie Jo Skalabrin, Judy Smaha, Ruth Steindorf, and Alice Vaeth.

For practical users, this technical information fills a void: Never have industrial dyehouses made such information available to the layperson. De Anza College textile design instructors have decided to use this collection of materials to begin a textile dye resource center located on campus. The color charts of yarn and cloth will greatly expand existing knowledge of dye color theory and provide instructional materials for existing courses. Materials will also be available for public use and will be redesigned for credit in an independent study module. Information may be obtained by writing: Dean, Fine Arts Division, De Anza Community College, 21250 Stevens Creek Boulevard, Cupertino, California, 95014.

Another source of information on dyes and dye is W. Cushing Company, Kennebunkport, Maine 04046. "Casserole Spot Dying, How to Do It," by Joan Moshimes, might be of interest to people who want to dye small amounts of wool and make some unusual hues where the colors meet. For example, 12′ (30 cm.) hooked rug strips make approximately 3′ (7.5 cm.) of finished hooked area. This spot dye method could be used for dyeing yarn as well as fabric.

Valuable articles appear occasionally in guild newsletters and fibers periodicals.

General Advice about Color

Any mixture of hues can be beautiful. Visual contrast is important. Key words to remember for contrasts are *light–dark*, *bright–dull*, and *warm–cool*. Various combinations of hues with these contrasts can make a pleasing pattern of color throughout the rug. In the color insert plates, you will notice that, though usually one hue is dominant in a rug, many variations are added to provide design sparkle and interest.

Look for sources that carry a wide spectrum of colored yarns, including a range of eight or more shades and tints. When a company has a stock of 200 or more choices, you are able to enrich the areas of color in your rug with subtle variations of value and vividness.

You may add to your color selection by dyeing white yarn or fabric and by overdyeing colored yarn or printed fabric. Craftspeople are using microwave ovens in their studios for small spot dyeing and steaming of fabrics.

Before you think that you must use hundreds of hues in one rug, consider the following comments made by a reviewer of the Houston Designer–Craftsmen 1976 exhibit in Blaffer Gallery of the University of Houston. Jane Vander Lee said that a few colors had the effect of many colors in Bruce Bunderstadt's hooked "Rug with a Blue Border," a Merit Award

Rug. This effect was the result of placement within a contrasting area which causes that color to appear different. The rhythm of connected triangular and rectangular shapes of pattern accent and counteract the color vibration.*

A color is influenced by the hue surrounding it, or by the neutrals, black, white, or grey. Areas of hue enclosed by areas of black seem to sparkle like stained glass. Surrounding areas of white seem to cause areas of a hue to expand and lighten. There are many color relationships to look at and to explore in pursuit of ideas for your rug.

Finishing Techniques

The beauty of the design and the durability of a rug are increased by finishing the edges and the underside, then joining and blocking.

Edges are sometimes finished when the rug has been completed. For example, an oval braided rug has tapered ends tucked into the fold of a braid. A crochet rug is slip-stitched to end it. Crochet finishes add strength to the edges. You can make edges structural by weaving warp yarns back into the cloth or by turning the rug canvas back before making the knot that goes around both layers of mesh. You bind off the knit rug when taking the stitches off the needles.

Some of the finishing techniques used are fringing, knotting, or stitching. Fringes and tassles can soften the hard edges of a flat rug, complement the color scheme, or add interest to the rug.

Stitching the edges should be neatly executed without any knots or loose ends showing. The rough edges of the rug canvas are turned back and covered with binding tape before any glue or rubber backing is used. Corners are not bumpy because a right angle or miter is made and the excess material cut off. The folded edge joins at an angle and is sewn with small, evenly placed stitches; overcast stitches, like the whip stitch and the buttonhole stitch, are made close together (refer back to Figure 3-9). The hue of the yarn may either match the dominant background hue to visually blend the edge into the mass, or it may contrast with the background, for emphasis.

The underside should be neat, free from knots and threads and finished to give added strength where needed.

*Jana Vander Lee, "Houston Designer-Craftsmen Exhibit," in "Hang Ups" (Review Section), *Fiber Arts*, Volume 3, Number 4, 1976.

For example, a pile rug that is looped and not tied, or is stitched on a wide mesh, may have a rabbit skin glue or liquid latex finish. An unbleached, cotton dust jacket sewn to the back of the tapestry prevents wear. Even subtle air currents in a building cause friction between tapestry and wall. Circular latch hook or pile rugs need firm support, which can be provided with thin wood or a welded rod. When the rug is hung as a wall decoration, finishing with a casing for the hanging rod can add longer life to the rug. Using Velcro material across the width of the rug provides solid support for a wall display. The backings used in museums are made of unbleached cotton or linen fabric. The natural material contains no chemicals that might react with the dye or fibers to cause their disintegration.

Join the rug backing or pieces of the rug design with small, evenly spaced stitches that blend into the texture or direction of the stitches on the front face. Work the ends into the backing or make them invisible.

Blocking with cold water or hot steam gives a finished, professional quality to the final shape. During the process, any dust or dirt that have accumulated during the construction of the rug is washed out with biodegradable soap. When you don't have a large, flat surface, like plywood or particle board, on which to arrange your damp rug, a frame can be constructed of wood, reinforced with angle bars to take the weight of the rug. Cloth strips wound around the frame permit fastening the damp rug to the frame. Or finishing nails placed at short, even intervals make it possible to stretch the rug on the frame. Do one side first, then the opposite side, working from the center out to the edges. Leave the damp rug to dry for several days.

Caring for Your Rugs

Handmade rugs are as versatile and sturdy as they are beautiful. Give them the same care as you would any woolen carpet. Sweep them daily in heavy traffic areas before dirt, pet hair, and grit are ground in. The surface of the yarn should be treated with a chemical sealer like Scotchguard to prevent dirt and liquids from soiling the rug easily. Vacuum once or twice a week. Turn the rug around, reversing the ends, to ensure that it wears evenly, not only from foot traffic, but also from the sunlight coming in through the windows.

Rugs may be dry cleaned, cleaned with rug shampoo once or twice a year, or cleaned with a naptha solvent at a commercial cleaners. If you live in a cold climate, brush in dry snow and sweep thoroughly with a broom.

Quick and correct treatment will prevent permanent stains from marring your rug. The general procedure is to remove the excess staining material.

Cleaning Methods for Spots and Spills

Liquids. Blot up any liquids. Pour ordinary kitchen salt on wet stains to absorb them. Or stand on a damp turkish towel placed over the stain—the moisture is absorbed more quickly by damp material and the weight helps force the liquid up from the shag or braid.

Urine spots, after the initial treatment of blotting and sponging with cool water, are sponged with a mixture of one teaspoon of white vinegar and one teaspoon of mild detergent in a quart of warm water. They're then blotted again. Use cold water on blood spots.

Solids. Solids like mud, gum, wax and butter are scraped up. Usually sponging with cool water and blotting with a clean towel are enough. Certain things are cleaned up more thoroughly after the initial blotting.

Grease. Cover grease spots with dry talcum powder or cornstarch and leave them for a few hours. Perfume and alcohol-based antiseptics or showering aid spots are sponged with a dilution of alcohol and water. Blot them quickly and apply the diluted alcohol and water solution until no stain color is absorbed.

Gum needs a spot cleaner or dry-cleaning solvent. Mud, after the initial scraping, should be allowed to dry completely. Then vacuum. Shampoo the area with a foam-type or concentrated liquid rug shampoo. Dry the area with a blow dryer set on cool or allow to air dry thoroughly, and vacuum. Always pretest the cleaner on an inconspicuous spot.

Moth-proofing

Commercially spun yarns are usually moth-proofed, and you can moth-proof handspun yarns in your home by applying moth-proofing sprays. However, turning the rug over on the floor or wall every month, vacuuming or brushing out the dust, and using it in well-lit areas usually protects it from moths and silverfish.

Fleas from your pets are another problem. Infestations are handled by testing any solution on the back of the rug to see if the colors bleed or bleach out. Treat the rug outside in a shaded area. A good herbal remedy for fleas is to make a weak tea of pennyroyal or to boil cedar chips in water and mix this in with the soap you wash the rug with each year.

Storage   At times you may want to store your rug temporarily. If so, vacuum the rug beforehand and repair any broken threads; then store it, rolled up, in an airy, open place. Never wrap it in plastic because plastic doesn't breathe. Moisture condenses on the inside, causing mildew. Do as museums do: Wrap the rug in unbleached muslin or acid-free tissue paper. Tie the paper or cloth in place with cloth tape. Metal pins may cause rust stains. Never store for years.

With dense pile rugs backed with latex, store the rug face side out to prevent the latex backing from cracking.

Frequently inspect your rug for damage from mice, nesting moths, or other insects. Moth flakes or cedar chips may be kept in the storage area. Never, however, place moth chips directly on the rug. The dye might react with them.

Fire Retardation   While fire retardant treatments reduce the flammability of fabrics, none is effective in preventing damage due to sustained heat. Surprisingly, treating rugs and carpeting to prevent burn damage from cigarettes is useless because no treatments available today can make combustible materials immune to fire or heat exposure. Sufficient contact with a burning cigarette will char and damage any treated material.

The use of rugs in commercial buildings, both on the floor and on the wall, may necessitate a fire retardant treatment. For natural fibers this treatment includes the use of a solution of water and chemicals, total immersion or wetting of the rug, and a thorough drying in a horizontal position. Most treatments today do not change the color or texture of natural fibers, except for a slight stiffening of the pile.

When synthetic fibers like orlon, nylon, dacron, and fortrel are used, wholly or in a mixture of yarns, special consideration and knowledge must be applied. Two classes of synthetic fibers, not commonly used by the craftsperson, are flame retardant: modacrylic and vinylidene chloride. The great majority of decorative textiles woven primarily of these two fibers also incorporate 15 to 25 percent rayon fiber.

Obviously, no attempt should be made to treat any fabric unless its fiber content is known or determined by analysis. For home use, an awareness that cigarettes can cause the rug to flame whether treated or not is sufficient. When working on commissioned pieces for use in public buildings, planning ahead for the fire-retardant treatment is a prime concern.

Your local fire department can give you information. Consult the Yellow Pages in your telephone directory for companies that treat fabrics with flame retardants. You can also check your local library or write the National Bureau of Standards, Washington, D.C.

The Undercarpet

Padding is essential to protect your rugs. Pads placed underneath area rugs add to the durability by 40 to 60 percent because of the resiliency. Pads also absorb sound, add insulation (especially when you have a concrete slab floor), and prevent slipping. Certain types of polymer pads have a high tolerance to wear, heat, cold, moisture, and sunlight. A jute hair padding may be better than a synthetic rubber pad. The choice of padding depends on the flooring and the heating system: For example, radiant floor heat has a detrimental effect on rubber padding.

Urethane foam padding is vermin- and mildew-proof and non-allergenic. When you doubt the effect of the rug in contact with the padding because of the chemicals it contains, an unbleached cotton backing can be sewn to the underside of the rug.

Marketing, the Law, and the Craftsperson

If you want to sell, the opportunities are getting better all the time. There are many outlets for you—galleries, department stores, personal contacts, crafts fairs, and the architectural and interior design trade. The National Endowment for the Arts is granting more awards to fiber artists. Local, state, and regional slide bank registries are being formed as resources for architects and people seeking art work, usually for public places.

Galleries can be a good outlet for the artist looking to sell his or her work. A person browsing in a gallery may see a finished piece shown (or taken on consignment) and buy it, in which case the gallery in a metropolitan area would usually take 45 to 50 percent of the total retail price in return for the costs of insurance, advertising, photography, and possibly bankruptcy.

Rugmakers and fiber artists run into problems because they produce one-of-a-kind pieces whose size requires a year or more to complete. Keeping an inventory of stock ready for sale ties up a great deal of capital. Because of the cost of the materials involved in producing a large piece, not many craftspeople can afford to maintain a large inventory. So whereas a contract with a gallery can keep rugs off the general market, the gallery outlet advertises, displays, and relieves you of the worry of selling. You can do what you do best—make rugs.

If somebody has seen and admired your work, you could receive a commission. They might want to see renderings custom-designed to their taste, especially if they have unusual space or color needs. The rendering fee would eventually be assimilated into the total cost of the commission. The importance of communication between the artist and the client cannot be overemphasized. It would be a good idea to view the space for the rug to get a feeling for the client's likes and dislikes and show your past works to get the client's reactions.

For work commissioned by a corporate client, a professional decorator might contact a gallery, view slides of the gallery's "stable" of artists, and chose an artist for the assignment. Usually the decorator has already coordinated the colors and textures, ordered the furniture, rugs, and drapes, decided on a wall treatment, and gotten an idea of the style the client wants. The gallery person, the decorator, and the artist would meet, then the artist would execute some drawings. Decisions would be reached and changes made, and the drawings would be returned to the artist to use as working models.

The craftsperson must plan for many things when accepting a public commission. The materials chosen should be lightfast, colorfast, and permanent and should be able to be fireproofed without danger of shrinkage and textural change. Natural fibers should be used whenever possible because they are more easily fireproofed; wool, too, which smoulders for the longest time before it bursts into flame needs to be fireproofed. You should contact the local fire department and find out what the local ordinances and laws are before you begin. Patti Henry advises that you should "be very sure that any space for which you accept a commission is either free from fireproofing laws or that every material you work with can be flame retarded before or after the piece is done. The only way to deal with the problem is to have a written contract with the client putting the responsibility upon the buyer."

Contracts become a part of the professional's life: contracts with galleries, museums, insurance companies and leases, for studio space and equipment. All these matters require legal expertise. Not all of us have had enough experience with these agencies to know when the piece of paper we've signed gives all the benefits we're entitled to. Consult your local information sources. Many large cities in the United States have associations of lawyers that artists can contact for legal advice. You may find that there's a Lawyers for the Arts Association in your area. To quote Patti Henry, "In . . . matters, like taxes, contracts, gallery relationships, and legal aid of any sort, contact a legal aid group, like the Bay Area Lawyers for the Arts (BALA). Gallery owners are businessmen, while artists are usually, by nature, opposed to marketing. Expect anything." BALA has also published several pamphlets to help artists, including a model contract. Help is available for a modest charge—and often no charge at all—from the lawyers for their services.

In this age of mass exposure, mass production, and mass advertising, the fiber artist needs the protection of a contract that spells out everything, including marketing, insurance, fire, theft, and bankruptcy provisions. Generally, local craftspeople tend to work with local galleries and to do local commissions. You must decide what you want to do with the opportunities.

You could also set up your own rug shop. You really have to be interested in being an entrepreneur if you are going to start a small business. One-third of your time is spent gathering materials and ideas; another third involves making the art object itself; the rest of your time is spent advertising, exhibiting, pricing, obtaining licenses from the local community to sell your work, figuring out your taxes, and performing other business functions. And, as exciting as it is to run your own business, you have to recognize that you're going into business to make a living. You must decide whether you're going to market a product that's well crafted, of high quality, with an overall style that's yours or you're going to compromise by making things that sell to a more general market.

Certain commitments must be made if you're going into the wholesale business. You need capital to begin with, as well as a knowledge of the laws of the place in which you're going to work. Consideration must be given to national, state, and local taxes, resale license,* wages, employee benefits,

*Guidelines, available from the Copyright Office concerning the Copyright Revision Act of 1976, became effective January 1, 1978. The California Legislature enacted a 5 percent resale proceeds right for the artist effective January 1, 1977 (California Civil Code Section 986, p. 38). The work must sell for over $1,000 and the sale must take place in the artist's lifetime. The

vendors' licenses, rent, utilities, insurance, returns, and suppliers. Problems of supply could become serious in the future: The cost of natural fibers and wool cloth are increasing as demand begins to exceed supply. Some states require a fiber content and fiber care label to be fixed to textiles for sale. Contacts must be made for supply sources; inventory must be kept. If you have people working for you, there are often regulations about taxes, health policies, and safety standards to be met.

Appraising and Photographing Your Rug

How much is your rug worth? You can estimate the cost of the materials and your labor per square foot. You may also consult a professional appraiser from a museum or antique dealers' association. The professional will describe the color and design of the rug in detail, list the materials, discuss the technique, maybe make a comment relating the rug to other rugs that have been produced by regional craftspeople, and attest to the originality of the design. A dollar value is assigned to the rug. This appraisal is important when your rug is a large room-size rug. You will need this information for your homeowner's insurance if you have a theft or fire: Don't take chances with something you've spent several years making. You also need this information when you exhibit the rug at a crafts competition or in an exhibition. Talk over protecting your work with your insurance agent and with other craftspersons.

Photographing your rug, with the dimensions listed on the margin, provides another useful record. Even an amateur can make a record of the rug for insurance purposes or sentiment. However, for either a sales portfolio or a slide to send a juried exhibit, you need a photograph or slide that shows the pattern and texture as well as the color. When the rug is photographed in your home on the floor, the services of a professional photographer who has a camera with wide-angle lenses and lighting equipment may result in a better picture.

Here's some advice: hang the rug on a wall in daylight against a plain, light-colored background whenever possible. Hammer finishing nails between warps or loops. Look at the shadow pattern the light creates on the rug. If it doesn't emphasize the texture, have a friend hold white cardboard to

artist receives 5 percent of the gross sale price within ninety days of the sale. The proceeds are deposited with the California Arts Council when an artist cannot be located within ninety days. After seven years, if the money hasn't been collected by the artist, it may be used by the Council.

reflect additional light on it and thus create a more dimensional texture.

Now, focus the rug in the center of the viewfinder. You want an accurate record, not an unusual composition. The esthetic impact of the rug photo comes from the pattern, texture, and variations of the rug itself. You may need to take two photographs: one for size, another to show detail. If you're unsure of your exposure, bracket your shots by changing the exposure slightly for three shots of the same view. When your pictures are developed, you can choose the best of the three. Finally, either use a tripod or rest the camera on a stationary object; if you can't be sure of steadying the camera enough, use fast film and a fast shutter speed.

Some color film records ranges of red more accurately than blue. Know the quality of the color film and its limits. You can check the Kodak guide to find out about film.

Ask for glossy prints when you have your pictures printed. A glossy photograph is required if the photo is to be published in black and white, as in an exhibition catalog. Look at some of the photographs that Shirley Fisher made for this book, and see how texture and pattern in the rugs are emphasized.

A Final Word

In today's society—be it primitive, agrarian, or technological—a person needs to organize his own or her own surroundings and express himself or herself through gestures, sounds, movements, and forms that communicate without words. Qualitative thinking in symbol and image is the source of these forms: the arts.

You who are concerned with the process of making a beautiful or useful handmade rug are answering an intrinsic need both for the pleasure of handling materials and textures and for expressing yourself in a qualitative way. You now have the basis for a relaxing hobby or perhaps a profitable career. What you don't yet know about esthetic and technical considerations, you'll undoubtably learn from the growing accumulation of reference sources, from others in the field, and from experience.

Use your native talents, your imagination, your time,

and the materials and tools of the trade to make beautiful things. Be daring. The ABC's of rugmaking are Always Be Creative.

You're on your own now. Relax and enjoy it!

Appendix

Conversion of US Measure to Meters and Kilograms
Yards to meters: multiply by .914
Pounds to Kilo: multiply by .453
Ounces to grams: multiply by 28.349

COMMON RUG YARN COUNT

FIBER CONTENT-SIZE	APPROXIMATE YARDS (METERS)/POUND	MISCELLANEOUS
Linen, grey, 6 cord	350 yds. (320 m.)	4 setts per in.
Linen 8/4 Rug Warp	560 yds. (512 m.)	5, 6, 8 setts per in.
Cotton 8/8 Rug Warp	840 yds. (768 m.)	3, 4, 5 setts per in.
Cotton 8/4 Carpet Warp	1,680 yds. (1,535 m.)	double strand 6 setts per in.
Cotton Crochet Thread		6 setts per in.
New Twist Cotton Craft Cord, 3-ply, #18	840 yds. (768 m.)	4, 5, 6 setts per in.

213

Mattwarp 12/9	840 yds. (768 m.)	4, 5, 6 setts per in.
Fiskyarn 12/6	840 yds. (768 m.)	4, 5, 6 setts per in.
Wool Mill Ends, Band 4-ply	350 yds. (320 m.)	4 setts per in.
Rya Wool (Scandinavia)	570 yds. (521 m.)	6 setts per in.
Berber Wools	450 yds. (411 m.)	4 setts per in.
Belgian Smyrnalaine		5-9 value range each color
50% wool, 50% nylon	550 yds. (503 m.)	3/16″ strand
3-ply (4 mm.) acrylic, "wool tone"	440 yds. (403 m.)	variegated strands give more "natural" texture and color.
4-ply acrylic	560 yds. (512 m.)	slight shine
4-ply (6 mm.) 100% polyester	640 yds. (685 m.)	made in heather or tweedy fiber mix.
3-ply (8 mm.) twisted polyolifin	440 yds. (402 m.)	satin sheen 3 values
3-ply 75% rayon, 25% cotton	500 yds. (457 m.)	3-5 values of color; slight shine
4-ply cotton roving, heavy	110 yds. (101 m.)	natural color
2-ply 1/16″ strand synthetic	960 yds. (877 m.)	

Glossary

Balance Equal visual weight.

   Asymmetrical Off-center visual emphasis.

   Symmetrical Mirror-like visual weight.

Bargello Mesh canvas embroidery. A type of needlepoint done by counting as you make the stitches. Also called *satin stitch* in sewing.

Blocking Squaring up the mesh canvas by dampening the completed object and stretching it back into shape.

Canvas Open-mesh cloth for needlepointing, embroidery, etc.

   Mono Tan, yellow, or white cotton or linen woven mesh. The spaces are counted to give the size for the number of stitches in needlepoint.

   Penelope Tan, yellow, or white cotton or linen mesh woven of pairs of threads, making a stronger canvas. You may work small stitches, like petit point, between the threads.

Cartoon Drawing on heavy paper used as a design for your rug. Scale is same size as rug.

Chroma Amount of vividness and greyness of the color. Brightness or dullness.

215

Coiling   Twisting into a circular, spiral, or winding shape.

Crochet   Using a single thread to form looped patterns by fingers or hook. Abbreviations of stitches and directions are CH-chain; SL-slip stitch; SC-single crochet; DC-double crochet; HDC-half double crochet; TR-triple crochet: YOH-yarn over hook; ST., STS.-stitch, stitches; INC-increase; DEC-decrease.

Design   The overall plan of the rug: texture, color, patterns, dark and light, motif or repeated shape.

Dominance   What the eye sees first.

Emphasis   Any stress applied to a given part or parts.

Frequency   A word used by scientists to mean hue.

Gauge   The number of stitches or rows per inch (2.5 cm.). In knitting or crocheting, a way of measuring the number of stitches per inch. Sometimes the rows which make up a specific area. Directions list the gauge obtained by the rugmaker when making the rug using a specific hook or yarn.

Ghiordes Knot   A girth hitch, half hitch or lark's head type knot used in Iranian (Persia) carpets. Called *turkey knot* and *rya knot*.

Lithography   The art or process of making a design or drawing on lithographic stone so that impressions in ink can be taken from it.

Miter   Diagonal join at corners of the hem.

Motif   The distinctive feature of a design; the dominant idea for your rug; the unit of shapes repeated.

Needlepoint   Mesh canvas embroidery. The stitches fill in the drawing on the canvas and cover the mesh. A type of count thread embroidery.

Pattern   How the eye travels across the surface of the design by grouping elements, for example, dark/light, dull/bright.

Plaiting   Three or more interlaced strands forming a braid.

Ply   The number of strands of spun fiber.

Pounce wheel   A metal tracing wheel with sharp prongs that punch small holes along the drawing lines of the cartoon. Pouncing chalk or charcoal dust over the holes leaves a dotted outline that is traced with indelible felt tip markers preparatory to working rug design.

Pull skeins   The end of the yarn strand pulls out from the center of the ball of yarn.

Rya knot   Ghiordes or Turkey knot. A Swedish and Norwegian word from the "Ry" and "Ryijy" Finnish word that means a shaggy covering. The long, many-colored strands make a larger knot than the single-strand knot of Iranian carpets. A half hitch knot.

Scrim   A cotton leno rug canvas fabric whose mesh or open weave is usually 3 1/2 to 5 openings per inch (2.5 cm).

Selvedge   The edge of a piece of woven material finished in such a way as to prevent ravelling out of the weft.

Shed To divide (the warp threads). The opening between alternating warp threads through which you throw your weft (or fill) threads.

Tabby weave Plain weave. Every other warp strand is interlaced with the weft.

Tone Overall value impact of the design. The general light or dark color effect of the form, shape, or area.

Value The relative lightness or darkness of color.

Warp The threads which are extended lengthwise (vertically) in the loom.

Weft The threads that cross from side to side (horizontally) of a web at right angles to the warp threads through which they are woven.

Yarn Fiber spun into threads for Weaving, Knitting, etc.

French tapestry Single-strand, four-ply needlepoint yarn. Usually 8 meters or 8 3/4 yards in each skein.

Persian yarn Loosely twisted strands of smooth, two-ply thread. Easily separated into single strands for accent in other areas. 8 oz. skein contains approx. 320 yards (344 meters). Sold by ounce or gram.

Rug yarn Tightly twisted four-ply wool or synthetic strands. Wool is usually heavier than synthetic rug yarn.

Sources
of Supplies

U.S. Suppliers

Braiding Equipment   HARRY M. FRASER CO.
192 Hartford Rd.
Manchester, Connecticut 06040

Linen Rug Backing   FREDERICK J. FAWCETT, INC.   THE HANDWEAVER
129 South St.   1643 San Pablo Ave.
Boston, Massachusetts 02111   Berkeley, California 94702

Fleece   GOLDEN FLEECE WOOLENS   GREENTREE RANCH
Box 123   Rte. 3, Box 461
Agincourt, Ontario, Canada   Loveland, Colorado 80537

Dyes   CUSHING'S PERFECTION DYES   STRAW INTO GOLD
W. Cushing and Co.   5533 College Ave.
Dover-Foxcraft, Maine 04426   Oakland, California 94618
(also books, cordage, feathers, spindles, fleece, yarns)

PUTNAM FADELESS DYES
Monroe Chemical Co.
301 Oak Street
Quincy, Illinois 62302

Rug Hooking NORDEN PRODUCTS
P.O. Box 1, 222 Waukegan Rd.
Glenview, Illinois 60025

RUG CRAFTERS
3895 S. Main
Santa Ana, California 92704
*(speed tufter, Montell hooker, other
equipment)*

RITTERMERE CRAFTS STUDIO LTD.
P.O. Box 240
Vineland, Ontario, Canada

YARN PAINTER ELECTRIC HOOKER
P.O. Box 4564
Fresno, California 93744

Needles THE BOYE NEEDLE CO.
4335 N. Ravenswood Ave.
Chicago, Illinois 60613

Weaving LIVING DESIGNS
7535 Sunset Way
Aptos, California 95003
*(tapestry yarns, Navajo looms, hand-
hewn tools)*

PENGUIN QUILL
Sunshine Canyon
Boulder, Colorado 80302
(looms)

CREATIVE HANDWEAVERS
Sunset Blvd.
Los Angeles, California
*(yarns and other things for the hand-
weaver)*

CASA DE LAS TEJEDORAS
1619 E. Edinger
Santa Ana, California 92705
*(roving, Navajo type yarns, handspun
and other yarns)*

DHARMA TRADING CO.
Box 1288
Berkeley, California 94701
(table looms, small hand looms, yarns)

THE HANDWEAVER
1643 San Pablo Ave.
Berkeley, California 94702
(looms, yarns, silk, cotton, cum yarns)

General BOUTIQUE MARGOT
26 W. 54th St.
New York, New York 10019

Paint CAL-WESTERN PAINTS, INC.
Sante Fe Springs, California
90670
*(water base, interior–exterior acrylic
paint and nontoxic water-clear varnish,
basic 24 colors)*

Yarns AMERICAN CREWEL STUDIO
Box 553
Westfield, New Jersey 07091

AMERICAN THREAD CORP.
90 Park Ave.
New York, New York

BUCKY KING EMBROIDERIES UN-
LIMITED
121 South Drive
Pittsburgh, Pennsylvania 15238

WILLIAM CONDON & SONS LTD.
65 Queen St.
P.O. Box 129
Charlottetown, Prince Edward
Island, Canada

CRAFT YARNS OF RHODE ISLAND, INC.
603 Mineral Springs Ave.
P.O. Box 385
Pawtucket, Rhode Island 02862
(rug wool, homespun, linen)

CREATIVE HANDWEAVERS
Sunset Blvd.
Los Angeles, California

THE COUNTRYSIDE HANDWEAVERS
Box 1225
Mission, Kansas 66222
(Swiss linen yarns)

HOUSE OF KLEEN
P.O. Box 58
Essex, Connecticut 06426
(Swedish yarns)

FREDERICK J. FAWCETT, INC.
129 South St.
Boston, Massachusetts 02111
(imported linen yarns)

LILY MILLS CO.
Shelby, North Carolina 28150
(cotton, wool, metallic, rayon yarns; embroidery threads)

MEXISKEIN
P.O. Box 1624
Missoula, Montana 59801
(Mexican handspun wool)

PATERNAYAN BROS., INC.
312 E. 95th St.
New York, New York 10028
(rug wool, monk's cloth)

WOOLWORKS, INC.
838 Madison Avenue
New York, New York 10021

THE YARN DEPOT
545 Sutter St.
San Francisco, California 94102
(rug wool, cotton, novelty yarns)

Foreign Suppliers

Yarns & Thread

BORGS OF LUND
Box 96
LUND, SWEDEN
(rya and flossa yarns)

C & F HANDICRAFT SUPPLIERS
246 Stag Lane
Kingsbury, London NW 9
England

T.M. HUNTER
Sutherland Mills
Brora, Scotland

THE NEEDLEWOMAN SHOP
146-148 Regent St.
London W1R6BA England

Fabrics

DICKSONS & CO., LTD.
Dungannon, County Tyrone
Northern Ireland

LOCKHART & SONS LTD.
Linktown Works
Kirkcaldy KY11QH

NOTTINGHAM HANDICRAFT CO.
Milton Road
West Bridford, Nottingham, England

Needles   J.P. COATES LTD.
155 St. Vincent St.
Glasgow, England

Kits and Catalogs

Knitting and Crochet   SHELBURNE SPINNERS
2 Howard Street
Burlington, Vermont 05401
(hats, caps, mittens and socks, yarns, crewel embroidery)

Needlepoint   ELSA WILLIAMS, INC.
445 Main St.
West Townsend, Massachusetts
01474
(outstanding designs, mostly Oriental, and highest quality materials; order full color catalog for $1—full of useful information and a pleasure to look at)

PAPILLON
56 E. Andrews Dr., N.W.
Atlanta, Georgia 30305
(lovely hand-painted designs—natural looking shells and Oriental; comes with Paternayan Persian needlepoint yarn)

JANE WHITMIRE
2353 S. Meade St.
Arlington, Virginia 22202
(good quality designs)

ELAINE MAGNIN NEEDLEPOINT
DESIGN CATALOG
3063 Fillmore St.
San Francisco, California 94123

Pile Rugs   NORDISKAS DESIGN
Skon Rugcraft
53 Lambert Lane
New Rochelle, New York 10804
or
NORDISKAS DESIGN
Nordiska Industriab
Box 141, 421 22
Vastra Frolunda, Sweden

WOOL DESIGN, INC.
P.O. Box 15891
Charlotte, North Carolina 28210

General Crafts   AMERICAN HANDICRAFTS
Dept. HBC
2808 Shamrock
Fort Worth, Texas 76107

Bibliography

Rugmaking—General

BOYLES, MARGARET. *The Art of Rugmaking. Latch Hook, Rya, Punch Needle, Needlepoint and Crochet.* New York: Columbia Minerva Corporation, 1974.
(Excellent diagrams on how to crochet, needlepoint, punch hook, latch hook. Hints on designing your own rugs and enlarging are encouraging for a beginner.)

FELCHER, CECILIA. *The Complete Book of Rugmaking: Folk Methods and Ethnic Designs.* New York: Hawthorne Books, Inc., 1975.

LAURY, JEAN RAY, AND JOYCE AIKEN. *Handmade Rugs From Practically Anything.* New York: Countryside Press, a division of Farm Journal, Inc., Philadelphia. Distributed to the trade by Doubleday and Company, Inc., Garden City, New York, 1971, 1972.

MARINOFF, KATHRYN A. *Getting Started in Handmade Rugs.* New York: Bruce Publishing Co., 1957, 1971.

McCalls's editorial staff, Rugmaking. New York: McCall's Pattern Co., 1974.

SILVER, LONA B. *Rugs from Rags.* New York: Drake Publishers, Inc., 1976.

ZNAMIEROWSKI, NELL. *Step by Step Rugmaking*. New York: Golden Press, Western Publishing Co., Inc., 1972.

Braided Rugs   CARTY, SALLY CLARKE. *How to Make Braided Rugs*. New York: McGraw-Hill Book Co., Inc., 1977.
(Good book for the novice. Specific guidelines for buying new wool, lacing together, variations of three-strand braid. Checklist for stain removal, advice for going into business.)

FAMILY CREATIVE WORKSHOP, Vol. 3. *Braided Rugs*. New York: Plenary Publishers International, Inc., 1974.
(The individual areas in these encyclopedic-like books are written by experienced craftspersons. The color illustrations are clear and show details well.)

PUTNAM, DOROTHY PARKS. *Beautiful Braiding*. Stow, Massachusetts: Action Press, Inc., Eighth Printing, Revised Edition, 1960.
(Detailed instructions for seventeen rugs. Excellent reference for technique.)

Fabric Construction Using a Single Strand   DAWSON, MARY. *Complete Guide to Crochet Stitches*. New York: Crown Publishers, 1973.

FOUGNER, DAVE. *The Manly Art of Knitting*. Santa Rosa, Cal.: Threshold, 1973.

KIEWE, HEINZE EDGAR. *The Sacred History of Knitting*. Oxford, England: Art Needlework Industries Ltd., 1971.

Mon Tricot, compilers. *Knitting Dictionary: 1030 Stitches and Patterns and Knitting, Crochet and Jacquard Techniques*. New York: Crown Publishers, 1973.

NORBURY, JAMES. *Traditional Knitting Patterns from Scandinavia, the British Isles, France, Italy and Other European Countries*. New York: Dover Publications, 1962.

PHILLIPS, MARY WALKER. *Creative Knitting: A New Art Form*. New York: Van Nostrand Reinhold Co., 1971.
(Exciting examples of variations in knitting.)

Step-by-Step Knitting: A Complete Introduction to the Craft of Knitting. New York: Golden Press, 1967.
(Good book for beginners, and inexpensive.)

STRATFORD, AUDRIE. *Introducing Knitting*. London: B. T. Batsford Ltd. New York: Drake Publishers, Inc., 1972.

Needlework and Stitchery   BEINEKE, MARY ANN. *Basic Needlery Stitches on Mesh Fabrics*. New York: Dover Publications, 1973.
(Easy-to-follow book on needlepoint.)

CAULFIELD, SOPHIA AND BLANCHE SAWARD. *The Dictionary of Needlework*. New York: Arno Press, 1972.
(Facsimile of 1882 edition. Interesting old-time approach.)

CHRISTENSEN, JO IPPOLITO. *The Needlepoint Book: 303 Stitches with Patterns and Projects*. Englewood Cliffs, N. J.: Prentice-Hall, Inc., 1976.
(Good illustrations of techniques.)

———. *Teach Yourself Needlepoint*. Englewood Cliffs, N. J.: Prentice-Hall, Inc., 1978.

DE DILLMONT, THERESE. *Encyclopedia of Needlework*. Mulhouse, France: D.M.C. Library; in U.S., distributed by Joan Toggitt, Ltd., New York.
(For the beginner, this is all you need to get started.)

FREW, HANNAH. *Three-Dimensional Embroidery*. London: Van Nostrand Reinhold Co. International Offices, 1975.
(Great for ideas, inspiration. Nice color photographs.)

GUILD, VERA P. *Good Housekeeping New Complete Book of Needlecraft*. New York: Hearst Corporation, 1959, 1971.

HINES, MILLIE. *American Heirloom Bargello: Designs from Quilts, Coverlets, and Navajo Rugs*. New York: Crown Publishers, 1977.

HULBERT, REGINA. *Left-Handed Needlepoint*. New York: Van Nostrand Reinhold Co., 1972.

ILLES, ROBERT E. *Men in Stitches*. New York: Van Nostrand Reinhold Co., 1975.

LANE, MAGGIE. *More Needlepoint by Design*. New York: Charles Scribner's Sons, 1972.

————. *Chinese Rugs Designed for Needlepoint*. New York: Charles Scribner's Sons, 1975.
(A beautiful book with ten excellent graphed designs and ideas for borders.)

LANE, ROSE WILDER. *Woman's Day Book of American Needlework*. New York: A Fireside Book, Simon and Schuster, 1963.
(A beautiful, marvelous book. Dozens of color plates, and the text is absolutely inspiring.)

One Hundred Embroidery Stitches. England: J. & P. Coats, Ltd., 1967.
(Comprehensive and inexpensive.)

SIEGLER, SUSAN. *Needlework Patterns from the Metropolitan Museum of Art*. New York: The Metropolitan Museum of Art, 1976.
(Gorgeous book full of patterns taken from ancient works of art. Photos of originals accompany the patterns from Pre-Columbian, Egyptian, Chinese, and European textiles.

Sunset Books editorial staff, compilers. *Needlepoint Techniques and Projects*. Menlo Park: Lane Publishing Co., 1977.
(Great for left-handed needleworkers.)

Pile Rugs   KOPP, JOEL AND KATE. *American Hooked and Sewn Rugs: Folk Art Underfoot*. New York: E. P. Dutton & Co., Inc., 1975.

PARKER, XENIA LEY. *Hooked Rugs and Ryas*. Chicago: Henry Regnery Co., 1973.
(Details of New England style folded border, p. 100.)

WISEMAN, ANN. *Rag Tapestries and Wool Tapestries*. New York and London: Van Nostrand Reinhold Co., 1969.
(From simple rag rug welcome mats to a 14-ft. mural of bold texture and intriguing effects, utilizing tweed and plaid rug strips and multi-twisted yarns, tufted, and cut looks.)

WILLCOX, DONALD J. *Techniques of Rya Knotting.* New York: Van Nostrand Reinhold Co., 1971.

WILSON, JEAN. *The Pile Weaves.* New York: Van Nostrand Reinhold Co., 1974.
(Fresh ideas, superbly presented. Detailed instructions with twenty-six techniques.)

Weaving   ATWATER, MARY MEIGS. *Byways in Handweaving.* New York: The Macmillan Co., 1954. 5th printing, 1972.
(The classic on handweaving—inkle, tablet, Estonia weave, Chilcat twined weaving.)

BEUTLICH, TADEK. *The Technique of Woven Tapestry.* London: Batator. New York: Watson–Guptill, 1971.
(Book for beginners or experts contains step-by-step instruction on designing, correcting mistakes, making looms.)

BENNET, NOEL AND TIANA BIGHORSE. *Working with the Wool.* Flagstaff, Arizona: Northland Press, 1971.
(Authentic treatment and directions for Navajo weaving.)

BLUMENAU, LILI. *The Art and Craft of Hand Weaving, including Design.* New York: Crown Publishers, Inc., 1964.
(The accent is on imaginative self-development based on an understanding of the basic weaves and some of the many possibilities they suggest.)

BROWN, RACHEL. *The Weaving, Spinning and Dyeing Book.* New York: Alfred A. Knopf, 1978.
(Good on all off-loom and loom techniques. Good diagrams of finishing techniques.)

BURT, BEN. *Weaving.* London: British Museum Publications, Ltd., 1976.
(Descriptions and photographs of some of the many kinds of looms that have been used throughout the world.)

COLLINGWOOD, PETER. *His Weaves and Weaving.* Santa Ana, Cal.: The Shuttle Craft Guild, 1963.

———. *The Techniques of Rug Weaving.* London: Faber & Faber, Ltd., 1968. New York: Watson–Guptill Publications, 1971.

GOODLOE, WILLIAM H. *Coconut Palm Frond Weaving.* Rutland, Vt.: Charles E. Tuttle Co., 1972.

HELD, SHIRLEY E. *Weaving, a Handbook for Fiber Craftsmen.* New York: Holt, Rinehart & Winston, Revised edition, 1978.
(Good book, goes into more depth than Birrell's book. Modern examples. Fine color plates.)

PARKER, XENIA LEY. *Creative Handweaving.* New York: Dial Press, 1976.
(Simple loom construction. Introduction to natural man-made fibers.)

RAINEY, SARITA. *Weaving without a Loom.* Englewood Cliffs, N.J.: Prentice-Hall, Inc., 1977.

REGENSTEINER, ELSE. *Weaver's Study Course: Ideas and Techniques.* New York: Van Nostrand Reinhold Co., 1975.
(Advanced course emphasizing patterns and fabrics.)

SEAGROATT, MARGARET. *Rug Weaving for Beginners*. New York: Watson–Gupthill Publications, 1972.

WILSON, JEAN. *Weaving is Fun*. New York: Litton Educational Publications, Van Nostrand Reinhold Co., 1971.
(Written for beginners. Excellent illustrations. Simplicity.)

Other Techniques

ANDES, EUGENE. *Far Beyond the Fringe: Three Dimensional Knotting Techniques Using Macramé and Nautical Ropework*. New York: Van Nostrand Reinhold Co., 1973.

HARVEY, VIRGINIA I. *The Techniques of Basketry*. New York: Van Nostrand Reinhold Co., 1974.

JANVIER, JACQUELINE. *Felt Crafting*. New York: Sterling Publishing Co., 1970.

SCHWALBACH, MATHILDA V. AND JAMES A. *Screen-Process Printing for the Serigrapher and Textile Designer*. New York: Van Nostrand Reinhold Co., 1970.
(Deals comprehensively with the design and printing of textiles and the fine art of serigraphy.)

Collecting and Preserving Rugs

ERDMAN, KURT. American edition translated by G. Ellis. *Oriental Carpets*. New York: University Books, Inc., 1960.

GREGORIAN, ARTHUR T. *Oriental Rugs and the Stories They Tell*. Boston, Mass.: The Nimrod Press, 1967.
(Mr. Gregorian's deep love for the land of his birth expressed itself in his belief that the simple rug weavers are uniquely gifted artistically. To illuminate the artistic tradition, he draws on his vast personal experience and familiarity with village, city, and tribal weavers.)

LEENE, J. E., ed. *Textile Conservation*. Washington, D.C.: Smithsonian Institution, 1972.

RODRIS, ROTH. *Floor Coverings in 18th Century America*. Washington, D.C.: Smithsonian Press. U.S. National Museum Bulletin #250. Contributions from the Museum of History & Technology Paper 59, pp. 1–64, 1967.
(Floor coverings were the exception rather than the rule in eighteenth-century America. This book details this period.)

WEEKS, JEANNE G. AND DONALD TREGANOWAN. *Rugs and Carpets of Europe and the Western World*. New York: Chilton Book Co., 1969.

Of General Interest to the Craftsperson

AMERICAN CRAFTS COUNCIL, compilers. *Contemporary Crafts Marketplace, 1977–1978*. 8352–0920–2 (May 1977).
(Source of American suppliers, shops, galleries, craft organizations, periodicals and newsletters, audiovisual materials, crafts events and their sponsors, degrees and courses of study at colleges, universities and other schools. Reference books in all craft media. Each listing gives you the current information needed to utilize and contact the firm or person—name, address, telephone number, key people, specialty, and the like.)

BIRRELL, VERLA LEONE. *The Textile Arts: A Handbook of Weaving, Braiding, Printing and other Textile Techniques*. New York: Schocken Books, 1973. (orig. pub. by Harper, 1959).
(Encyclopedic survey.)

COLIN, PAUL AND DEBORAH LIPPMAN. *Craft Sources, the Ultimate Catalog for Craftspeople*. New York: M. Evans and Co., Inc., 1975.
(Like the Whole Earth Catalog, *informative and entertaining to read.)*

CONSTANTINE, MILDRED AND JACK LENOR LARSON. *Beyond Craft, the Art of Fabric*. New York: Van Nostrand Reinhold Co., 1972.
(Graphically illustrates the innovative concept of weaving as an art form. Each artist's technique analyzed.)

CRAWFORD, TAD. *Legal Guide for the Visual Artist*. New York: Hawthorne Publishers, Inc., 1977.
(A handbook for painters, sculptors, illustrators, printmakers, photographers and all other visual artists.)

EMERY, IRENE. *The Primary Structures of Fabrics*. Washington, D.C.: The Textile Museum, 1966.
(Definitive dictionary of fiber arts terminology related to anthropology, industry, and education.)

GLASSMAN, JUDITH. *National Guide to Craft Supplies*. New York: Litton Educational Publishing, Inc., 1975.
("The Craft Yellow Pages.")

HARTUNG, ROLF. *Creative Textile Craft*. Ravensburg, Germany, 1963. New York: Reinhold Publishing Co., 1964.
(The basic structure of fibers and the many ways they can be manipulated. Twisting, looping, twining. Simplified version of The Primary Structure of Fabrics *using exploration and discovery approach.)*

HOLZ, LORETTA. *How to Sell Your Art and Crafts. A Marketing Guide for Creative People*. New York: Charles Scribner's Sons, 1977.

NEWMAN, THELMA. *Contemporary African Crafts*. New York: Crown Publishers, 1974.
(The author gives credit to the individual artist as shown in these photographs of craftspersons involved in the process of creating.)

O'BANION, NANCE, AND CINDY SAGAN. *Fiberfinder: A Guide to Bay Area Sources*. Berkeley: Fiberworks Center for the Textile Arts, 1977.
(Excellent annotated source book, includes information about basketry, classes, dyes, weaving equipment, galleries, needlework, quilts, rugs, yardage, and services.)

PAQUE, JOAN MICHAELS. *Design Principles and Fiber Techniques*. Shorewood, Wis.: Joan & Henry Paque, 1973.
(Book of diagrams illustrating knotting, looping, wrapping, and finishing techniques. For those with a more advanced interest.)

PAZ, OCTAVIO, AND THE WORLD CRAFTS COUNCIL. *In Praise of Hands*. Conn.: The World Graphic Society, 1974.
(A picture book of an international exhibition of contemporary crafts at the Ontario Science Center in 1974.)

SIDES AND SMITH. *Decorative Art of the Southwestern Indians*. With annotations by Clarice Martin Smith and a Foreword by Frederick Webb Hodge. New York: Dover Publications, 1961.

Legal Matters BAY AREA LAWYERS
FOR THE ARTS, INC.
25 Taylor Street
San Francisco, Cal. 95014
(Arts law handbooks and arts law guidebooks and pamphlets for visual artists, performing artists.)

ART AND THE LAW
36 West 44th Street
New York, N.Y. 10036
(Volunteer lawyers for the Arts publication. 10 issues yearly. Subscription by contributions.)

Periodicals AMERICAN FABRICS MAGAZINE
24 East 38th St.
New York, N.Y. 10016

HANDWEAVER AND CRAFTSMAN
246 Fifth Ave.
New York, N.Y. 10001
(Fibers, shows, books, interviews. Bimonthly.)

AMERICAN CRAFT
22 W. 55th St.
New York, N.Y. 10019
(Formerly Crafts Horizons. Bimonthly publication. Articles, reviews, show news. Subscription included with membership to American Crafts Council.)

THE RUG HOOKER, NEWS AND VIEWS
W. Cushing & Co.
Kennebunkport, Mne. 04046
(Small newsletter shares ideas from rug hookers about dyeing, advice about design, guild information, supplies. Bimonthly.)

CRAFTS MAGAZINE
28 Haymarket
London, SW1Y 4SU, England

SHUTTLE, SPINDLE & DYEPOT
1013 Farmington Ave.
West Hartford, Conn. 06107
(Quarterly publication of Handweaver's Guild of America, Inc. Articles on spinning, dyeing and weaving.)

FIBERARTS
50 College St.
Asheville, N.C. 28801
(Articles about fiber artists and exhibits, books, sources. Bimonthly.)

VISUAL DIALOG
1380 Country Club Dr.
Los Altos, Cal. 94022
(Quarterly publication with interviews and news about shows, various media.)

THE GOODFELLOW NEWSLETTER
P.O Box 4520
Berkeley, Cal. 94704
(Articles on crafts, exhibits, book reviews, good advice by West Coast craftspeople. Catalog published yearly.)

WORKING CRAFTSMAN
Box 42
Northbrook, Ill. 60062
(Trends, outlooks, competitions, fairs, grants, new products, health hazards.)

Index

A

Additive color, 198
African tribes, 8
American Indians, 2, 8, 35
Appraisals, 209
Aran Islands, 121
"Arciform" (Johnson), 186–87
Art Protis method, 31, 33–34

B

Back Stitch, 103
Backstrap style looms, 72
Bargello stitch, 165–66
Basketry, 60
Basketweave pattern, 64
Basketweave stitch, 166, 167, 169
"Bedroom, Circa 1900" (Henry), 183, 184
Blocking, 114, 129, 159, 174, 203

Braided rag rugs, 50–59
   braiding, 52–53
   color and shape, 51
   estimating amount of fabric, 51–52
   finishing, 57
   lacing, 54–55
   materials for, 50
   variations on traditional, 57–59
Brick stitch, 165
British Museum, 8
Brosnan, Maggie, 27, 200
Brushes
   cleaning, 21
   for painted floorcloths, 16–17
Bunderstadt, Bruce, 201–2

C

Campbell, Terence, 198, 199
Card-weaving looms, 72
Care of rugs, 203–6

Casting on loops, 99, 100, 103, 122, 125
Chain stitch, 99, 100
Chase, Constance, 135
Circular crocheted rugs, 106–15
Cleaning methods, 204
Clove hitch, 91
Cluster stitch, 99, 103
Cochran, Samantha, 27
Coiling, 62–63
Color, 197–202
    additive, 198
    in braided rag rugs, 51
    dyes, 199–201
    general advice on, 201–2
    lighting and, 199
    for painted floorcloths 15–16
    partitive, 198–99
    subtractive, 198
Commissions, 207
Compound ikat, 68
Continental tent stitch, 166–67
Contracts, 207–9
Cooper, Berkeley, 3, 50–52, 54–55, 57
Crewe, Leonard C., Jr., 9
Crocheted rugs, 94–119, 176–79
    basic stitches, 99–100
    basic yarns, 96–97
    blocking, 114
    circular, 106–15
    estimating amount of yarn, 97–98
    finishing, 106–114
    hexagonal, 104–6
    increasing, 112–13
    joining yarn, 113–14
    making initial loop, 100, 103
    materials for, 104
    planning, 94–95
    preparation, 95–97
    variations on, 114–19
Cutler, Dorothy P., 147, 155
"Czechoslovakian Romance" (Freimark), 31

D

Decorative stitches, 169–71
De Mouthe, Frank, 57

Design, 192–95
    of cartoon, 196–97
    definition of, 192
    planning, 194–95
    sources for, 192–95 (see also Pattern design)
Diagonal stitches, 166–69
Directories, 193–94
Double crochet stitch, 95, 99, 110, 116
Double ikat, 68
Dyes, 199–201

E

Eight-harness floor looms, 72
Electric speed tufted rugs, 182–90
Enlarging motifs, 18–20
Estimating amounts:
    for braided rag rugs, 51–52
    for crocheted rugs, 97–98
    for knitted rugs, 97–98
    for needlepoint rugs, 162–63
    for punch hook pile rugs, 146
    for rya rugs, 133
    for woven rugs, 68–72
Extending felting, 33–34

F

Felted rugs, 7, 25–34
    extending felting, 33–34
    felting process, 27, 28–31
    materials for, 28
Finishes, for painted floorcloths, 16, 18, 21
Finishing techniques, 202–3
    braided rag rugs, 57
    crocheted rugs, 106, 114
    hooked rag rugs, 47–50
    knitted rugs, 129
    latch hook rugs, 142
    needlepoint rugs, 160, 174
    woven rugs, 90–94
Fire retardation, 205–6
Fisher, Shirley, 210
Fowler, Jane, 40, 42

Frame looms, 72, 75–76
Freimark, Robert, 31–34
French tapestry, 161–62

G

Garter stitch, 99, 125–26
Geometric designs, 6, 81–84
Gluing pieced carpets, 24–25
Gobelin stitch, 165
Graham, Deborah, 192, 193
Granda reds, 87
Gros point, 163

H

Half-drop repeat pattern, 137
Half hitch, 91
Henry, Patti, 182–84, 199, 207, 208
Hexagonal crocheted rugs, 104–6
Hiding the stitch, 113
Hooked rag rugs, 36–50
  finishing, 47–50
  hooking, 46–47
  materials for, 42
  pattern design, 42–45
  pattern making and transfer to backing, 45–46
Hopi Indians, 35, 60
Hundertwasser, F., 184

I

Inlay patterns, woven rugs and, 81–82

J

Jersey (stocking) stitch, 100
Johnson, Judy Miller, 22
Johnson, Lynden Keith, 184–90

K

Kits, 1
Klagetos, 87
Knit stitch, 95, 99, 121
Knitted rugs, 94–103, 119–29
  adding, dropping and ending stitches, 128
  basic stitches, 99–100
  basic yarns, 96–97
  casting on loops, 99, 100, 103, 122, 125
  estimating amount of yarn, 97–98
  finishing, 129
  materials for, 121–22, 128
  origins of knitting, 121
  planning, 94–95
  preparation, 95–97
Knitting Dictionary Stitches and Patterns (Mon Tricot), 99
Knotting, 113, 133–34, 140–41
Koren, Nancy, 176–79, 199

L

Lacing braided rag rugs, 54–55
Latch hook rugs, 1, 130, 136–44, 179–81
  finishing, 142
  knotting, 140–41
  materials for, 138–39, 143
  pattern design, 137–38
  transfering design to canvas, 139–40
  variations on, 142–43
Lark's head knot, 91
Lazy stitch, 62
Lee, Jane Vander, 201
Lee, Josephine, 154
Lee, William, 121
Leno canvas, 160
Lininger, Anna Marie, 136
Looms, 72, 75–76
Looped crochet stitch, 99

M

Marketing, 206–9

Maryland Institute College of
Art, 9
Materials:
for braided rag rugs, 50
for crocheted rugs, 104
for felted rugs, 28
for hooked rag rugs, 42
for knitted rugs, 121–22, 128
for latch hook rugs, 138–39,
143
for needlepoint rugs, 158–62
for painted floorcloths, 11, 13,
16–18
for pieced carpets, 23
for punch hook pile rugs,
144–46
for rya rugs, 131–32
sources of, 218–21
Mono canvas, 160
Moshimes, Joan, 201
Moss stitch, 103
Moth-proofing, 204–5
Mouthe, Jean de, 6
"My Moon Map" (Johnson), 186

N

National Endowment for the
Arts, 206
Naturalistic designs of woven
rugs, 81–84
Navajo Indians, 35, 84–86
Needlepoint rugs, 130, 156–75,
197
decorative stitches, 169–71
diagonal stitches, 166–69
estimating amount of yarn,
162–63
finishing, 160, 174
materials for, 158–62
pattern design, 172–73
stitching, 173–74
straight stitches, 165–66
Needles, for needlepoint rugs,
161
Norsemen, 2
Numdah rugs, 26

O

Oaxaca, Mexico, 86

Oriental rugs, 87–88
Overhand knot, 91

P

Paint, for painted floorcloths,
16, 18
Painted floorcloths, 7, 8–21
color, selection of, 15–16
enlarging motif, 18–20
finishes for, 16, 18, 21
materials for, 11, 13, 16–18
painting canvas, 20–21
pattern design, 15
preparing canvas, 13–15
Paper weaving, 63–66
Partitive color, 198–99
Pattern design:
for braided rag rugs, 51
for hooked rag rugs, 42–45
for latch hook rugs, 137–38
for needlepoint rugs, 172–73
for painted floorcloths, 15
for pieced carpets, 23–24
for rya rugs, 131
for woven rugs, 66–68, 81–87
Pazyrk carpet, 87
Penelope canvas, 160–61
Periodicals, 228–29
Persian knot, 88
"Persian Prayer Garden"
(Henry), 184
Persian-type yarn, 161
Petit point, 163
Photographing rugs, 209–10
Pieced carpets, 7, 22–25
gluing, 24–25
materials for, 23
pattern design, 23–24
Pile rugs, 87–90
Pilgrims, 35
Plaid weave, 66, 67
Plain weave, 64, 67, 76
Plaiting, 60, 61
Plumb, Annie Bird, 3, 36–40,
42–47
Plying, 113–14
Popcorn stitch, 103
Pottery, 60
Pounce bag, 45
Pounce wheel, 45

Pre-shrinking, 14
Punch hook pile rugs, 144–55
    backing and frame, 151–52
    drawing pattern, 152–53
    estimating amount of yarn,
        146
    materials for, 144–46
    using tools, 147, 149–50
    variations on, 153–55
Purl stitch, 95, 99, 121, 126

Q

Quick point, 163
Quirke, Mortimer, 37–38, 42–46

R

Regional designs of woven rugs,
    84–87
Rollers, 18
Rubbings, 12
Rug collage (see Pieced carpets)
Rugmaking, origins of, 2
"Rug with a Blue Border" (Bun-
    derstadt, 201–2
Rya knot, 88, 91
Rya rugs, 2, 88, 130, 131–36
    estimating amount of yarn,
        133
    estimating canvas, 132
    knotting, 133–34
    materials for, 131–32
    pattern design, 131
    variations on, 135–36

S

Satin stitch, 165
Senna knot, 88
Shell stitch, 103
Shrimp stitch, 179
Shrinking, 14
Shuttle hook rugs, 179–81
Single crochet stitch, 95, 99,
    103, 108–10, 116, 118
Slip stitch, 99
Smithsonian Museum, 8

South Sea Islands, 8
Square knot, 91
Squaring up canvas, 14–15
Stitched needlepoint rugs (see
    Needlepoint rugs)
Stitches:
    basic crochet and knitting,
        99–100
    basic needlepoint, 163–71
Stockinette stitch, 95, 126
Storage of rugs, 205
"Storm" patterns, 87
Straight stitches, 165–66
Strasbourg Guild of Knitters, 120
String heddles, 75
Subtractive color, 198
Supplies, sources of, 218–21

T

Tabby weave, 64, 67, 68, 76
Tapestry weave, 81
Texture, 195–97
"Tide Pools" (Warner), 180–81
Triple crochet stitch, 116
Tufted rugs, electric speed,
    182–90
Turkish knot, 88
Twill pattern, 65
"Two Grey Hills" weaving re-
    gion, 86

U

Undercarpets, 206

V

Varathane, 16, 18, 21
Victoria and Albert Museum,
    119–20
V'Soske, Stanislaus, 185

W

Warner, Howard Milton, 179–
    81, 197

Warp, 63, 68–70
Warp ikat, 68
Warping, 76–79
Weft, 62–64, 71
Wilson, Erica, 158
Winterthur Museum, 8–9
Wissa-Wassef, Ramses, 81
Woven rugs, 63–94
    estimating amount of yarn, 68–72
    finishing, 90–94
    looms, 72, 75–76
    pattern design, 66–68, 81–87

Woven rugs *(cont.)*
    patterns, visualizing, 64–66
    pile rugs, 87–90
    warping, 76–79
    weaving, 80–81

Y

Yarn (*see* Estimating amounts)
Yeibechais-style rugs, 86
Yeis-style rugs, 86